THE STORY OF TRIUMPH SPORTS CARS

THE STORY OF TRIUMPH SPORTS CARS

by

Graham Robson

MOTOR RACING PUBLICATIONS

MOTOR RACING PUBLICATIONS LTD
56 Fitzjames Avenue, Croydon, Surrey, CR0 5DD

First published 1973
2nd impression 1974
ISBN 0 900549 23 8

Sole United States distribution by
Motorbooks International Inc.,
3501 Hennepin Avenue South,
Minneapolis, Minnesota 55408, USA

Library of Congress Catalog
Card Number 73-88323

Photosetting by Seventy Set Ltd., London
Printed in Great Britain by Taylor-Bloxham Ltd., Leicester

Contents

To John Lloyd

without whose original encouragement
this book might never have been started

ERRATUM

The references made to the Triumph Twelve in the first paragraph on Page 64 should refer to the Standard Flying Twelve/Fourteen released in the autumn of 1935. Similarly, the upper caption on Page 65 should make reference to this earlier model as being the inspiration for the first post-war Triumph saloon.

Introduction

AS FAR as the historian is concerned, the Triumph *marque* has always appeared to have been neglected. In spite of the worldwide sales successes and large post-war dollar earnings, not to mention competitions successes at all levels, there has always been a substantial amount of ignorance about the cars. The legends that did exist, where documented, had often become distorted with age, and many of the people intimately involved were hardly known

The year 1973 marked not only the twenty-first birthday of the phenomenally-successful Triumph TR sports cars, but also the fiftieth anniversary of the release of the very first Triumph car, and the seventieth anniversary of the formation of the Standard Motor Company, which eventually resurrected Triumph from financial obscurity. With all these anniversaries falling together, it became apparent that an authentic chronicle of the fortunes and failings of the cars should be compiled.

A book about every Triumph ever made would be huge, difficult to categorise, and perhaps dull in parts, particularly in respect of the more recent years when Triumph saloons have really been better-class Standards under a different name. Since 1945 the name of Triumph has returned to prominence because of the sports cars, on which, therefore, it has been decided to concentrate this book. In the earlier years of the company, the sports and sporting cars bore a much closer relationship to the saloons than they do now, and I have tried at all junctures to relate the development and family lineage. Those readers, however, who are looking for a detailed account of the Glorias, Dolomites, Heralds, 2000s and Vitesses will, I'm afraid, have to look elsewhere.

Of all the sports and sporting cars, some, like the TRs, the Spitfires and the Stag, have succeeded beyond even their sponsors' wildest hopes, while others, like the fabulous and nearly mythical straight-eight Dolomite of 1934, only serve to illustrate what might have been possible had the finance been available to back up the good ideas. One or two of the sporting cars have met with a very mixed response – the TRX of 1950 being a very good example – often because there were too many fingers in the design pie. A few of the sporting cars listed, like the controversial but elegant pre-war Dolomite Roadsters, bordered on the touring rather than the sports car definition, even though they achieved both sales and competitions successes at the time. Any hide-bound sports car fanatic who will only consider two-seater cars for his own definition would have a thin time in listing the pre-war cars; there are several cars in this book which combined the fun of motoring with an ability to carry at least four people in adequate comfort.

It is important to realise that there have been several distinct phases in the history of development of the Triumph car. At first the name was not even carried by cars, but by pedal-cycles and motor-cycles. Cars came along hesitantly in 1923, and were of a ploddingly mundane nature until the influence of Lt-Col Claude Holbrook was felt. The age of elegance (Holbrook's 'Smartest Cars in the Land' period) stretched from 1933 until the company went into liquidation in 1939. Triumph then had a brief and shadowy war-time existence under the wing of Thomas W. Ward Ltd, when the company was effectively moribund and no cars were built. Glorious revival took place in 1945, when the company's assets were bought for Standard by the dynamic and little-liked Sir John Black, leading to a period of growth when the most notable individual successes were gained. Finally came the decade of the takeovers, when Standard-Triumph was first swallowed by the Leyland Group, and latterly merged into the British Leyland Motor Corporation of 1968. Pedal-cycle and motor-cycle interests had been hived off in 1936, but the Triumph name still survives in the two-wheeled field on highly-priced and very rapid machines built by BSA.

Unhappily for the historian, for accuracy and for detailed information, Triumph's entire pre-war records, whether of production or of significant commercial and financial events, have been destroyed. Coventry's disastrous blitz of 1940 saw to that, and since the same treatment was also handed out to Coventry's libraries and newspaper offices, the account of happenings at Priory Street, Clay Lane and Holbrooks Lane are all subject to the vagaries of memory, and the mainly technical information to be found in the principal motoring journals. I am therefore particularly indebted to Tony Cook of the Pre-1940 Triumph Owners Club, for allowing me to study his own considerable researches about the original cars, and to Walter Belgrove and Donald Healey for their reminiscences. Without the superbly detailed records available at the British Museum's Newspaper Library in Colindale I would have been unable to trace the financial ups and downs of the original company. Naturally it would have been very difficult to make any sense of the technical development of the cars through the years without referring to the ever-invaluable records held by *The Autocar* (now *Autocar*), *The Motor* (now *Motor*), and *Motor Sport.* To them, and to the staff of the National Motor Museum at Beaulieu, I would merely say that such an undertaking would have been out of the question without their help.

Apart from Donald Healey's exciting straight-eight Dolomite and the pretty little Southern Crosses, the pre-war cars were sporting rather than out-and-out sports cars. However, their successes in road events as lengthy and arduous as the Monte Carlo Rally and Alpine Trials of the 1930s cannot be denied, even if that other famous sports car manufacturer – the one based at Abingdon – steadfastly refused to acknowledge their existence! Post-war Triumphs, since the TR2 at least, have bowed their head to none, and the fact that Abingdon types were said to detest the rival product very heartily must have indicated a grudging but very healthy respect for the competition. That MG and Triumph are now both answerable to the same Board of Directors must be considered ironic in the extreme!

From the day that I first witnessed 100 mph on the speedometer of a car – in an early, noisy and very exciting TR2 – I suppose it was inevitable that I would want to write this book. After spending hundreds of hours in the navigator's seat of TR3s in rallies throughout Britain, and seen the incredible punishment that these rugged cars could soak up from the worst of rallying roads, there could be no denying my commitment. Ruggedness and reliability have been the hallmark of Triumphs for many years, but it is also appropriate to point out that the sports cars have often been British and sometimes world pioneers of engineering innovations. The TR3A was certainly the world's first car in volume production to be equipped with disc brakes (and a nod to Jensen for their parallel, if limited, enterprise); the TR4 was probably the first to incorporate face-level ventilation; the Spitfire was the first cheap sports car to boast independent rear suspension; and the TR5 was Britain's first motor vehicle with a fuel-injected engine. The Stag's built-in roll-protection bar was actually pre-dated by a similar feature in the hardtop of a TR4, while the 2000 Roadster was, paradoxically, the last production car in the world to be equipped with a dickey seat!

When judging the first of the post-war Triumph sports cars, it is well to remember that they originated in a factory that had had no previous experience in designing or building fast two-seaters. Their instant success demonstrates yet again that good sense, adaptability and speed-to-learn are all hallmarks of a motor industry engineer from Coventry. Technical complexity and mechanical elegance might be somewhat difficult to achieve, but commercial success is even harder. Whatever the merits of the various cars' technical specifications, few would argue with the commercial benefits they conferred upon Standard-Triumph.

With the world's motoring climate apparently changing rapidly at this time, in the face of persistent and not always well-founded anti-pollution and ecological lobbyists, public taste appears to be moving away from the raucous pleasures of driving a TR2, to the more sybaritic delights of conducting a Stag. One can only hope that there *will* be future generations of sports car enthusiasts who will appreciate this breed of car. In particular one can also hope that British Leyland will continue to recognise the prestige – and the profits – that such extrovert products can bring to their image; at the close of this book I record Lord Stokes' thoughts on the subject, and it is good to know how much he favours the sports car and its enthusiasts. The true enthusiast has rarely been faced with so many uncertainties as to his future transport; I hope that future legislation and fashion will not conspire to kill off the fun-car business altogether.

I would like to acknowledge the information, facts and opinions referring to the Triumph company which I found expressed in the following books and magazines:

The Autocar (latterly *Autocar*); British Sports Cars – by Gregor Grant (Published by Foulis); The Car Makers – by Graham Turner (Published by Eyre and Spottiswoode); The Cars that Got Away – by Michael Frostick (Published by Cassell); The Daimler Tradition – by Brian Smith (Published by Transport Bookman); Georges Roesch and the Invincible Talbots – by Anthony Blight (Published by Grenville); Harry Ferguson, Inventor and Pioneer – by Colin Fraser (Published by John Murray); Healeys and Austin-Healeys – by Peter Browning and Les Needham (Published by Foulis); The Leyland Papers – by Graham Turner (Published by Eyre and Spottiswoode); Morgan, First and Last of the Real Sports Cars – by Gregory Houston Bowden (Published by Gentry Books); *The Motor* (latterly *Motor*); *Motor Sport*; Post-war British Thoroughbreds – by Bruce Hudson (Published by Foulis); Riley – by Dr. A.T. Birmingham (Published by Foulis); Sleepless Knights – by John Sprinzel (Published by Motor Racing Publications); The Standard Motor Company – by John Davy (Published by Sherbourne Press); The Story of the MG Sports Car – by F.Wilson McComb (Published by Dent); The Triumph Companion – by Kenneth Ullyett (Published by Stanley Paul); The Triumph Guide – by Dave Allen and Dick Strome (Published in America by Allen, Strome); Twentieth Century Coventry – by Kenneth Richardson (Published by MacMillan).

Many other individuals have also given unsparingly of their time and their memories to help satisfy my thirst for the truth. I have already mentioned Tony Cook of the Pre-1940 TOC, but I am perhaps equally indebted to the British Leyland public relations offices, especially to Keith Hopkins and James Gee, for their help and for the way in which they have encouraged Triumph engineers and other employees to open their files and their memories for my benefit. All photographs used to illustrate the following pages have been drawn from Triumph files other than those which have been credited to other sources. It would be quite impossible to mention everyone who has helped, but I would like to list the following:

Warren Allport, Walter Belgrove, Gordon Birtwistle, Anthony Blight, William Boddy (Editor of *Motor Sport*), Bill Bradley, Charles Bulmer (Former Editor of *Motor*), Frank Callaby, Tony Cook (Pre-1940 Triumph Owners Club), Peter Cox, Bob Currie, Neil Dangerfield, Alick Dick, Peter Garnier (Editor of *Autocar*), Ian Hall, Donald Healey, Ray Henderson, John Lloyd, Lyndon Mills, Peter Morgan, Ken Richardson, Michael Sedgwick, Lord Stokes of Leyland, Harry Webster, Andrew Whyte.

Brampton, Cumberland,
May 1973 *A.A.G.R.*

CHAPTER 1

Bicycles to cars

TODAY ONE might well think of Triumph in terms of fuel-injected engines, all-independent suspensions, and racing and rallying successes, not to mention large-scale North American sales. They all sound like typical modern sports car attributes, and no-one would deny that Triumph have had their share of these. But the export successes have been almost exclusively post-war. Sports car successes are of post-war extraction, too, though there were several well-liked sports models in the 1920s and 1930s. Triumph was an independent company until 1939, and in many ways typical of Coventry's sprawling complex of motor firms of the 1930s. Unhappily, there were times when no sports car appeared in the Triumph line-up, times when the oft-changing management turned its back resolutely on any other than middle-class motoring, and times when sales were by no means substantial. But the earliest Triumphs were not even mechanically-propelled machines of any description.

The Triumph name can, in fact, be traced back into the last few years of the nineteenth century, to Coventry where there lived – as was to become so typical of the origins of Coventry's great motor industry – a humble maker of pedal-cycles. Siegfried Bettman, born in Nuremberg, Germany, in 1863 of Jewish parents, came to England in 1883, first of all to work for the Kelly's Directories publishing company. But soon Bettman's sharp business mind turned to thoughts of his own company, and settled on the idea of making his fortune by producing and selling pedal-cycles, which in the last quarter of the century had become socially acceptable things to own. Mechanically-driven devices, whether powered by steam or more precariously by one of the new-fangled 'explosion engines', had yet to achieve any form of reliability. Bettman's company was founded before any 'autocar' or powered two-wheeler had found its way on to the still-atrociously surfaced British highways, and there seems to be little doubt that his business horizons at the time were firmly limited to the sale of pedal-cycles. Bettman and Co was joined, in 1887, by Mauritz Johann Schulte, another expatriate German, who was soon to become the company's guiding genius. Schulte was always interested in expanding the partnership, and in getting involved in the exciting possibilities of the new internal combustion engines, about which he had heard so many extraordinary stories from France and Germany.

Bettman's first pedal-cycles were built on his behalf by a William Andrews of Birmingham, and it was not until 1890 that Siegfried Bettman and Mauritz Schulte themselves moved north to Coventry, where manufacture of pedal-cycles eventually started in a small factory in Coventry's Much Park Street, very close to the eventual site chosen by Walter Maudslay's Standard Motor Company, which was also to begin its days in Coventry. It is coincidences and juxtapositions such as this which make Coventry's industrial development so fascinating; names and geographical locations intermingle regularly, and the miracle of it all is that so many firms stayed independent for so long! To gain immediate expansion and commercial expertise, Bettman approached a Mr Sawyer, then Manager of the White Sewing Machine Company, to give backing to his enterprise. Sawyer agreed, the initial capital was set at £10,000, whereupon Sawyer was appointed Chairman, with Bettman and Schulte as joint Managing Directors.

The Triumph *marque* appears to have been evolved at this very early stage, not for any particularly vainglorious reason, or because the company had anything in particular to boast about. It was more likely to be because of Bettman's commendably ambitious Teutonic nature; additionally the name is reputed to have been chosen because it was a suitably forceful name which sounded much the same, and had similar connotations, in a variety of European languages. Exports, it seems, were already in Bettman's plans.

The first time that the originators and predecessors of the Triumph Cycle Company became involved with the internal combustion engine was in 1895 (not long after Bettman had acquired the larger Priory Street site that was to play such a part in Triumph's fortunes over the years) when Schulte imported one of the earliest motor-cycles, a Wolfmuller, from Germany. This device could not legally be driven on British roads at more than 4 mph before the end of 1896, when the man employed to walk ahead of mechanically propelled devices was finally made redundant (incidentally, the 'red flag' requirement had been rescinded some years earlier though nevertheless one was invariably carried) so Schulte was obliged to carry out early trials on the local Coventry cycle racing track. Experiments were then initiated into the building of a Triumph motor-cycle, though these took a surprisingly long time to mature by the standards of the late 1890s.

However, in the manner of many such expanding businesses in such prosperous times, there were all kinds of commercial changes in the make-up of the company. 1895 saw Harvey du Gros (Chairman and Managing Director of the Dunlop Company) persuaded to provide Dunlop capital to allow for expansion; the new capital employed was then £45,000, and the old company's goodwill was set at £13,369. Only two years later, in 1897, came another reshuffle. Bettman and Co was re-formed as the New Triumph Cycle Company Limited, a title soon altered to the Triumph Cycle Company Limited. Bettman and Schulte were joined as directors in this venture by P. Schloss, Alfred Fridlander and Alderman Albert Tomson. Commercial undercurrents detectable here were that Albert Tomson had been the owner of the Much Park Street works before Bettman had started to use it, while both Schloss and Fridlander were active members of Coventry's Jewish community, through which activities they had come to know Bettman. Tomson was to be the Triumph Cycle Company's first Chairman, with Bettman and Schulte joint Managing Directors as before. Thus Triumph came to be established, and proceeded to make an early name for itself, as a manufacturer of one-man-power machines.

Schulte's very first Triumph motor-cycle used a Beeston Cycle Co engine, and was exported to Australia, but by all accounts it was not a success. Indeed, it was not until 1902 that the first motor-cycle was offered for sale, this being a specially modified and strengthened pedal-cycle frame to which an imported $2\frac{1}{4}$ hp Belgian Minerva engine had been fastened, thence transmitting its power to the rear wheels by belt. Minerva, like several other famous names in the fledgling motor industry (Adler, Pierce, Fiat and Renault to name but a few others) had originally become manufacturers by courtesy of engines supplied from the dominant French firm de Dion Bouton. Indirectly, therefore, Triumph may be seen to have been influenced by that doyen of all French companies from whom Minerva, and therefore Triumph, gleaned their original commercial successes.

Triumph employees topped 100 almost at once, this figure building up rapidly as both pedal-cycle and motor-cycle sales boomed. Imported engines sufficed for a time, but Mr J.A. Prestwich's JAP concern also supplied engines for a while, as did Fafrin. Motor-cycle sales soon took over the bulk of the business, though in 1906, when Triumph's own engine was first offered, this only amounted to 533 machines. That there were, at that time, no fewer than twenty-two motor-cycle manufacturers in Coventry *alone*, gives some idea of the way in which the motor industry was at that time fragmented, precarious and motivated by hope. Triumph motor-cycle production, however, rose steadily, topping 1,000 units in 1907, doubling in 1908, and exceeding 3,000 in 1909.

During this time Bettman had really integrated himself into the mainstream of Coventry's business community, joining the City Council in 1903. Following the death of Albert Tomson, Bettman became Chairman of his own company, and in 1911 also took on the chairmanship of the Standard Motor Company, thus establishing an early – if spiritual – link between the two companies that was not to develop into anything more concrete for a further generation.

Standard had been founded by Reginald Walter Maudslay in 1903, operating from premises in Much Park Street. His financial partner, Charles (later Sir Charles) Friswell, quarrelled with him in 1911, so Friswell's share of the Standard business was purchased by Bettman with the help of Charles Band, later to become Standard's Chairman himself. Following this by becoming Mayor of the City of Coventry in 1913 and 1914 (the first non-British subject to hold this position) Bettman could truly be said to have reached the pinnacle of business achievement. The Great War, however, which soon generated anti-German hysteria which was even applied without thought to long-dead composers like Beethoven, as well as to anyone known to have German relations, soon put paid to Bettman's larger ambitions. He was effectively frozen out of the chairmanship of Standards, though nothing could oust him from his own company.

During the Edwardian era, Triumph's fortunes had gone from strength to strength. The machines were soon to become known as 'Trusty Triumphs', a popularity greatly to be augmented during the Great War by the performance and record of the Model H used by despatch riders in such large numbers. Production of the 550 cc three-speed belt-driven machines was pushed up from 50 to 70 every week at Triumph, and 30,000 examples were supplied to the British Army alone. The first overhead-valve Triumph engine came about at this time when Sir Harry Ricardo began his lengthy association with the company; the new 'Ricardo' engine not only had valves overhead, but no fewer than four of them, an attribute considered daring in air-cooled engines at the time, though soon to become very popular in water-cooled car engines, notably in W.O. Bentley's post-war products. Ricardo's expertise was also to be used when the company ventured into motor-car production, but the association had lapsed some time before the company's financial failure in 1939. In spite of the stories banded around at the time, the Ricardo - Triumph link was *not* resumed in the 1960s for the Dolomite/Stag engines, there having been much confusion on this point due to the somewhat convoluted relationship between Triumph and Saab, Saab and Ricardo.

Bettman's Triumph company, like so many others at the time, had profited greatly in the Great War, and immediately after the 1919 Armistice had decided to enter the car manufacturing business. The time was ripe, it was thought, for an assault on the middle-class market, whose motorised experiences in the Great War had led them to desire their own transport in the peace that was to follow. Triumph were in no hurry to release a new design that might be unreliable, but the same could not be said of many others. In that post-war boom year of 1920 no fewer than 59 new motor manufacturing concerns came into being. That Triumph persisted in developing cars, even in the face of such crowded competition, and survived where scores failed, must have been due partly to chance, but mostly to the sound financial backing and commercial expertise engendered by the motor-cycle products. As to their prospects for the future, I can do no better than to quote Bunny Tubbs' feature written in 1973 as part of *Autocar*'s '100 Motoring Years' Supplement:

'Never has there been more variety than in the boom year of 1920. Good pre-Great War cars changed hands at colossal prices for those days, and new cars were at a premium. Everywhere, new firms sprung up; some of them designing cycle cars, a crude form of motorised joke, some with lush engineering designed for a luxury market, and yet others with cars mainly assembled from bought-out components . . . Between 1919 and 1924 the number of cars on the road in Britain multiplied by four times, and between 1924 and 1930 it doubled again, topping the million mark. New car buyers were trooping through the showrooms all the time, most of them wanting cars that were comfortable, weather-tight, and easy to drive . . . '

At that time (1920) there was no hint of the slump years that were speedily to threaten post-

The first Triumph – the 10/20 open two-seater with dickey seat for one, a 1,393 cc, 23 bhp engine and rear brakes only. It was released in 1923

war prosperity, nor of the way in which prosperity in the 1930s was at best a tenuous and ill-nourished flower. No fewer than 100 British car manufacturers were listed as attending the Olympia Motor Show that year, yet there was no way of knowing that this number would be reduced to a mere 31 by the end of the Vintage years. Yet paradoxically enough, even the economic blizzard of the early 1930s failed to kill off many more, and a slightly higher number of makes – 37 – existed on the outbreak of the Second World War in 1939.

The design of the first Triumph car appears to have been started during 1920, though it is doubtful if Bettman and his team had much idea as to where they would eventually assemble production examples. Certainly the original intention was to make as many as possible of the new car's mechanical components within the well-equipped Priory Street factories, yet these buildings, each being crowded and no less than seven stories high, were quite unsuited for final vehicle assembly. Bettman, however, was astute enough to realise that additional factory premises might become available to him as one or other of Coventry's hopeful new manufacturers folded up.

Public release of the first Triumph car was delayed until early 1923, partly because of the problems of finding a home for the product, but the first news came in the form of controlled leaks in the 'establishment' motoring press. *The Autocar*, for instance, who at that time never stepped out of line unless encouraged to do so by a publicity-conscious car maker, stated in December 1921 that '. . . it has been known for some time past that the Triumph Cycle Company Ltd was interesting itself in the production of a light car'. The magazine then went on to confirm that Bettman's business sense had been justified and they remarked that Triumph had gone so far as to purchase the works and fittings of the Dawson Car Company, also of Coventry. It was presumed that these purchases of machinery and a factory in Clay Lane, Stoke, Coventry, would be the first concrete step towards series production. Certainly it had become abundantly clear that assembly would not be at Priory Street, especially as the motor-cycles' success was, if anything, even greater than during the War itself. *The Autocar* hazarded a guess that there were probably more Triumph motor-cycles on the road than any other make.

Production of mechanical components, then, was to be at Priory Street, by now one of the biggest motor industry complexes in Coventry. One must remember that in 1921 there was no vast and concentrated motor industry; the huge Chrysler UK factory at Ryton, the Standard plant at Canley, and the Jaguar factories in Allesley were all mere gleams in some civil servant's eye, not to appear before the late 1930s and even then being intended as 'shadow' factories for production of war machines. Humber and Hillman made cars alongside each other in Humber Road, Standard were in business at Canley in a smaller way, and other important names now long gone included Riley, Singer and Lea-Francis. Triumph's Priory Street premises were right in the heart of the city, and were always to figure strongly in the history of the concern, right up to its dying gasps during the Second World War. Priory Street was, however, virtually obliterated on the night of November 14th/15th 1940, when a massed raid of German bombers did its best to raze Coventry to the ground; after that there wasn't a lot left. The city's fourteenth-century perpendicular-style cathedral church of St Michael also faced out onto Priory Street, and became its most famous (or notorious) casualty, though in truth the whole of Priory Street was effectively flattened. Coventry has been completely rebuilt, and redesigned, in the last thirty years; apart from a length of road alongside the dramatically-fashioned new cathedral, Priory Street has ceased to exist. The Triumph site, once occupied by a priory (which explains the derivation of the name) is now covered by the Halls of Residence for the Lanchester College of Technology, and by the Olympic-standard municipal swimming-pool.

The 10/20 sports making a re-start on the Test Hill at Brooklands in 1924 (Picture: Autocar)

Despite the fact that times became progressively harder in Coventry during 1921 – unemployment in the city's engineering trades topped 33 per cent in the autumn of 1921 – Bettman and Schulte were brave enough to persist in their planning. Yet when Billy Morris' fledgling Morris Motors concern ran into financial trouble a short time afterwards Bettman refused to inherit an already known design by buying him out, thus failing to change the shape of Britain's motor industry for many years to come. In the terminology of the present day, he appeared quite determined to 'do his own thing', and there might indeed have been an element of spite in this, for Bettman was never to forget the snubs cast upon him by the anti-German citizens of Coventry a few years previously.

The site chosen for four-wheeler assembly, the old Dawson factory at Clay Lane, was perhaps half-a-mile from Priory Street, and a mere hefty stone's throw from the city's football stadium in Highfield Road. At the time, Clay Lane was on the very edge of the city's built-up area – another two miles of housing have been added since then – and it was not for several years more that Briton Road was to be built behind the factory, thus giving it its final address of the 1930s. Of the Dawson car, what should one say? Like many of the other post-war projects, it was neither a technical nor a financial success, and there is absolutely no reason to suppose that Triumph bought the concern to get at the mechanical niceties of the Dawson car. Very few, if any, Dawson cars survive, and although there were certain general similarities between the Dawson and Triumph layout these were merely symptomatic of the period. There was no badge-engineering as such (a phrase still unknown in the naive 1920s) and any firm link can be discounted. Dawson, as a maker of cars, had certainly perished before Triumph bought Clay Lane.

Having bought and equipped their new factory, Triumph were then ready to show their car to the public. April 1923 saw the release of the new car, which in fairness can hardly have been called 'long-awaited' because the motoring public had no reason to suspect that a Triumph would be any more viable than had several other light cars shown around the same time. Called the 10/20 hp model (this referred to the new-fangled and already hated Treasury Rating of 10 horsepower – based on a formula which considered cylinder bore but not stroke – and to an actual developed power of around twice that figure). In the manner of the day, the new car was offered at first only as an open 2/3-seater tourer, though a sports version and Weymann-bodied saloons and tourers were soon to be added. It was obvious from the first descriptions that there was no technical innovation to be seen from any corner of the car's specification. It looked, and was intended to be, a thoroughly conventional, respectable, and reliable middle-class car. *The Autocar*'s observation that 'Possibly the name of Triumph is better known to motor-cyclists than to users of cars, but wherever it is recognised at all it is connected with a reputation for superlatively fine workmanship' seemed to sum up the desired effect perfectly.

The three years of experimental work, delayed somewhat by a search for premises, had not given rise to anything startling, especially as it became known that Triumph were not the designers of their engines, neither were they intending to undertake manufacture of bodies at first. No less an authority than Sir Harry Ricardo had been retained to design the engine – a conventional looking side-valve four-cylinder – no doubt because of the high regard in which his motor-cycle engines were now held. Though overhead valves had already been applied to the motor-cycles, nothing so advanced (or expensive ?) was to be given to the car's engine and in almost every way its layout was unexceptional. The cylinder bore and stroke were respectively 63.5 x 110 mm, equal to a swept volume of no more than 1,393 cc; this stroke, incidentally, was in excess of that of any British engine in production fifty years later, but was considered quite normal in the 1920s when the fiscal charges were thought more serious than the revving capability of a design. With a 10 hp Treasury Rating, the annual road fund tax was £10, which may seem little enough half a century later, but in fact was the equivalent of five times as much at contemporary values. The actual power output claimed was 23.5 bhp (gross, no doubt) at 3,000 rpm – a creditable rate of revolutions for a long-stroke design of the early 1920s, helped along by Ricardo's latest thinking in the cylinder-head department, and by updraught Zenith carburation. Lubrication was of the then universally accepted variety with no pressure-fed oil to the crankshaft bearings, but a dip bath and splash arrangement to transfer oil from the shallow sump to the cylinder walls and main bearings. This was achieved by means of dippers in the big-end bosses of the connecting rods arranged to scoop oil from the bath at the bottom of their travel and hurl it up the cylinder walls later in the revolution.

The engine construction was rather more complex than was to become usual in later years. The cylinder block itself, incorporating a water jacket, was separate from the crankcase, and on assembly was dropped into and fastened to the crankcase rather like a linked set of wet liners. The cylinder head, because of the side-valve layout, was a simple and shallow casting with generous water passages. The crankcase looked very rigid, with side walls extending downwards several inches below the crankshaft centre-line, and was closed by a shallow oil pan. The side camshaft drive was from a gear on the nose of the crankshaft, via a Fabroil intermediate gear, which also provided a drive to the oscillating-plunger oil pump. There were H-section connecting rods of great length, white metal shell-type big-end bearings, and slipper-pattern aluminium-alloy pistons.

The chassis, too, was unexceptional, comprising channel-section side-members with cross-members riveted rather than welded into place. Suspension was by half-elliptic leaf springs front and rear, and there appeared to be no shock absorbers at all. Artillery-pattern road wheels were specified, and in the manner of the day, though soon to become unfashionable, only rear-wheel brakes were provided. As the progenitor of a breed, this Triumph was unique in one respect in that it was the only model ever to be marketed without four-wheel brakes, or more particularly without hydraulic brakes. The wheelbase was 8ft 6in, and both tracks 3ft 10in. The unladen weight appears to have gone unrecorded in contemporary literature, and only two cars survive, but a fair guess would have been approximately 1,800 to 2,000 lb dry weight. The four-speed gearbox was mounted centrally, remote from the engine, and there was a right-hand gearchange. The rear axle was a conventional spiral-bevel type, the batteries were stored under the seats, and there was neither fan nor water pump – all typical design features in the early 1920s.

The basic tourer body, to be built for Triumph by the Regent Carriage Company of Fulham Road, London, was panelled in steel, had separate front seats, plus a feature that lasted longer on Triumphs than on any other make of car – a dickey seat. Since the new car's track was narrow and the body similarly styled, it is not surprising that the dickey was only laid out to accommodate one willing (and chilly, no doubt) passenger. With the hood erected this poor individual had little view and no opportunity of conversation with those up front – yet such seats were popular in many makes in Vintage years. No saloon version was offered at first, as conventional coachbuilt steel bodies exacted awful weight and performance penalties as then conceived.

The normal bodywork was erected from wooden framing with steel panels, but an early option was the first car to emanate from Triumph called a sports model, being a strictly two-seater version without the dickey, having front and rear wings flared into the running boards, and being clothed in aluminium. Reminiscent in more than one way of the 30/98 Vauxhall, the 10/20 sports model was not endowed with any noticeable engine tuning, although reputedly it was given a cylinder-head with modified combustion chambers and improved breathing.

Chronologically this car appeared at just about the same time as the first Morris Garages Specials, the forerunners of the MGs, and that Triumph did not instantly persevere with the development of sporting cars is certainly due to the absence of another Cecil Kimber on their staff, for the 10/20 sports model was both as attractive and potentially as rapid as the Morris Garages cars. *The Autocar*'s April 1924 road test talked in terms of '. . . a comparatively small unit sufficient to propel the sporting car in the region of a mile a minute'. That region might, in the diplomatic manner of the day, have meant a rather breathless 55 mph, but from such a 1,393 cc engine it was creditable enough.

But high-volume sales were unlikely to be achieved, even if the product had been of world-shattering performance, for Triumph had no wish to attack the none-too-certain low-price markets. Their middle-class leanings ensured that the 10/20 tourer sold for a solid £430, and the aluminium-panelled sports model for £425. Since the value of money has changed so much in the subsequent fifty years, one might reflect that such an example of the automobile designer's work would cost in the region of £2,000 in today's terms, for which privilege one would pay the Government well over £50 in Road Fund licence fees annually! Certainly by comparison with other established makes, the 10/20 was not cheap. Billy Morris' 11.9 hp Cowley cost £198 at the time (to be slashed to £150 the following year), a Standard 11 cost £235, a Wolseley 10 £250, and the more substantial Austin 12 £375. As far as the sports model was concerned, an open two-seater Morris Garages Special sold for £350. No doubt Bettman was right in his marketing approach, for the company, once established as car makers, did not falter in its intent. The first four-seater version of the 10/20 arrived during 1924 when Triumph enterprisingly wedded four seats in a tourer layout to the Weymann method of flexible panel assembly. This car also displayed one feature that many would appreciate today – a single door on the driver's side of the car, and two doors on the kerb side!

Having established a name in the industry, the next step was to expand the range, which duly happened at the 1924 Olympia Motor Show in the shape of a 12.8 hp five-seater tourer. Here, no doubt, was a more substantial car on which sporting bodywork could be erected, but Triumph did not pursue this. Mechanically the 12.8 resembled the 10/20 in many respects, with a much enlarged engine displacing 1,873 cc, and a bore and stroke of 72 x 115 mm. There was a longer wheelbase, wider tracks, and a three-speed gearbox. The 12.8's only claim to fame was as the very first British car to be advertised and sold with the revolutionary Lockheed hydraulic brakes, which had contracting bands instead of the later internally-expanding variety. The new engine had a combined block and crankcase and the significant advance of pressure-fed oil to the big-end and camshaft bearings. The new unit boasted 36 bhp.

The original Triumph 10/20 lasted a mere two years in the showrooms, and the 12.8 hp model was soon supplemented by the yet larger and more middle-class Light 15. Although the new car had an engine of 15 Treasury Rating horsepower, it was by no means light, and certainly never exhibited any sporting pretensions; both these cars may be pushed aside firmly for study by the chronicler of the definitive history of the more mundane Triumph models.

By 1927, four years after the first car had been shown to the public, Triumph were ready to look to wider markets. They appeared to have a secure name, and needed to fill out the capacity of their Clay Lanes facility, which had been expanded since its acquisition in 1921. Early models had been well-built and of high quality, but they were expensive, and it was thought that the time had now come to start making smaller (and by definition cheaper) models. A few years earlier there would have been no respectable precedent of how this should be tackled, but since Herbert Austin's cheeky little Austin Seven had been setting new sales records ever since its release to a startled motoring world in 1922 a new standard had been set. Triumph, therefore, determined to make their own quality-first version of a Seven, though as Billy Morris had also had the same idea it was clear that sales of Triumph Sevens would not casually be achieved.

The Super Seven sports car dates from 1927. This is a 1931 model (Picture: Autocar)

Imitation, it is often proclaimed, is the sincerest form of flattery, and in the case of the new small Triumph it was quite obvious that Triumph were flattering the Austin Seven. Herbert Austin's best-selling baby, it will be remembered, was reputedly conceived, drawn and detailed by a single draughtsman in the billiards room of Austin's own home, and eventually reached the public *via* the Olympia Show at the end of 1922. By 1926, when the Triumph Super Seven was started, the Austin Seven was already a great success, and had dragged the financial threshold of motoring down very significantly. No-one, surely, would say that all the Austin's engineering was sound – idiosyncratic is probably a better word for some of its features – but there was no doubt of its appeal, especially in terms of size, fuel consumption and price. Bettman therefore decided that here was the sort of car that could

Interiors were sparse in those days. This was the Supercharged Super Seven. There were no doors to the bodywork – you clambered in or out (Picture: Autocar)

fill out his factories, expand sales, and bring the name of Triumph to a wider public; more important, it would help to bridge the gap between the Triumph motor-cycle and car owners, and it was hoped that the motor-cyclist would be encouraged to 'trade up' to a Super Seven.

Designing the new car was going to be no less of a problem than it had been for the first four-wheelers, for there was still no effective engine and transmission design department, no stylists, and no body layout draughtsmen! The lack of a body design office had not been thought serious at first, for cars were almost universally square-rigged and had their bodies wrapped firmly and squarely round the seats and rudimentary facia. However, the advent of viable saloon car styles, and the continued trend to lowered roofs and higher performance, made attention to body shapes worthwhile. The Super Seven was not to receive such attentions, but by the time it was released there had been a sign of change in this respect.

One of the earliest employees in the design section was Walter Belgrove, who figures strongly in many later models which crop up in Triumph's sports car history. Belgrove joined Triumph towards the end of 1927 and was surprised to learn that '. . . the company lacked a body drawing office and design section in those days. The models, like Topsy in "Uncle Tom's Cabin" just growed. This was, however, to be rectified about 1931, I think, when Frank Warner joined the company as Chief Body Engineer, following a change of policy by the company.'

Chassis design and general layout went ahead rapidly during the winter of 1926/27, while the body designs 'just growed'. The engine layout would have to be all-new, and once again was to be entrusted to Harry Ricardo, though it was to be produced *in toto* by the well-equipped machine shops in Priory Street. On accouncement in time for Olympia, in September 1927, the Super Seven (all Triumphs of this family were to be Supers for some years) was seen to resemble the Austin Seven fairly closely as to styling, and in general mechanical layout, yet was considerably better equipped and therefore more expensive. Even if the car's engineering had been pared down to the same limitations as the Austin Seven, Triumph could never have sold it at the same price (the cheapest Austin Seven sold for £135) and made a profit, because there was no way that their small factory could have turned out as many cars. They were under-capitalised as always, neither were they blessed with the sort of dealer organisation that Herbert Austin enjoyed. The Super Seven was to run alongside the 12.8s and Light 15s for a time, the original 10/20 model having run out at the end of 1925. The Super Seven was advertised as being the last word in its class, and to have equipment not to be found on any other Sevens then on the market.

The Super Seven was in all respects a very small car. The wheelbase of 6ft 9in and tracks of 3ft 6in saw to that, while an overall length of a mere 9ft 10in for the saloon (less than that of the BMC Minis) gave promise of no more passenger space other than provision for four people, sitting bolt upright, rubbing shoulders closely, and in considerable discomfort; in other words it gave very much the same sort of habitability as the Austin Seven. Comfort and adequate passenger space were not thought essential for the sort of people who could afford this sort of car – they would, no doubt, be grateful to be able to travel in relative comfort, instead of braving the elements in their own motor-cycle combinations. The thought that the marginal motorist came in a smaller size than the more prosperous one was a tenet which persisted in the British motor industry for at least another thirty years.

Mechanically the new car was conventional. The chassis frame, in the vogue of the period, was simple and none-too-rigid, with channel-section pressed side-members linked by a minimum of cross-bracing (of which the engine/gearbox unit also played its part), and stopped short of the rear axle line after the manner of the Austin Seven. Front suspension was conventional, by half-elliptic leaf springs damped by a single transverse friction damper, but at the rear Triumph again aped the Austin with trailing quarter-elliptic springs supporting a worm-drive back axle. The four-wheel brakes, definitely in advance of the Austin, were of impressively large dimensions – $9\frac{1}{2}$ in diameter, hydraulically-operated, and now of the conventional internal-expanding type. There was a separate transmission handbrake. The Ricardo-designed engine had four cylinders, a bore and stroke of 56.5 x 83 mm (equivalent to a fiscal rating of 7.9 hp and a swept volume of 832 cc), and had the luxury for such a small engine of a three-bearing crankshaft. The engine also boasted a cooling fan, but in other respects was completely conventional. Side valves were, of course, specified, though the cylinder block and crankcase were cast in one piece. There was pressure-fed oil to the bearings of the crankshaft and camshaft, splash lubrication being retained for the pistons and cylinder walls. Power output, probably around 15 bhp, was not disclosed. A non-synchromesh three-speed gearbox was in unit with the engine, fitted with a long, central control, change lever. Although 19 in artillery-style road wheels were specified, the rear axle ratio was as high, numerically, as 5.25 to 1, such gearing being necessary to ensure adequate performance, even though the saloon's unladen weight was a mere 1,250 lb.

Two-door coachbuilt saloons (£192) and two-door Weymann-bodied saloons (£187) were offered, but for the more sporty-minded there was an attractive little two-seater sports version, which sold for £167 10s, though the cheapest version of all was a four-seater tourer for which £149 10s was asked. The sports two-seater had no pretensions to extra-special styling, looking remarkably like the Austin Seven two-seaters from some angles, having a 1920s-standard duck-tail style with flat deck.

As to performance the Super Seven saloon was no ball of fire. *The Autocar* recorded 46 to 48 mph in its test the following spring, but commented that the car showed two outstanding features – good springing and good brakes. Nevertheless there was the comment: 'When the car is first occupied there is an impression of slight rolling in the suspension, although in half an hour the feeling is forgotten'. Forgotten by the testers, no doubt, but presumably an indication that the car was a little high and narrow, without really effective damping. Fuel consumption in the saloon was a frugal 42 mpg, and the hydraulic brakes were said to be really effective.

Though the sports two-seater was not particularly fast, there was a limited-production version fitted with a supercharged engine which was a very bright little car. Supercharging was by courtesy of a Cozette blower, drawing its air-fuel mixture through a Zenith carburettor mounted inaccessibly low and behind it. As far as competitions are concerned, Triumph were not particularly interested, and although the supercharged cars were entered for a variety of Brooklands races (notably driven by Vic Horsman, at times winning outer circuit handicap races at up to 80 mph) they were usually overshadowed by the more specialised racing Austin Sevens and the MG Midgets. Nevertheless the Supercharged Seven was fast, if temperamental; *The Autocar*'s testers said: 'The supercharged Super Seven is capable of close on 70 mph . . . The effect of the Cozette supercharger is to improve the acceleration at low speeds a little, and the acceleration at high speeds a very great deal. The engine is rendered smoother, it gains an astonishing verve, and settles down to pull at 55 to 60 mph as if it had an unlimited number of cylinders'. It is interesting to remind oneself of what was acceptable in the late 1920s, though, for the bodywork was not equipped with doors, the sides being flush-fitting.

Vic Horsman raced a single-seater version of a Supercharged Super Seven with some success. This picture was taken after the car had won a Brooklands Long Handicap at 78.25 mph in 1929 (Picture: C. Posthumus)

There was a considerable price penalty for anyone who required the privilege of specifying individual coachwork and supercharging – the Supercharged Seven cost £250. Reading between the lines of the tests it may be inferred that the engines were always liable to suffer from sooted-up sparking plugs unless driven in an enterprising manner at all times, and they must have been fairly difficult to keep in perfect tune.

Although the Sevens broke no records on the track, they did achieve a modicum of success in rallies. It was in a perfectly standard Super Seven saloon that a young motor trader from Cornwall – no less a person than Donald Healey, whose name was to become much more closely linked with Triumph in later years – competed in the 1929 Monte Carlo Rally. Due to start from Riga, but unable even to get there because of the appalling weather and deep snow, Healey then elected to start from Berlin. Weather conditions throughout Europe that year were nothing short of 'ice-age', and although it would be nice to add a fairy tale ending to this particular paragraph it must be said that Healey's little car ran out of time in France's many snow drifts, finally arriving in Monte Carlo a mere two minutes outside the time limit for qualification.

Nothing daunted by this, Healey then entered the same little car for the 1930 event, drove through another series of difficult sections (winters appeared to be much more severe forty years ago in Europe) and finished a very creditable seventh overall, the best performance by a British car. This must have been a truly heroic performance, especially in a car that must have been pushed to achieve a maximum speed of 50 mph, and in which heating and comfort might charitably be said to have been non-existent. There was little reaction from Triumph to this success, one understands, with the predictable result that Healey then abandoned the marque the following year, when he drove an Invicta to a splendid outright victory. In the meantime, however, Healey had collected Lands End Trials Gold Medals in a sports Triumph, and used one to win the Brighton Rally outright in 1930.

Even so, by the end of 1930 it would still be untrue to suggest that Triumph had succeeded in establishing themselves as manufacturers of sports cars. Unlike MG at Abingdon, who had decided to make nothing but sporting cars, Triumph were still committed to making small saloon and touring cars of undeniable quality, the sporting products being very much of a sideline. The economic blizzard that struck Britain in 1931 must surely have put them off such frivolous pastimes for good, if logical economic thinking had been applied, but in Coventry's motor industry such logical thought was often absent. The company, still buoyed-up by the considerable reputation and profitable activities of the motorcycle division, was in any case contemplating radically new policies and designs, one of which was that future sporting cars were to be more specialised, even if they were not prepared to embrace a competitions department and a racing programme like MG were doing at Abingdon, or Singer on the other side of Coventry. The main reason for this was that the company's founder, Siegfried Bettman, was now looking forward to retirement, and was organising a new management team around him before doing so. He had already quarrelled with Mauritz Schulte, who had left the company, and the most favoured personality to take over the reins was an ex-Army officer called Holbrook, whom Bettman had recruited during the 1920s. Lt-Col Claude Vivian Holbrook (the third son of Sir Arthur Holbrook, himself a noted soldier) was 45 years old in 1931, and had served with distinction in World War One. Credited with the CBE in 1919, he had first met and impressed Bettman over dealings concerning the supply of Triumph motor-cycles to the Armed Forces during the war. Holbrook's principal attribute was organisation, and this was rewarded in 1931 when he became Assistant Managing Director. At the same time Bettman invited the influential local landowner Lord Leigh (the 75 year old 3rd Baron of Stoneleigh) to become the company's Chairman; Lord Leigh had already been connected with other Coventry car manufacturers, and had at one time lent the name of 'Stoneleigh' to a car produced by Armstrong Siddeley. Lord Leigh had been Lord Lieutenant of Warwickshire since 1921, and his Triumph appointment was thought to bring prestige to the company.

In the same year, the admission that cars were commercially as important as motor-cycles became formalised when the company's title was changed to The Triumph Company Limited, all reference to cycles being dropped. That year's company report pointed out that the Clay Lane factory had been expanded to include a building in Briton Road which – being back-to-back with the Clay Lane works – could be rapidly integrated into it. The new complex was seven times as large as the original ex-Dawson plant bought ten years earlier, it brought the number of Triumph factories in Coventry up to six, and it ensured employment in those difficult days for no fewer than 3,000 people, a very large work-force indeed for Coventry's motor industry at the time. No production records remain, but probably up to 100 or 150 cars a week was the best ever achieved by Triumph in this period when the Super Seven was selling in healthy numbers. Putting this achievement in perspective, it is worth remembering that in 1931 there were no fewer than eleven separate car-producing concerns in Coventry (Alvis, Armstrong-Siddeley, Daimler-Lanchester-BSA, Hillman-Humber, Lea-Francis, Riley, Rover, Singer, Standard, Swift, Triumph – and SS was soon to join in), while a further forty had been started, had risen, and had then fallen away in the years since 1919.

1931 was certainly a year for staff and product changes. Claude Holbrook, once he was firmly esconced as the 'heir-apparent', was determined to change the course of Triumph's model marketing. He was not particularly interested in the motor-cycle side of the business, which nevertheless had supplied the major part of the company's profits during the 1920s, and he was not happy with the stodgy, rather boxy image presented by the cars. Holbrook was determined to develop the cars into the most elegant, at least, in Coventry, and his first move in this respect was to set up a proper body design and styling department under Frank Warner, Bill Thornton (later to join SS to work closely with William Lyons for the next thirty years) and Walter Belgrove. Experimental work began on a completely new range of cars, in which modern styling, good handling and high performance were due to predominate. Decisions also had to be made about future engine designs. With a new range of heavier and, hopefully, faster models in view, new engines would be required for further development of the little four-cylinder Super Seven/Super Eight engine, or the six-cylinder Scorpion unit which was related to it, was neither possible nor desirable. Since Triumph were capable neither of designing nor of financing new designs of their own at that stage, it became necessary to look around for proprietary units which would fill the bill. Fortunately there were several companies supplying the motor industry's engine needs in the early 1930s, and Triumph's choice fell upon a local firm, Coventry Climax, whose factories were situated only a mile or so away. Climax could offer several engines, and since Holbrook was looking for a related range between perhaps one-litre and two-litres, they seemed to be an obvious choice. The snag was that Coventry Climax were not able to supply the quantities which Holbrook was forecasting (this was at the height of the depression of 1931, and it must have been a brave man who even considered his company's existence in the following years), so the transition would have to take place slowly.

First fruits of this arrangement came in the autumn of 1931, when the new Super Nine saloon was announced. There was no mention in the new car's description of the engine being anything other than a Triumph design, but with its bore and stroke of 60 x 90 mm, and a swept volume of 1,018 cc (Treasury Rating of 8.9 hp) the *cognoscenti* recognised its parentage at once. The engine itself had a three-bearing crankshaft and side camshaft, but an interesting cylinder-head arrangement, where the inlet valves were overhead, operated via pushrods and rockers, while the exhaust valves were in the normal (or should one say obsolescent?) position at the side, with the sparking plug directly over the exhaust valve and main combustion chamber. Camshaft and dynamo shared the same chain drive, chain adjustment being by tensioning the dynamo away from the cylinder block on an adjustable clamp; coil ignition was standardised. The Super Nine, as announced, was no sports car, but in the spring of the following year Triumph showed off a true sporting derivative of it, based very closely on the same chassis and mechanical layout and called the 'Southern Cross' (after the star formation seen over Australia, then one of Triumph's best export markets).

The Southern Cross chassis, like that of the Nine, used half-elliptic leaf springs to suspend

The Super Seven Sports – smart and simply finished (Picture: Motor, ex Light Car)

Triumph's first bigger sporting car – the 1932 Southern Cross. It used a Super Nine chassis, and a Coventry Climax-designed engine (Picture: Autocar)

both axles, and had Lockheed hydraulic brakes (now no longer much of a novelty). It also had additional cross-bracing behind the gearbox, and like the Nine and other future Triumph cars the Southern Cross was fitted with wire-spoked wheels. Wheelbase and track were 7ft 8½in and 3ft 9in, respectively, making them identical with the saloon's chassis, and there was a four-speed gearbox with long whippy central control change lever, and a worm-drive axle.

The smart, though high-waisted open body, had its spare wheel mounted externally at the rear, and was panelled throughout in aluminium. Although the car was a four-seater, the rear seats could be and often were covered by a tonneau; they were situated immediately above the axle, and consequently were placed several inches higher than the separate front seats. Body design was by Ratcliffe, but built by Salmons and Son, whose trade name was Tickford, at Newport Pagnell. The price was set at £225, which probably represented better value than any previous Triumph with sporting inclinations, including as it did a fold-flat windscreen, Brooklands steering wheel, a full array of impressive-looking instruments, and an unladen weight of no more than 1,790 lb. Performance tests do not appear to have been published for this car, but road impressions suggest that it could reach at least 70 mph in top gear, with upwards of 50 mph in third. The Coventry Climax engine was basically identical with that fitted in the Super Nine when the Southern Cross was announced, but before the end of the summer it had been joined by the more powerful option of an 1,122 cc version, this being the same engine bored out from 60 mm to 63 mm; Treasury Rating went up to 10 hp.

It was at about this time that Triumph joined the fashion of meeting an apparent public demand for tiny-capacity six-cylinder-engined saloons by producing the Triumph Scorpion. Like the other six-cylinder mongrels, the Scorpion was nothing more than the Super Nine's chassis and body with a six-cylinder version of the old side-valve Eight hung out over the front axle. The

The Southern Cross chassis. Note the transmission handbrake drum behind the gearbox and the worm-drive axle (Picture: Autocar)

engine size was 1,203 cc, the rear-axle ratio no less than 5.25 to 1, and the handling about as abysmal as could be expected. I am deeply indebted to Tony Cook for a reminder that the best thing ever said of the Scorpion was that 'those who bought one usually felt that they had been stung!'. At least Triumph never committed the Wolseley-sin of making a small 'sports car' out of such an undeveloped combination. The Scorpion is best forgotten, as indeed it was very quickly forgotten by the clientele.

There were financial straws in the wind that appear to have been brushed aside at the time. The company's large reserves, built up assidiously by Bettman during the last couple of decades, had suffered badly during the depression. It was necessary to take out a Debenture in favour of Lloyds Bank in 1933 to secure a large bank overdraft, the Ordinary shareholders had seen no dividend since 1930, while the Preference shares bore fruit for the last time in May 1932. There had been losses before, but the accounts for the year ending August 1932 exposed the awful deficit of £145,856. This was a dreadfully disappointing result, even though it could be accommodated by the dwindling reserves. But had Holbrook known it there was worse to come, although in the meantime two very important developments were to take place. Siegfried Bettman finally retired, and 'Gloria' arrived.

CHAPTER 2

The age of elegance

LOOKING BACK, 1933 is seen as a definite watershed in the affairs and development of the Triumph company. In that year Siegfried Bettman retired from active day-to-day management, and a completely new range of cars that was to typify the company's intentions for the rest of the 1930s was announced. Unhappily, 1933 was also a year in which the financial losses reached an all-time record for Triumph, and was the first year in which the company's liquid reserves were exhausted. Not to put too fine a point on it, from 1933 onwards the company's reputation for cars of good design, styling and performance began to pick up, while its finances began to slide inexorably downwards.

Siegfried Bettman resigned as Managing Director on his seventieth birthday, in April 1933, handing over immediately to Lt-Col Claude Holbrook. As Lord Leigh was already Chairman, Bettman could not kick himself upstairs completely, so he took over the honorary position of Vice-Chairman for the time being. This was not to last for long, however, as he retired completely from the Board of Directors towards the end of 1934, when a management shake-up became necessary.

Triumph's policy in marketing one model range with a proprietary and none-too-cheap engine had not made public sense for a time after the Super Nine/Ten cars were announced, but all became clear when a completely new range of delicately styled saloons and tourers was shown in the autumn of 1933. Holbrook's intention to change the whole direction of Triumph car development became apparent when the time came to inspect the new Gloria; the older, smaller and more staid models already in production, some of them since the late 1920s, were clearly destined to take a back seat and were presumed to be due for withdrawal shortly. Whereas the Eights, Nines and Tens, even the Southern Cross sports car, were stubby and perhaps a little dull, the new range of cars were long-wheelbased, rakish, relatively low-slung and undeniably different from all previous Triumphs. The Super Eight, Super Ten and Southern Cross were all to continue, but the only common component in the Glorias was a developed version of the four-cylinder Coventry Climax engine.

The Gloria chassis frames were conventional in layout and came in two wheelbases, depending on the engines fitted. They were rigid, cross-braced with cruciform structures under the passenger cabin, and passed underneath the line of the rear axle to aid the body styling possibilities. Whether or not this did in fact aid styling, the legacy of an underslung frame was to be passed down from model to model, via Walter Belgrove's Dolomite Roadsters and the post-war Triumph 1800 Roadster, until the TR sports prototype was conceived. By 1952, however, it had long since outlived its usefulness, for it had always carried certain disadvantages, including limitation of rear-wheel movement which was to be the subject of strong criticism of the TR2s. The Gloria's front and rear suspension was by half-elliptic leaf springs, and the Lockheed hydraulic brakes were no less than 12 inches in diameter, though the transmission hand brake had been dropped. There was to be a choice of Coventry Climax-designed engines, the basic design being the four-cylinder unit, this time using a slightly smaller cylinder bore (62 mm, giving a swept volume of 1,087 cc) than had been used for the Southern Cross, and the alternative a very similar six-cylinder unit of 1,476 cc. The 'six' shared many components, including connecting rods and valve gear, with the 'four', and had a common stroke of 90 mm, though to keep the Treasury Rating down below 13 hp the cylinder bore was reduced to 59 mm. Students of rationalisation will see that in the space of two short years Triumph had committed themselves to using pistons of identical design, but of 59 mm, 60 mm, 62 mm and 63 mm in diameter! Naturally the six-cylinder engine was considerably longer than the 'four', a difference which was accommodated by providing a 9ft 8in wheelbase, eight inches longer than that of the basic car. The extra eight inches were added to the chassis frame ahead of the passenger compartment, of course, which meant that the 'six' had the longer and intrinsically more rakish bonnet and front wings. Overall lengths also differed by eight inches, but front and rear tracks remained the same at 4ft 0in.

For such an important range of cars, for which a considerable sales volume was forecast, Coventry Climax were in no position to supply built-up engines, and since Triumph already possessed scores of modern machines at Priory Street which had been used to produce the old Ricardo-designed engines they were most anxious to keep them in commission. It was fortunate that Coventry Climax were willing to discuss the question of manufacture under licence as this suited Triumph's needs admirably, as well as allowing Climax to continue supplying engines to their other customers. Under the mutually advantageous agreement Climax received licence payments, supplied castings and forgings, sometimes direct from their own suppliers, and agreed to the attachment on each engine of a label stating that the engine was a 'Triumph by arrangement with Coventry Climax Limited'. Triumph completed all machining, assembly and testing operations at Priory Street. Contemporary sources suggest that the 1,122 cc engine used in the later Southern Cross was supplied complete from Coventry Climax because it had their 'standard' capacity, but all other Triumph-destined engines were built by the car manufacturer.

Gearboxes and rear axles were of ENV manufacture. The four-speed gearbox had no synchromesh – this was still an *avant-garde* feature in Britain, pioneered by Vauxhall in 1932 – but there was the much-advertised and fashionable 'twin-top' feature, which was to say that although first and second gears still had to be engaged by means of sliding pinions, third and top gears were always in constant mesh, engagement to the output shaft being by face-dog teeth. There was an optional free-wheel, claimed to be a help in achieving silent gear-changing, which could be locked in or out of action by a handwheel mounted on the facia; it was automatically locked out of action when reverse gear was engaged. A remote control gear-change mechanism was adopted for the very first time, bringing the short gear-change lever back to the line of the front seats in the best sporting tradition.

There were to be three model variations on the same basic chassis, each with the choice of wheelbase and engine specification. The standard four-door, four-light saloons were supplemented by the Specials (which had slightly tuned engines and rather more standardised equipment) while there was also to be an extremely smooth-looking open tourer, which had four seats, two doors, a fold-flat windscreen and a well-equipped interior. The quoted prices indicated just how much extra engineering and equipment had been put into this new range. Whereas the Southern Cross, continued into 1934, sold at only £215, the Gloria Speed Tourer needed £285 with the same basic engine and probably very similar performance, while the larger Gloria Six Speed Tourer was priced at £325. To get these prices into perspective, the 1100's £285 price-tag compared with the same asking price for an L-Type MG Magna and a Riley Imp at £298. The Gloria Six Tourer cost £325, and sold against a Riley Lynx at £348, a 1½-litre Singer at £285 or an MG Magnette KD at £390.

There was no evidence, therefore, that the Glorias were over-priced, and indeed there was further justification for their pricing when the list of equipment was considered. Upholstery was in real leather, there were permanently-fitted jacks all round, as well as the weirdly complex Startix engine starting system, and Biflex headlamps. One interesting styling detail introduced by Frank

Warner, which as far as is known was never used by any other manufacturer, was the 'adjustable' door profile on the tourers. When the side windows, hood and windscreen were all lowered or removed (the windscreen folded forward) the door looked sleek and well proportioned, partly because the top-of-door line was straight, blending completely with bonnet and rear seat surround lines. However, for those who wanted to use their Glorias in a more sporting manner, perhaps in driving tests where a lot of elbow-winding was inevitable, or even if only to achieve a more sporting appearance, there was a hinged portion that could be folded down. This converted a full-depth door into one having the fashionable cutaway style. There was no difficulty in providing this feature as there were no wind-up door glasses, only removable side-screens, which could be stored in the back when not required.

There has been lively speculation, both at the time and subsequently in Vintage magazines, as to the reason for choosing the name of Gloria, particularly as much publicity was made (and photographs taken) of the new cars with a very well-known fashion model of the period – Miss Gloria, of Selfridges, the London department store – seated in the cars. Were the cars named after her, perhaps? A romantic notion, certainly, but the truth is likely to be much more mundane than this. Gloria was a name that had already figured in Triumph's history for many years – the early pedal-cycle factory in Much Park Street had been called the Gloria works – and it seems that Claude Holbrook merely took a fancy to that name. Certainly it seems highly unlikely that a new factory would also be named after the same fashion model – yet the one purchased in 1935 was also to be called the Gloria works!

Co-incident with the new cars came new management. Holbrook was under no illusions as to his own motor industry expertise, and to achieve his often advertised aim of producing the 'Smartest Cars in the Land' he set about finding people to assist him. The Gloria range was already finalised and ready for production, so Holbrook's search was for experts to improve and develop on this theme. Of paramount importance was a really good experimental engineer, and it is here that Holbrook made the wise choice of employing a good practical man rather than a

Donald Healey's finest Monte Carlo Rally performance for Triumph was in 1934. Using an old-type Southern Cross chassis, a much-altered Monte Carlo tourer body and oversized tyres, Healey finished third overall with Tommy Wisdom and R. C. Clement-Brookes (in rear seat) as co-drivers (Picture: Autocar)

boffin. It is at this point in the story that the remarkable personality of Donald Healey re-appears. As recorded earlier, Healey had already performed with credit in Triumphs in the Monte Carlo Rally and had driven them with distinction in many British rallies and long-distance trials like the Lands End and the Exeter. Incidentally, it had been Healey who discovered Blue Hills Mine, near his home in Cornwall, and who had brought it to the attention of the Motor Cycling Club for their future Lands End Trials. After his Monte experiences in the Triumph, Healey quit his little garage in Perranporth to work part-time with Invicta in London, later taking one of the rather viciously-handling 4½-litre cars to an outright win in the Monte Carlo Rally in 1931. Then, tiring of the regular travel between Cornwall and Invicta, Healey decided to move himself to the motor industry Midlands, settling down in Barford (where his son Geoffrey still lives) and working for the Riley company in 1932 and 1933. Healey recalls: 'The first approach I had was from Charles Ridley, who was then Colonel Holbrook's deputy. I was attracted by the Gloria project, which looked better than Riley's own Nine. I also had good friends at Triumph – particularly Gordon Parnell, who was then Chief Designer. After I talked to Charles Ridley, I had an interview with Colonel Holbrook, and it was decided that I should join the company as Experimental Manager, which I did. My first job was cleaning up the Gloria range, which was just about ready for production. There was no Technical Director as such. I reported direct to Charles Ridley for a time, and after about a year became Technical Director myself'. There was also to be a proper Triumph-backed rallying programme for the first time, and rather than overburden Healey with too much at first, Charles Ridley's son, Jack, was made Competition Manager; in Healey's opinion Ridley was also a very fine driver, as his performance in future Montes and Alpine Trials was to show. To back up the engineers, Holbrook had chosen Frank Warner as his body engineering chief, but Warner soon moved to Humber-Hillman, after which Bill Thornton became responsible for the bodies. His deputy was Walter Belgrove, who became Chief Body Engineer early in 1935, and was to remain connected with Triumph until the end of 1955.

The four-cylinder Coventry Climax engine used in various forms by Triumph from 1931 to 1936. This is the twin-carburettor 1,232 cc version as fitted to the Monte Carlo Tourer and Southern Cross (Picture: Autocar)

Right from the start, the Healey influence became apparent at Priory Street, where all development and design was carried out. Conversations between Healey, Colonel Holbrook and journalist/sports car driver Tommy Wisdom had centred around the lack of a really competitive sports car built in Britain to challenge the Italians and French. The outcome of these discussions was the exciting straight-eight Dolomite project – a story so remarkable that I have felt it necessary to devote a separate chapter to its evolution. Conceived late in 1933, the straight-eight Dolomite first ran in the summer of 1934, and was wound-up early in 1935. Widely canvassed as the first car to carry the name of Dolomite, this is not, in fact, true. At the Olympia Motor Show in 1933, immediately after Donald Healey's appointment, the company announced that although they had nothing to show, they were working on a new two-seater which would have a highly-tuned version of the 1,100 cc Climax engine, would cost no less than £500, and would be called a Dolomite Special. This car never appeared in that specification, nor at that price, nor even with the same name, but instead it bequeathed its name to the magnificent straight-eight car, and appeared alongside it, much cheaper and in two guises, as the Gloria-based Southern Cross two-seater.

Meantime, the company's finances had suffered a further blow. The £146,000 loss in 1932 had been bad enough, but at least there had been reserves. By the middle of 1933 the expense of preparing for the Glorias, plus a parallel expense in launching a new range of Triumph motorcycles, had taken a heavy toll. At the end of the year the company announced that they had lost a 'record' £168,705, and that to cover this all the cash reserves had gone; for the first time in many years the company had to carry forward an adverse balance of £78,316. A commentary of the company's finances throughout the 1930s could be dull, and may be largely unintelligible to those only interested in the cars themselves, but consideration of these successively grim figures usually gives a clue as to the failure to capitalise on certain promising projects.

However, it took a lot to hold down Donald Healey's sporting instincts, and an immediate benefit of this was seen in the shape of an additional model in January 1934. Called at first merely a 'Sports Gloria', it was to all intents and purposes a slightly modified version of the Gloria Speed Tourers seen a few months earlier. The new car was identical with the Speed Tourer ahead of the passenger compartment, though at the rear the Speed Tourer's swept and neatly rounded tail had been discarded in favour of a very MG-type stub tail, complete with a 17-gallon slab fuel tank, twin-spare-wheels and twin number-plates, one attached to each rear wing. The engine, on announcement, was the 1,087 cc four-cylinder unit and the usual Lockheed brakes were fitted. The engine had twin downdraught 30 mm Zenith carburettors mounted over the engine, effectively one each side of the rocker boxes. The throttle linkage was arranged so that only one instrument, the nearside one over the exhaust system, was in use for starting up and slow running, the second being brought into use by a delayed linkage rather after the style of the compound double-choke carburettors used in modern British Fords. However, it must be recorded that this linkage could get itself seriously out of adjustment, the result being less performance than expected, considerably higher fuel consumption, and greatly increased profits for one's local garage; the free-wheel offered on normal Glorias was not available on this car. Inside the car, the facia panel was all that could be desired, with a full array of instruments including large matching dials for the rev-counter and speedometer, and there was a remote control gear-lever and fly-off hand-brake lever.

The price on announcement was £325 – £40 more than the Gloria Speed Tourer, but trading somewhat on Donald Healey's reputation. However, it was not put into production at once, as Healey first had to prove certain features on the much-modified Triumphs prepared for the Monte Carlo Rally. A few months later, therefore, there were specification changes when yet another engine size appeared – 1,232 cc, aided by a cylinder bore increase to 66 mm – André Telecontrol suspension dampers were added, and

The Monte Carlo Tourer, as modified from the Gloria Tourer. Changes were mainly at the tail, with an exposed slab fuel tank, twin spare wheels and twin number plates. The door top panels are folded away in this view (Picture: Autocar)

Miss Gloria, the Selfridge's fashion model, in the Gloria Speed Six Tourer at the 1933 Olympia Show (Picture: Motor)

the wings became aluminium instead of steel. The car then went into small-scale production at the same price of £325, with the 1,087 cc engine remaining as an option that no-one seemed to take up.

1934 was an outstandingly successful rallying year, for the company's own cars achieved splendid results in the Monte Carlo Rally and in the Alpine Trial. Five special cars were prepared for the Monte Carlo event, being called Glorias but actually using the old Southern Cross chassis frames and outsize wheels to increase ground clearance. Though there was no flat-out mountain circuit or special stages in those days, there was still well over 2,300 miles to be covered in deep snow, without studded tyres, with only rudimentary heating, and with no reconnaisance. Healey took along Tommy Wisdom and R. C. Clement-Brookes, starting with the other team cars from Athens. A route through blizzards, on very primitive tracks through the Balkans, led through Salonica, Sofia and Belgrade to Szeged in Hungary. The following sections through Budapest, Vienna and Stuttgart to Strasbourg seemed almost futuristic by comparison, and even the run through the Maritime Alps to Monte Carlo must have seemed like a rest cure. The rally, for those unpenalised on the road sections, was settled by a 110 metre speed test followed by braking in the shortest possible distance. Healey's virtuoso performance was rewarded by third best performance in the rally which, following his seventh place in 1930, an outright win in 1931, and second overall in the same Invicta in 1932, gave him a remarkably consistent record. Other team Triumphs were also well-placed, with Jack Ridley's car sixth overall, Beck's car tenth, and Jack Hobbs' twelfth; Beck's car also took third place in the post-rally *Concours d'Elegance.* Healey rubbed in his successes by making fastest time in the Monte wiggle-woggle tests that followed the event, and there was so much disbelief over the Triumphs' performances that Healey's engine was stripped in response to a protest – and found to be entirely legal.

Spurred-on by this success, an attack was made on the 1934 Alpine Trial, which is still remembered as one the hardest of the pre-war Alpines, in which the Triumphs and of course the Talbots did so well for Britain. There had been Triumph 10s in the 1933 Alpine Trial, but they had achieved no great success. The 1934 entry used the smaller 1,087 cc engines to bring the cars within the 1,100 cc class limit, the cars being basically Southern Cross Tourers. The team entry comprised Jack Ridley, sales manager Vic Leverett and Lt-Col Holbrook himself, while other cars were driven by Donald Healey, London Triumph distributor Maurice Newnham and Miss Joan Richmond. All the well-known passes were used, including the Stelvio, the Izoard and the Austrian horror of Turracher Höhe (which was described as a super-long version of Beggars' Roost). Switzerland, Jugoslavia and Austria were always part of the Trial in those days, the event starting from Nice and finishing in Munich. Triumph, like Talbot, had a phenomenally successful event, being the winner of the *Coupe des Alpes* team prize in their category. All completed the road section without loss of road marks, though the Ladies' crew had to be disqualified after changing one of the sealed and marked components. Both Maurice Newnham and Donald Healey won individual *Coupes des Glaciers.*

This, however, was to be the last appearance of the little Southern Cross, which had been based on the Super Nine, for Donald Healey had been working on a new car. Announced very coyly just before the 1934 Motor Show, and naturally completely overshadowed by the blaze of publicity enjoyed by the straight-eight Dolomite, was a new Southern Cross based on the mechanical components of the Glorias which, for the 1935 season, had taken advantage of recent reductions in the 'horsepower tax' by having enlarged four and six-cylinder engines. The original 1,087 cc unit went up to the 1,232 cc size first seen in the Monte Carlo Tourer earlier in the year, while the 1,476 cc unit was taken right out to 1,991 cc by increasing both bore and stroke to 65 x 100 mm, respectively. The new chassis was similar to that of the Glorias, although the wheelbase had been shortened by a foot in each case. This time the shortening had been effected at the rear, for the new Southern Cross was a two-seater car, with styling by Walter Belgrove. A true side view comparison between the Monte Carlo Tourer and the Southern Cross for 1935 shows a great similarity. Nose, wings and scuttle were the same on the four-cylinder models (the 'six', of course, had the longer nose section), and the doors were unaltered, but the main body shortening had been achieved by cutting out provision for the rear seats and moving the rear axle line forward, along with the big fuel tank and the twin spare wheels. Apart from the promise of good performance, especially from the 2-litre version, the new Southern Cross was also good value for money. In an attempt to generate more sales the 1,232 cc Southern Cross was marketed at £275, while the six-cylinder car sold for £335, only £10 more than the Monte Carlo, despite offering much more performance and sporting success potential. Assuming that Triumph could stay in business at these prices, no-one was likely to complain.

For a long time it has been fashionable to suggest that no pre-war sporting Triumph could really justify that title, but on the evidence of the Southern Cross this is simply not so. The car soon earned itself a good reputation as a rally car, and was certainly endowed with very good looks. Its main competitors were the SS sports cars (which were, admittedly, both faster and better value for money) and the 2-litre SA MG, which cost £375 at the time. By 1935 standards the Southern Cross was as desirable as the Standard-inspired TR2 was to prove many years later, and probably a good deal more attractive into the bargain. *The Autocar* laid their hands on a very early example of the 2-litre Southern Cross in 1935 and found that they could achieve a flat-out maximum speed with hood and sidescreens erect of more than 80 mph. An absolute maximum of 83.33 mph was recorded over a flying quarter mile at Brooklands with the hood, sidescreens and windscreen removed, but with aero screens in position. Acceleration from rest to 50 mph occupied 13.4 seconds, and to 60 mph 19 seconds, at which point the engine was just about peaking in third gear. Of equal interest to potential buyers was its performance as a trials or rally car.

The Autocar testers, whose spiritual home in those days appeared to be in the West Country, said of the car: '. . . it should be a most useful trails machine, possessing an excellent turn of acceleration, and showing all the necessary power for the ascent of hills. With this aspect in view the car was taken over a number of trials gradients during the test and *without* competition tyres climbed Dover Hay, Beggars' Roost, Station Hill, Lyn Hill and Tarr Steps, all on or near Exmoor. It was raining at the time so that the surface was slippery, but Station Hill, Lynton was twice ascended on second gear with two up, all the way. . . . Second gear indeed proved most useful, for even on Beggars' Roost first gear was needed only for a very short space, and with the quick change to second available much unnecessary revving on first gear could be avoided. . . .' However, what often made such impartial road tests less than informative was the way in which the testers donned the mantle of diplomats so completely that it was difficult to learn very much from them. What, for instance, should one think of the remark that: '. . . the gearbox is of the type sometimes called an 'ordinary crash box' without any synchromesh or other special mechanism. Without paying the manufacturers an undue compliment it may be said that in this particular box any such mechanism would be unnecessary. . . .' The fact that the Southern Cross still didn't have synchromesh was nothing of which to be ashamed; no MG, for instance, was so equipped until 1936.

But although the Southern Cross and Donald Healey's superb straight-eight Dolomite were fine cars, they represented just about the high point of Triumph's pre-war sporting ambitions. Although the company's trading record in 1934 had eased somewhat, with a loss of a mere £1,220, other losses had to be added in, and the total loss in the year to August 1934 was nearly £56,000. Bettman retired, probably happy to leave his old company that appeared to be folding around him, and it was thought advisable to make further Board changes. Although the Gloria range had established itself well during the year, not enough of them had been delivered, and strict economies were necessary. The new Board of Directors, which included Lloyds Bank nominee H. Howe Graham as Financial Adviser, put out a statement that they were setting about 'complete re-organisation of the company's affairs. Arrangements are being made to instal an up-to-date costing system and other systems, and factories will be working under strict budgetary control.' One is tempted to inquire why the factories were not already operating in this manner?

The company's principal problem was that it was running out of space at Clay Lane to produce the larger and more complex Glorias and their derivatives, and of course that large debts had been run up in the lean years following the

The Southern Cross (Gloria-based) and Monte Carlo had near-identical interiors. The sprung steering wheel was standard, while a freewheel (not fitted to this car) was optional. The control was usually on the floor near the gearlever. (Picture: Autocar)

depression of 1930/31. Raising money in the City in those circumstances and at that time was difficult, even though the company was agreed to be under-capitalised. Therefore it seemed that the only way to liquidate the debts, and find space to build more cars, was to sell off some of the assets. Lt-Col Holbrook, now in sole executive charge since Bettman's retirement, had little interest nor much liking for the two-wheeler side of the business, and found an enthusiastic supporter in Maurice Newnham, newly appointed to the Board. They were only really interested in making more of the 'Smartest Cars in the Land', and were convinced that these elegant sporting saloons and their derivatives could yield good profits and would soon do so. The simple non-sentimental accountant's answer was to sell-off the motor-cycle and cycle businesses, which were of no further interest, to raise capital to re-structure the car side of Triumph. That the motor-cycles had often been the mainstay of the company cannot be denied – before the depression Triumph motor-cycles were selling at a rate of at least 1,000 machines every week. At the same time the straight-eight Dolomite project was killed, and the competition programme curtailed.

Selling off the motor-cycle factories in Priory Street would mean moving out all the car activities contained therein, including the design and development departments, the machinery used to make engines, and that part of the tool room which would be retained for the cars. The engineering departments were not large, but in

The Gloria-based Southern Cross. This is the 8ft chassis car with the 1,232 cc engine. Aero-screens and a folding windscreen were standard *(Picture: Walter Belgrove)*

1934, when the straight-eight Dolomite was being built, Donald Healey estimated that there would be up to 100 people in design, development, testing and toolroom activities. This was drastically reduced later, as Walter Belgrove confirmed when he said that at the last factory only about twenty could be mustered in entire engine, chassis, body and tooling drawing offices. Holbrook therefore needed a new factory in which to assemble the Glorias as Clay Lane and Briton Road would be impossibly cramped. Fortunately (or perhaps unfortunately as far as the shareholders were concerned later) an opportunity occurred in the spring of 1935 when the old engine manufacturing plant of White and Poppe Ltd came on to the market. This factory, soon to be re-named the Gloria Works, was situated in Holbrooks Lane, which had nothing to do with Colonel Holbrook – there had been a Holbrooks Lane for many more years than there had been a Triumph factory, as the old maps of the city make clear. It had been the site of a Government shell-filling plant during the Great War, and had been taken over by White and Poppe in order to make larger quantities of their engines, which they supplied to Morris Motors amongst others. White and Poppe were taken over by Dennis Brothers of Guildford, and when their activities declined in 1934 they moved all their remaining work to Guildford.

As factories go, the new works was a typically red-brick erection behind high walls. It was next door to the Dunlop factory which made vehicle wheels, and over the back wall, probably not too far away for industrial espionage to operate in its 1930s form, was William Lyons' prosperous SS Cars Ltd. Colonel Holbrook was sufficiently impressed with the new premises to buy them in April 1935 and complete the transfer of assembly lines from Stoke by the end of August. In his annual message to Triumph dealers he said: 'In early April, therefore, an offer was made for the purchase of a fine modern factory in Holbrooks Lane, Coventry, which would provide ideal facilities for the manufacturing of chassis and the mounting of bodies for the car side of the business, so that the older factories could then concentrate entirely upon the other products. . .

On the 9th August – the date of the announcement of the new season's programme – the factory was in full production, working with the most modern facilities. The shops had in the meantime been repainted from top to bottom, no less than 400 heavy machines had been transferred from the old works, or new ones purchased, new furnaces had been installed, stores erected and tracks laid down. During this period production of the current season's models continued without any serious break and the new season's programme was being steadily advanced. During the three weeks ending 31st August, output of the new season's models will have exceeded the number delivered during the first three months of the 1935 season, and supplies will continue regularly. . . .'

Reading between the lines after all these years suggests that if three weeks' production at Holbrooks Lane could exceed three months' supplies from Clay Lane, it was no wonder that things had been sticky in the previous year or so.

It is also interesting to pluck this phrase out of context: '. . . so that the older factories could then concentrate entirely on the other products . . .'. Holbrook was filleting his factories carefully, so that when the time came there would be nothing of value to the car side still inside the oldest Priory Street factories. This new factory, the machinery *and* the long-term debts had to be paid for somehow – and soon – if Triumph were to survive. Little had been done to the Gloria model range in the preceding year, except that the Vitesse series had now become a range of Glorias in its own right with the specially tuned engine, high-lift camshaft, larger valves and twin-carburettor details already fitted to the Southern Crosses. When the 1936 programme was released there was no mention of the six-cylinder Southern Cross, though plenty of publicity for the four-cylinder version; nevertheless the larger-engine car remained in production. The 1935 financial results, announced at the end of the year, were again awful, a trading loss of £16,891 being bumped up to a total of £90,088 when all other factors were taken into consideration. This brought the total debts up to £238,756, which made it inevitable that there would be no dividends, and remarkable that no creditor should force the company into bankruptcy.

At the time of the annual meeting there had been no comment regarding the sale of assets, so it came as somewhat of a surprise in January 1936 to see an announcement that the motor-cycle and cycle businesses were to be sold off. The cycle business, remarkably, was sold to none other than Siegfried Bettman, who came out of retirement at 73 years of age to run Coventry Cycles Limited. Raleigh Cycles, of Nottingham, soon took over production and rights to the name, keeping a Triumph pedal-cycle in their range until 1954. Once the re-sale to Raleigh had been accomplished, Bettman finally retired in 1939, enjoying twelve more years in his home at Stoke Park, Coventry, before his death in 1951 at the ripe old age of 88.

The motor-cycle business found a willing buyer in the shape of Jack Sangster, whose Ariel company already made motor-cycles in the Birmingham area. Motor-cycle production continued at Priory Street without a break after the remnants of the car business (including design and development) had moved to Holbrooks Lane, the motor-cycle firm becoming known as the Triumph Engineering Company. A section of Priory Street was leased back by the car side for a service and spares stock department. One of the personalities at Ariel was a gifted engineer called Edward Turner, then chief designer, who was drafted in to the re-formed motor-cycle company as Managing Director, along with another director – Siegfried Bettman! Bettman, it seemed, had a very soft spot for his two-wheelers. Incidentally, Edward Turner has usually been credited with the design of the first vertical-twin Triumph engine, which eventually appeard in the Speed Twins and Tiger 100s. In fact Mauritz Schulte built his first twin-cylinder engine in 1913, and when Triumph were sold off they were already using an advanced 650 cc vertical-twin unit designed by Val Page. Turner, however, killed this off, substituting his own design, which was certainly cheaper to make but not necessarily any more efficient. Turner was already noted as the designer of the now legendary Ariel Square-Four engine, and was to turn up many years later in connection with Triumph cars in most intriguing and still rather mysterious circumstances. The story is told in *Appendix I* in connection with the Daimler SP250 sports car; Turner became Managing Director of Daimler during the 1950s following a steady rise through Triumph, then BSA (when Triumph motor-cycles were sold to them in 1951) and into the Daimler side of BSA. The Triumph motor-cycle firm was to fare little

The general chassis layout of all new Triumphs built after 1933 until 1939. This is the six-cylinder Coventry Climax-engined Gloria Six Vitesse, which was substantially the same as later Dolomites. The Southern Cross chassis had a shorter wheelbase. (Picture: Walter Belgrove)

better than the Triumph car concern during the Second World War, their Priory Street premises being bombed-out on that same November night in 1940, after which production of two-wheelers was resumed on a small scale in rented premises in the Cape, Warwick (very close to the site of Donald Healey's first Healey factory after the war), until new premises could be built on the Coventry-Meriden road.

With Lord Leigh as his chairman, and Maurice Newnham and Charles Ridley as his co-directors, Claude Holbrook now felt secure in the business of making quality cars, with no diversions, however profitable, to cloud his horizons. Although the range looked fairly complex, a great degree of rationalisation had been carried out. There was a single basic chassis, in several lengths (this was possible with the minimum of tooling changes), a single family of engines (four- and six-cylinders in various guises), and about four different basic bodies. A further mechanical refinement announced after the main range had been publicised was the revised free-wheel, available for £5 5s (£5.25) extra. Mounted at the rear of the gearbox as a sandwich between the box and the propeller-shaft extension, this ingenious little mechanism, constructed according to Warren patents, was connected to the clutch pedal through an adjustable linkage; in normal gearchanging it was only necessary to depress the clutch pedal fully to the floor for the gearbox to be effectively isolated from the engine and propeller shaft, thereby allowing the non-synchromesh gearchange to operate in a more fool-proof manner than usual. The Warren device could also be operated purely as a free-wheel, merely by depressing the clutch to the floor once while simultaneously releasing the throttle pedal; the car then coasted until the accelerator pedal was once again pressed. There was a rash of such devices in Britain at around this time, just as there was to be a rash of two-pedal controls on offer during the mid-1950s. But they were of doubtful merit and very few lasted long, Triumph's surviving for only a year until the next set of major mechanical changes was released; very few were actually sold.

It was at the end of the summer of 1936 that Triumph's third phase of development became obvious. It will be remembered that the company had started out as car manufacturers in 1923 with engines designed for them by Harry Ricardo. This policy had continued with little change until 1931, when the release of the Super Nine ushered in the age of engines machined by Triumph but designed and largely supplied as raw castings and forgings by Coventry Climax. Although the Climax engines played their part in Triumph's development, they were always blessed with a particularly awkward combustion chamber shape and, as Donald Healey pointed out, a propensity for overheating their exhaust valves due to the difficulty of making provision for water cooling in that area. Eventually Triumph amassed enough experience of their own, and Healey settled down with Swetnam to design their own range, which were to be announced for fitment to the 1937 cars. In fact there was a gradual tapering-off of Coventry Climax supplies after the announcement until the middle of 1937, but once Triumph production was well under way they were speedily abandoned.

Four-cylinder and six-cylinder versions of the new engine were to be available, the six-cylinder unit having the same bore, stroke and 1,991 cc capacity as the abandoned Climax unit. Indeed, in many respects the internal dimensions of the two designs were identical, even down to such details as cylinder centres and main-bearing dimensions. Triumph had done the sensible thing, copying from Climax where they had thought it worthwhile, and making the maximum use of existing machine shop tooling for main castings and forgings in order to minimise on new investment. The cylinder-head layout, however, was completely different. The Climax inlet-over-exhaust-valve arrangement was discarded in favour of a conventional overhead-valve arrangement, with valves vertically disposed and in line. The new head was 'crossflow' in layout, with twin SU carburettors in each case. There was a torsional vibration damper on the crankshaft nose to add refinement to what was reputedly a very quiet engine.

The four-cylinder engine, however, was much larger, both physically and in swept volume, than that used previously. While the old 1,087/1,232 cc Climax engine was suitable for the Morgans, AJSs and Crossleys which it inhabited in other forms, there was little doubt that it was getting

Walter Belgrove's controversial style on the Dolomite Roadster Coupé. The grille was said to be inspired by the Hudson/Essex Terraplane, but Belgrove claims the rest as being original

short of breath in the latest Belgrove-styled coachbuilt Triumphs. In any case it was to be a related engine to the six-cylinder unit as the company could not afford to tool up for two engines. There were two different sizes – 1,496 cc and 1,767 cc.

As already observed, rationalisation was far advanced, and if Triumph had survived into the 1940s it was certain that larger versions of the engines would have followed; the six cylinder engine could have been taken out to 2,244 cc using the 69 mm pistons, and no less than 2,650 cc using the 75 mm pistons. There was space and built-in strength in the engine to accommodate this. But whereas Triumph's 2-litre engine was to bring most of the sporting successes in the future, it was the little 1500 which was to survive the longest.

The 1937 Triumph range was announced as early as July 1936, to allow for the production build-up of the new engines, though the company made the fatal mistake of having a lot of the Climax-engined cars in stock when the announcement came. Apart from the new engines and minor styling changes the Glorias, priced from £268 (including one which retained the old 1,232 cc Climax engine), and the Vitesses, starting at £318, were very much as before, but at the top of the range there was an entirely fresh line of Triumphs called Dolomites. There was absolutely no connection between Donald Healey's straight-eight sports car and this new range, for although Healey had been Technical Director since the turn of 1934/35, and therefore responsible for all that was designed thereafter, this was merely a new 'flagship' using a registered name that Triumph already owned. The new Dolomites used the same basic chassis to be found under the Glorias and Vitesses, and in the usual two wheelbase lengths. During the past year the Gloria and Vitesse tracks had been increased to 4ft 2in, but the Dolomites exceeded this with tracks of 4ft 4½in. The same 12-inch diameter brakes were specified, but behind the engines the old unsynchronised gearbox had been abandoned, as had the Warren-type free-wheel, and in their place there was a new Triumph-designed box with synchromesh on top, third and second gears. No-one was admitting to anything at the time, but in fact the internals of this gearbox were bought from Austin at Longbridge, ready machined, to be fitted into Triumph's own casing; this happens even in the '70s, of course, witness the case of the Austin Maxi internals supplied for the five-speed Lotus gearboxes.

However, the most controversial feature of the Dolomite, apart from its name and the much modified mechanical specification compared with previous years, was the new car's styling. While the general outline of the car was as stylish and nicely-detailed as one had come to expect from Walter Belgrove's drawing board, there was no doubt that it bore a striking similarity in some respects to the SS Jaguar (which preceded it by a full year) and it had a startling radiator grille variously described as a fencer's mask or a waterfall design. The general layout, particularly in the disposition of the styling features of the passenger compartment, the side windows, the rear quarters and the elegant sweep of the tail, all bore a similarity to the SS Jaguars, and it would be intriguing to know precisely how this happened. Donald Healey suggested to me that there was no mystery in this, because both he and Maurice Newnham were great admirers of the SS Jaguars, and sought to out-do the Lyons-designed cars at all times. Since it was possible to tool up a body shell from ash frames and hand-beaten aluminium panels in less than a year, it would be reasonable to assume that Belgrove had had a good look at the SS Jaguar in the autumn of 1935 before styling his own Dolomites. There is really no question of industrial espionage because there was no need for it, even though the two factories, as mentioned earlier, literally backed on to each other. Another clue to similarities was that Bill Thornton (Triumph's Chief Body Engineer until early 1935) had gone to work for William Lyons after leaving Triumph, and may have influenced the style of the SS Jaguar from ideas which were already brewing at Triumph before he left. Lyons was already noted for the way in which he personally master-minded the styling of all his products, but he often allowed his engineers to put up initial proposals for him to modify and finalise. There would be nothing more natural, therefore, than for Bill Thornton's artistic memory of the latest Triumph sketches to be translated into themes for the SS Jaguars. As to the new radiator grille design, 37 years later Belgrove expressed himself still happy with it, for he had been pushed to get away from the traditional British look, and to add a touch of Americanisation to the front of his cars. Within the Triumph factory the new car became known as 'Jumbo', which seems rather hard on a controversial though fairly successful treatment. As an aid to streamlining the new grille might have had something, had the massive headlamps not been stuck uncompromisingly out in the breeze, and the 28-inch diameter spare wheel not been housed on the front wing under a pressed-steel cover!

However, in spite of the hive of activity instanced by the new cars and the new engines, the financial facts of life at Triumph had continued to be grim. Even Healey's second Coupe des Glaciers success in the Alpine Trial (in a 2-litre Vitesse saloon) could do little to lighten the gloom. Lord Leigh, who was a very sick man, had resigned in April, whereupon Lt-Col Holbrook was elevated to Chairman, and Maurice Newnham became the new Managing Director. Nevertheless, when the accounts to the end of October 1936 were published, it became known that Triumph, for all their new factory and their fine cars, had shattered all previous 'records' by returning a total loss of no less than £212,104, which brought the total debts to £450,860. Even after certain 'financial adjustments', whatever that might have meant, the total indebtedness was still over £350,000, and with bank overdrafts and secured loans approaching the quarter-million mark it was clear that something would have to change. Remarkably, the bank were still indulgent enough to allow the company to continue trading, but set in train a complete appraisal of what was good and what was bad in the company. In the midst of all this gloom, the company report said: 'Discussions are now taking place with important financial interests for the complete re-organisation of the company's capital structure, and the provision of the necessary additional capital. . . . Despatches of cars in November and December 1936 are already double those of the previous year. . . . Further progress has been made in the concentration upon manufacturing cars of a specialised type as distinct from mass-produced machines. . .'

One of the casualities of the retrenchment that was necessary during the winter of 1936 was the pretty little Southern Cross sports car, which was withdrawn. By the middle of 1937 the last examples had left the factory (the last few cars having the Triumph-designed 1,767 cc engine and matched gearbox), and for the moment there was absolutely nothing in the range to interest the sports-car-minded enthusiast. During the 1937 season, Maurice Newnham made great efforts to shift the stock of Coventry Climax-engined cars, but eventually he had to take a loss on each and every one. It was, indeed, a miracle that the company still existed, but the promised financial reconstruction duly materialised in April 1937. As far as personalities were concerned, Claude Holbrook was shifted unceremoniously side-ways to become Vice-Chairman, while a little-known financier called H. A. Reincke became Chairman. The Ordinary shares were to be reduced in value from £1 to only 2s (10p), and since there were 400,000 of them this automatically reduced the company's nominal value to £40,000 and a lot of new capital was needed to pay off the debts. This was to be raised by asking all existing shareholders to subscribe to a new 'rights issue' of two new shares priced at 2s (10p) for every written-down share they held. The Preference shares were not to be altered, but holders of these were asked to waive their right to the 6½ per cent dividends not paid since 1932. A total of £360,000 would be raised by this 'rights issue', which would neatly pay off the accumulated debts of £353,993 and allow the company to carry on trading.

As far as the sports car enthusiast was concerned, when the 1938 programme was released in July 1937 it was a complete washout. There was not a sports or sporting car in sight, and none was immediately in prospect. After only four years in the limelight the Gloria range had virtually disappeared, with the single rather formal six-light saloon kept on for 1938. Mechanically there were few changes, although a system of central chassis lubrication (a fully automatic Luvax Bijur system) had been adopted, and there was now a tandem-master-cylinder braking layout.

On a happier note, however, increased sales during 1937 and further rationalisation had helped to create a much more favourable trading position. At the end of the year, with no expansive new models introduced, and the effects of Maurice Newnham's new broom becoming obvious, the financial situation had improved to the point where for the first time in five years there had been a profit on actual trading – a healthy one of £35,528 for the nine-month period which had followed the reconstruction. Indeed, so much more confidently were Triumph regarding their future prospects that they began to cast around for a commercial partner with whom to share a programme of expansion. There were several rumoured merger discussions (one must remember that Coventry was still made up of largely independent motor or motor body manufacturers, mostly of similar size and, one must say, of similar financial prospects) but the only one that ever looked likely to get off the ground was with that other producer of quality cars, Riley. Such a merger, which was canvassed by Donald Healey, who still had friends in Foleshill, would have been interesting and probably beneficial to both parties. The Riley name was quite literally 'as old as the industry', dating from the nineteenth century when the Riley family had been making pedal-cycles. Riley was still a family controlled firm, and their fortunes had looked rocky from time to time, but in the previous ten years they had developed a fine line of sporting saloons and outright sports cars. Freddie Dixon had made the Riley name famous at Brooklands, while the ERA racing cars had

If the devil cast his net . . . . . Billingham, Walter Belgrove, Donald Healey and two Triumph secretaries proving that a Dolomite Roadster really was a possible five-seater (Picture: Walter Belgrove)

used the six-cylinder high-camshaft Riley engines as the basis for their own *voiturette* units. However, although Riley had survived the depression with credit, they had also been caught by the decline in car sales in 1936 and 1937, so that they, too, declared a thumping loss towards the end of 1937.

In February 1938, when Triumph appeared to be getting back on their feet, Victor Riley, who was Chairman and Managing Director of Riley, said: 'The directors have given long and anxious consideration to the financial position of the company, and in view of the difficulties experienced in carrying on the business, they have felt constrained to ask the company's bankers to appoint a receiver to protect the assets in the interests of all concerned. . . . The company's position has been largely affected by the general falling-off of demand which, though considered temporary, has been experienced during the last few months.

'Certain negotiations have been carried on in connection with a proposed merger with another company (Triumph) and the board are most hopeful that with the co-operation of all parties concerned it will be possible to submit a reconstruction scheme, either by merger or otherwise, which will enable the company to preserve the interest of both creditors and shareholders and to resume again the leading position it has for so many years occupied in the motor industry.'

Riley, then, were in much the same position as Triumph had been a year or so earlier, but they carried on under the administration of a receiver. However, although exhaustive discussions took place, nothing further was heard of the proposed merger and in September 1938 Lord Nuffield stepped in by purchasing the Riley concern out of his personal fortune, subsequently re-selling it to Morris Motors and incorporating it into the Nuffield Organisation.

A Triumph-Riley merger, if it had come off, would have presented intriguing possibilities. Riley had very high-class and powerful engines – the 1½-litre and 2½-litre engines which were to power the post-war cars had been released in 1934 and 1937, respectively – and these would certainly have been superb foils to Triumph's Belgrove-styled coachwork; a new sports car with real performance would also have been an obvious result of the liaison. The future of the two companies, indeed, would have been completely different.

The talks with Riley, however, foundered after what was perhaps the last flare-up of commercial enterprise in the company. But in spite of this, there was still time for another fine car to be produced, and with the war clouds already beginning to gather over Europe came the announcement of the Dolomite Roadster Coupé, probably the most elegant piece of work ever to come from Walter Belgrove's department. Announced in April 1938, and available from May, the Dolomite Roadster Coupé would not correctly be described as an out-and-out sports car by anyone looking to MG or Singer for inspiration, but to the people who wanted a sports car for sporting occasions, and one in which 'fun' of almost every kind might be enjoyed, the Roadster definitely qualified. It did not have the square-rigged styling still yearned after by the die-hards, but in the context of the Bentleys, Lagondas and Continental machines then on the market, it was an up-to-date concept of a sports-tourer. Hardbitten two-seater enthusiasts would not like the Roadster because it was equipped with such unheard-of luxuries as wind-up glass side windows, and carpets on the floor, not to mention the possibility of carrying the third passenger in the middle of a bench-type seat. One unfortunate consequence of this on the early cars was that the saloon's remote-control gear-change had been discarded in favour of a long spindly lever acting directly on to the gearbox selectors. It might have been practical, but it was soon dropped by public demand.

Mechanically the Roadster was almost pure Dolomite saloon, with the same 1,767 cc engine in the same chassis (of which the wheelbase had mysteriously crept up to 9ft 2in) and having the same suspension, brakes and steering. A six-cylinder 1,991 cc version was expected, and duly arrived at the end of the summer with three SU carburettors instead of the twin instruments usually employed. In each case advertised power outputs were higher than for the saloons, the smaller 14/65 version boasting of 65 bhp and the six-cylinder car 75 bhp.

Just how quickly experimental work progressed in the 1930s is shown by the time scale of production for this car. Belgrove had the first one-eighth-scale illustration of the body style completed by Christmas 1937, the prototype was on the road within four weeks of the project's approval, was announced to the public two months later, and was in the showrooms a month after that. The secret behind this sort of speed lay in the use of a separate load-bearing chassis and a coachbuilt body, allied in this particular case to the fact that the entire front end, wings and running boards were lifted straight from the appropriate Dolomite saloons. But to design a new folding-hood arrangement, seats, boot and auxiliary details, and to get them on the road within four weeks still shows very quick reactions indeed. Belgrove is still proud of this car, as is Donald Healey of the full range. Belgrove comments that 'It was, of course, a batch-production vehicle, as against being fully tooled and volume-produced. We used Birmabright (aluminium alloy) panels on an ash frame. It won consistently in most of the *Concours d'Elegances* – in or out of its class – and it also took a coachwork Gold Medal at Earls Court in 1938. By the way, it has been inferred that I 'borrowed' the design of the Roadster from the Mercedes 170V sports-roadster, but as far as I was concerned I never saw it until after the styling job was finished.'

Certainly the Roadster had similar lines to those of the Mercedes, but this can be treated as no more than coincidence. At first sight it was purely a two/three seater, but inspection of the boot, by opening the lid, revealed that Triumph feature of 1923 – one that had all but disappeared in Europe at least – the dickey seat. Getting in and out of the dickey was something of an adventure, especially for the ladies, for unlike the later Standard-Triumph 1800 Roadster which succeeded it, there was no step-plate to assist as a launching pad. In its place there were let-down steps neatly concealed in the body sides, on to which one climbed from the rear of the running board to scale the flowing wing line, and hoped for the best. With the dickey panel closed down and the hood erect the Dolomite Roadster looked like a very large-booted two-seater coupé, where the spare wheel was recessed into an elegantly sweeping tail panel. The dickey panel, when erect, doubled as a back-rest, and passengers sat in almost the same location, if a little higher than rear-seat passengers in a Dolomite saloon.

Only one prototype of the Dolomite fixed-head coupé was made. It was not as attractive as the Roadster, and of course the dickey-seat had gone (Picture: A.C. Cook)

With the Roadster now in production, if on only a very small scale, the Dolomites really began to live up to their new images as 'businessmen's expresses'. In a way they were akin to the Bristols of later years, but of course very much cheaper. The four-cylinder Roadster sold for £348, and offered a lot more car, if not much more performance, than had the Southern Cross of only a couple of years earlier. Donald Healey and Maurice Newnham both took every opportunity to use the cars in the bigger British rallies, the six-cylinder version proving to be more than useful in both *Concours* and road sections. In the 1938 RAC Rally, for example, A. L. Pearce's car won its class (10 hp to 15 hp Treasury Rating) on the road section, while Donald Healey's car won its group (open cars) in the coachwork section. Pearce's success was repeated in 1939, when G. S. Davison's Dolomite won Group 4 in the same event, and the Welsh and Scottish rallies also received the attention of the Dolomites.

The six-cylinder Dolomite Roadster might not have had as much get-up-and-go as had the Southern Cross sports car, but those rallying successes showed it was no slouch. Road tests were not carried out until after the outbreak of war, when they usually demonstrated a maximum speed of between 78 and 80 mph. Much was made of the car's refinement, and its ability to keep up high cruising speeds for lengthy periods, 60 to 70 mph being considered normal and comfortable. Acceleration to 60 mph took about 23 seconds (perhaps four seconds slower than for the smaller Southern Cross).

Although car production was recovering compared with 1937, the increase in numbers delivered was not dramatic. When the Roadster was released in April 1938 Triumph claimed that

Architect of the 'Smartest Cars in the Land' was Lt-Col Claude Holbrook, Managing Director from 1933, Chairman from 1936, Vice-Chairman from 1937

production 'had increased by 56 per cent', but from what base was not made clear. Later, when the 1939 cars were shown, it was said that the total 1937 production figures had been exceeded by the end of April 1938. All of which makes it surprising to note that the 1938 accounts claimed only a $12\frac{1}{2}$ per cent increase in sales between 1937 and 1938 – which must have meant that the end of the 1937 financial year had been a very lean time for the company, and that things had become rapidly better in the early months of 1938. With the results for 1938 likely to be little better than for the previous year there seemed little likelihood that the 1939 season would see any radically different cars. Indeed, the announcement made it clear that further rationalisation was to take place, for in future all the cars would be Dolomites. There had been some styling changes; Walter Belgrove had taken a second look at his controversial radiator grille design, found it a little narrow for his latest styling tastes, and widened it significantly; there were still twenty vertical bars, but the air gaps were wider than before. The spare wheel had been removed from the front wing to a recess in the boot lid. He had also designed an impressive Dolomite Royal saloon, of larger and more generous body dimensions than the conventional saloon, while the $1\frac{1}{2}$-litre Special, the other saloons and the Tickford touring bodies carried on unchanged.

Maurice Newnham, having been in charge since the spring of 1936, now appeared to be reaping the benefits of further rationalisation, and there was no longer any doubt that the company's styling and engineering details were well liked. But – and it was a big 'but' – for 1939 there were to be solid and unexpected price increases across the range. As far as the sporting cars were concerned, the four-cylinder Roadster shot up from its £348 at announcement only three months previously to £395 (an increase of no less than 14 per cent), while the six-cylinder car weighed-in at no less than £450. These price increases, bad enough in themselves, also had to be compared with what SS were doing just over the wall; their $1\frac{1}{2}$-litre and $2\frac{1}{2}$-litre SS Jaguar dropheads were priced at only £318 and £415 respectively, their styling was thought to be at least the equal of the Triumph, and performance was equally as good. Even the fiercely fast $2\frac{1}{2}$-litre and $3\frac{1}{2}$-litre SS100 sports two-seaters only cost £395 and £445, respectively, so it was quite clear that Newnham's cars were being squeezed on both the performance and the price fronts. The commercial world, while kindly disposed to the cars, and noting the competitions successes, was nevertheless waiting for news about the company's financial fortunes, and when it arrived, in December 1938, it was bad news yet again.

True there had been a trading profit for the second consecutive year (of £13,878), but much money had to be written-off against tooling, development and launch costs for new models, and interest charges on old debts, the result being an overall loss of £41,950. That there had been an increase in turnover and trading since 1937 was little consolation, especially as the secured bank loan had risen once again to over £160,000. In the company's annual report, it was stated that the factory facilities were now thought to be too large for the car production envisaged, and that half of the production capacity of the machine shops would henceforth be turned over to the manufacture of aero-engine components in order to feed the government's new 'shadow' factories then being completed in Coventry.

So production of the Dolomites was restricted, and by the look of that statement would probably become more restricted still, for even at their new prices they were unlikely to bring much profit into Holbrooks Lane. So a further desperate gamble was needed, and in order to fill the production lines and keep the dealers happy a new, cheaper car would be necessary – or so the reasoning went. In a way this situation almost exactly paralleled Bentley's experiences in 1931, when he was prevailed upon to make and sell the 4-litre after the glories of the Speed Sixes and 8-litre cars. The fact that a cheaper car almost inevitably would be nastier, slower and less well equipped did not make much of an impression on the Board, who were more than ever dominated by Howe Graham, the 'cuckoo-in-the nest' from Lloyds Bank. The new car, when announced early in 1939, proved to be an unsporting little 12 hp saloon, with neither performance nor outstanding good looks to recommend it, though at £285 it was considerably cheaper than the other cars.

In spite of claims to the contrary in publicity, there was very little new in the car's engineering. The 9ft 0in Dolomite chassis, and 4ft 4½in wheel tracks were retained, as was the smallest (1,496 cc) version of Triumph's own engine, though it was in single-carburettor form. One immediately recognised economy was in the use of pressed-steel disc wheels, bought from the Dunlop factory around the corner from the Gloria works; this was not an advance, but definitely a departure, for all previous Triumphs in the Gloria-Vitesse-Dolomite family had been equipped with centre-lock wire wheels. In view of the desire to save money it was also surprising to see that the grouped grease nipple system of chassis lubrication had been retained. Belgrove's body style, however, was very restrained compared with his sweeping Dolomite shapes. The 'fencers' mask' grille had gone, and in its place stood a perfectly conventional shape, reminiscent of earlier Gloria and Vitesse styles, with a touch of MG and Lagonda moulded in for good measure. It was a specifically conventional four-door four-light saloon car aimed at people who were not interested in sports-saloon performance or behaviour; in other words, it was no longer the sort of Triumph which the enthusiastic motorist had come to expect, and it must have broken the hearts of the designers and craftsmen set to work on it. Looked at in hindsight, it is very difficult to see where Triumph were saving the money on the car in order to sell it at £285 and still make a profit. In the chassis, only some simplifications to the engine, and the use of pressed-steel wheels looked likely to help, and the bodywork showed little sign of penny-pinching in any area. It could only have been a saviour if the sales volume had soared dramatically.

By then the company's fortunes were at a very low ebb indeed; apart from the obvious money difficulties staff morale was seeping away as it became clear that car production was declining and policy was changing, while in the boardroom things were little better. Lt-Col Holbrook had been knighted during 1938 for services to the legal processes of Warwickshire (he had sat on the bench for some years) and he no longer held a position of executive power. Control was now firmly in the hands of the finance houses and bankers. It did not seem to spell much of a future for the company, and even Maurice Newnham's undoubted flair for salesmanship (aided by the efforts of his own garage chain in London) could not help. Newnham and Howe Graham quarrelled bitterly. The problem, as ever, had been the constant fight against under-capitalisation. Walter Belgrove's comment was: 'The closure of the old company is history now. The products were never better in performance and looks than in the latter years of the decade. The company never built for stock – every vehicle was virtually sold off the line. The trouble was that we could never build enough of them, and the finance for extensive production re-organisation did not exist. I think the company might have weathered this, but not the war as well.'

To those in the know, the end had been expected for some weeks following the launch of the 12 hp, of which production at a barely profitable price had barely begun. The announcement, when it came on June 7th 1939, was brief and to the point. A receiver had been appointed by Lloyds Bank under the powers contained in the company's debenture dated March 10th 1933. Mr H. Howe Graham who, in addition to his Triumph duties, was a director of Rover and a partner in the Birmingham accountancy business of Gibson & Ashford, was to be that receiver. The dream was over. Claude Holbrook's vision about the 'Smartest Cars in the Land' was shattered. Just sixteen years since the first Triumph car appeared, a once-great company was ruined.

CHAPTER 3

The straight-eight Dolomite

ALTHOUGH DONALD HEALEY joined the Triumph company in 1933 as experimental manager, there was never any doubt that his considerable sporting achievements and ambitions would be put to good use. Any company employing a member of the Healey family could be expected to take an interest in motor sport eventually, though reluctantly it must be agreed that Triumph took a little more convincing than most. Before Healey's arrival at Priory Street, there had been very few products that truly could be called sporting, and what cars were made found their way into rallies rather than track racing. In view of this, and the generally poverty-stricken atmosphere which persisted in Britain at the time (and was already developing at Triumph), the appearance of a genuine contender for sports-racing honours was bound to create a considerable stir. Therefore, the last minute appearance, weeks after Triumph's bread-and-butter range for 1935 had been announced, of the exotic and exciting straight-eight Dolomite caused a sensation among the press and sportsmen; it was an event that would be rivalled in the '70s only by Triumph suddenly revealing a 450 bhp mid-engined monster with which to take on Ferrari and Matra in sports-prototype racing!

British sports cars in the early 1930s fell into two distinct categories. Either they were small, high-revving and not particularly fast – like the Super Seven sports car had been, and as were the multitudinous MG Midgets, small Singers and dreadfully 'pseudo' Wolseley Hornets – or they were ponderous and lorry-like in the Bentley and

Donald Healey's exciting straight-eight Dolomite. Healey's own BRDC badge is on the dumb-iron of this car. Production cars would have had full-length flared wings, a fold-flat screen and a hood (Picture: Autocar)

Lagonda tradition. Perhaps the only car which could combine performance with reasonably light weight was the new $3\frac{1}{2}$-litre Bentley, just developed by Rolls-Royce as a much-improved version of their own 20/25. Rolls-Royce, it will be remembered, had taken over the ruins of Bentley in 1931, but were not really interested in competitions.

Indeed, Bentley successes in the late 1920s and early 1930s no doubt had made sports car enthusiasts unhappy with the lack of success which followed. Once the Bentley racing team had been disbanded, the Le Mans crown had been taken over by Alfa-Romeo of Milan, who also stamped their personality on the Mille Miglia race; their fleet and beautiful 2.3-litre 8C 2300 sports car also won classic races all over Europe, and by 1933 had definitely become the car to beat. Earl Howe, himself a very successful driver in a variety of expensive and competitive foreign cars, was clearly very impressed by the 8C Alfa which he co-drove with Sir Henry 'Tim' Birkin to win at Le Mans in 1931. Howe, who was well insulated from the rigours of living in a depressed Britain, lamented the lack of a similar car built at home, and said in a letter to Arthur Fox at the time:

'So glad you enjoyed your ride in the Alfa. Why it is that the British manufacturers are not more interested in such a car I cannot think. I should have thought that any British manufacturer would have been only too glad to try and get a run in such a car in order to find out what they really are like. Whenever I have these first-class foreign cars I have always been only too delighted to place them at the disposal of any English concern for the purpose of producing something really hot over here, but I have never been asked to do so.

'As a matter of fact, the seeds have already been planted with a certain number of people, which I hope in due course may possibly bear fruit, with the idea of producing an English edition of the Alfa in this country. It is useless I am afraid to expect anything from the British motor industry today – they are hypnotised, as it seems to me, by the prospects of mass production and do not, I think, realise how near saturation point this country is with regard to motor vehicles at anything like their present prices. If and when that point arrives Morris may yet fail to see whether he has been entirely right in eschewing and indeed doing everything in his power to pour cold water upon the value of racing in the motor car industry.'

Georges Roesch of Talbot, at least, was not uninterested in the Alfa, for in a letter to Fox connected with the above he said: 'Far from being disinterested in a car of the Alfa Romeo design you may be certain that it is the reverse and if his Lordship would be so kind as to allow me to try the car at any time, if only for a few minutes, I should be ever so grateful to him. Furthermore, if it is dismantled I should certainly be very glad to examine it in detail.

I would like you, however, to appreciate that whatever I see may serve as a guide for future design, but only as such, as I always have an urge to do better.'

This exchange tells us quite a lot about the personalities, and the times in which they were living. Firstly, Earl Howe clearly had no vision about the eventual growth of popular motoring; if Britain was thought to be near saturation point in 1931 with just over a million cars on our roads, what would he have thought of the 1970s, and more than 13 millions? Secondly, as a wealthy man, Howe clearly had no idea of the desperate straits in which the country – and the motor industry – found itself in the early 1930s. 1931 was actually the worst year for both, with car production turning down, companies like Bentley going to the wall, and more than three million able-bodied men unemployed. Howe was not one of them, and therefore could not be expected to realise that the very last sort of car likely to sell and make a profit for its sponsors would be a highly-tuned, temperamental two-seater sports-racing car for which a king's ransom was asked in payment. Georges Roesch, on the other hand, was clearly a typically 'thinking' engineer who, while quite prepared to be impressed by the Alfa's performance and specification, was not prepared to accept its excellence on trust. The engine, after all, had first appeared in its original form in the mid-1920s, and the ever-confident Roesch was sure he could improve on it.

However, Earl Howe had been talking hard to several people about an Alfa copy – though it was obvious that W.R. Morris had sent him away with a flea in his ear. The 'seeds bearing fruit' must have landed on poor, if not stony ground, and it was not for a further three years that the buds were seen to flower in public.

The sudden and unexpected appearance of the Dolomite straight-eight at Olympia in 1934 has always been clouded with mystery and intrigue, and without the fortuitous appearance of articles and letters in *Motor Sport* magazine during 1972 it might still not have been possible to quote the exact way in which the car came about. Donald Healey, who was mainly responsible for the design of the Dolomite, had been far too busy furthering his own career, and the Healey motor car, to bother to refute the often wild stories which had appeared in print about the failure of the car to go into production. In writing this book, I am doubly fortunate in being able to quote Donald Healey's own article in *Motor Sport* (August 1972), and in having had a chat with him during the course of research.

I would like to set the scene for the design of this outstandingly interesting and exciting British car by reprinting Healey's thoughts on the car published in the *Motor Sport* article; almost a year after that article was published, I find it necessary only to correct the great man on minor points. It was, in fact, late in 1933 (as soon as he had joined Triumph) that the project got under way; Claude Holbrook's knighthood did not in fact come through until 1938; and Walter Belgrove has denied styling the car. However, I have left Healey's narrative uncorrected:

'In 1934, after the great successes of the Triumph cars in the Alpine Trial, Sir Claude Holbrook, Chairman of the Triumph Company, Tommy Wisdom and myself were deploring the lack of a good British sports car able to compete with the Continental cars of that date. Tommy was then one of our top sports-car drivers at Brooklands and in rallies and the Alpine Trial. He suggested that we built a car similar to the then-most-successful racing car, the 2.3-litre Alfa Romeo. Sir Claude agreed and I was given immediately a very tight budget to build such a car in the least possible time. That budget would not have been enough to develop a scooter, today! To design and develop an engine of this type, with our limited knowledge of such a machine, would be a big undertaking, although we made the best motor-cycle engine of the day, and had developed a completely new range of engines for the current Triumph cars.

'Our production engines had to be designed and produced to normal time-schedules, but this job had to be done quickly, and as economically as possible. I decided to get an Alfa-Romeo and make a design study of the engine, and to keep as close to its design as possible.

'I have been accused of being a copyist, but it is the general practice of all car producers to carefully study competitors' products. One of the most famous cars in the world had its present engine developed from a well-known American engine and was originally a very close copy.

'So I purchased an Alfa-Romeo racing car, being lucky enough to be able to buy the 2.3-litre so successfully raced by Lord Essendon, then the Hon. Brian Lewis. I also visited Italy and discussed our intentions with Alfa's Chief Engineer, the famous Signor Jano. Alfa Romeo were very pleased and honoured that a Company as famous as Triumph had decided to follow their design – we even discussed the possibility of calling the car a Triumph-Alfa. They were very interested in our up-to-date range of motor-cycles and considered the possibility of making one of them in Italy. Signor Jano was very helpful. But we decided not to join up the names in any way.

'I was fortunate in that we had a first-class engine drawing office and probably the best tool-room in Coventry. With much overtime working and a lot of enthusiasm we had an engine running in under six months. It was made completely by 'knife-and-fork' methods; even the Roots blower rotors were hand-contoured. To our delight the engine gave over 120bhp without any tuning; this was later improved to 140 bhp. The beautiful block and head castings were made by High Duty Alloys but we made every other part ourselves. I had a discussion with Mr Robotham, the Chief Engineer of Rolls-Royce, on the new bearing metal just discovered, lead-bronze, but unfortunately our crankshaft was not hard enough and we badly scored and ruined the two halves of the crankshaft, probably respresenting 500 hours of skilled craftsmen's work. So we changed back to white-metal-lined shells and had no further trouble. A retrograde step probably, as the bearings were very narrow

The magnificent Triumph 2-litre straight-eight engine, acknowledged to be a copy of the 8C 2.3-litre Alfa Romeo unit. An Armstrong-Siddeley/Wilson preselector gearbox was used. The original twin-choke Zenith carburettor was later changed to an SU. Overhead-camshaft drive was by gears in the middle of the engine, which had two separate four-cylinder blocks (Picture: Autocar)

and theoretically very overloaded; if we had had time to further develop the crankshaft for lead-bronze bearings we could have raised the bmep considerably. But we could not afford to be pioneers.

'The chassis presented no difficulties. A normal gearbox could not be found to cope with the power we had – but Siddeley had done a lot of work in developing a racing epicyclic pre-selector box for ERA. I decided to use this and never experienced any kind of trouble. Alfa Romeo were then using aluminium brake drums of very large diameter and very narrow shoes and, against the recommendation of Gordon Parnell of Lockheeds, I had them made. Parnell had pointed out that the rubbing speed was far too high for the linings then available and they were never a success. Later on we changed to normal-sized brakes in cast iron drums, which proved as good as they could be got in those days. We used springs with an extra large number of leaves to increase the natural damping and these, coupled with Hartford dampers, gave an excellent hard ride, as we then thought desirable for a fast car. Later, I learnt, during four days and nights on a Monte Carlo Rally, how hard they really were! We had a lot of trouble with frothing of the oil in the pretty ribbed tank fitted between the front dumb-irons and for road and rally use reverted to a wet sump. The Roots blower was the same size as that on the 2.3 Alfa so we had a little more boost on our smaller 2-litre engine. Beyond the noise, this never gave any trouble with the SU carburettor used.

'The Dolomite's body was quite original. It was styled by the stylist of all the Triumph cars, Walter Belgrove, was made entirely in our coachwork factory, and was considered by experts to be very beautiful.

'On the road the car did all we expected. The testing was all done by Jack Ridley and myself. Tommy was the first racing driver to try it and his write-up described the car as excellent in every respect. We did a lot of testing at Brooklands but never achieved the lap speed of 120 mph which we hoped for – still, it got very close to this and, considering a rather wide touring body, we were quite pleased. One incident during testing – when doing something over 100 mph on the London road the car and I were spotted by a PC and reported to Coventry Police for dangerous driving. Fortunately my passenger was the Hon. Cyril Siddeley, the then Lord Lieut. of Warwickshire, and his word refuted the dangerous driving charge . . . .

'Having a car with a such superior performance I thought, here was a chance to repeat my Monte Carlo Rally win of 1931. Starting from Umea in Northern Sweden in the 1935 Rally, I demolished the front end of car No. 1 in a collision with a train. From the remains of this I built a car for the next Monte Carlo Rally but this time I ran without the blower and managed to finish eighth.

'During that year the Triumph Company got into financial difficulties. The motor-cycle business was sold and the Dolomite programme was cancelled completely and the name used on a production car we were introducing.

'People have made rude remarks about my *copy* of the Alfa Romeo and have suggested that Alfa threatened Triumph with legal action, etc – I can categorically deny this; actually they were extremely helpful, as I previously have mentioned.'

(Donald Healey's reference to the 'famous engine' copied from a well-known American engine is thought to refer to the V-8 fitted to Rolls-Royce and Bentley cars, which was released in the autumn of 1959, and at the time bore a distinct resemblance to a Cadillac V-8 engine, of which Rolls-Royce were known to have examples. However, this sort of cross-fertilisation of design ideas and non-patentable features has existed in the motor industry for years, and is nothing of which to be ashamed. As for the 3½-litre Rover V-8, this was quite openly bought from General Motors, and is an up-dated version of the Buick V-8.)

It is now difficult to understand why the 8C 2300 Alfa engine should have been chosen as a basis for the Triumph straight-eight, especially as it was a supercharged design. Presumably any such design would be expected to perform well in the major British races, not only at Brooklands, and it was a fact that at the close of 1933 the RAC decided to ban the use of superchargers from all future TT races! In addition, it would appear reasonable that Jano was willing to encourage Healey to perpetuate the design for, even though the Alfa engine was to soldier on until 1939 with 2.6-litres, 2.9-litres and finally 3.8-litres, as far as Jano was concerned it was already an old design; by 1934 he was far more interested in supplying Nuvolari's Grand Prix cars with bigger and more powerful engines with which to fight the German Mercedes and Auto-Union monsters.

To confirm Healey's minor mistake as to timing, and the concept of the Dolomite, he joined the company late in 1933, and the straight-eight project came into being almost at once. The first engine, therefore, probably ran on a test bed in May or June 1934, and all three Dolomite prototypes (for only three were ever built) were produced between mid-1934 and the end of the year. The actual Olympia Show car was not quite complete, but the prototype which was driven at Brooklands by Donald Healey and Brian Twist of *The Autocar* during September had already been running for some weeks.

The straight-eight Dolomite was an astonishingly attractive car. With its sleek and rakish-looking two-seater body hiding a 2-litre supercharged engine, it looked very fast, even when standing still. It was provisionally priced at £1,050 in chassis form, or £1,225 when supplied with the Triumph-built body. Here, truly, was Earl Howe's Alfa-beater, and certainly at an Alfa price! By comparison other British sports cars in 1934 were considerably cheaper. The SS1, with 68 bhp, cost £345, and though not in the Alfa class was good enough to perform with distinction in the Alpine Trial. The most expensive Frazer-Nash, with 78 bhp, sold for £545, while the LG45 Lagonda, with 135 bhp but a lot more weight, had an asking price of £1,000. The only car with the same sort of performance and distinction was the 3½-litre Rolls-Bentley, which produced approximately 120 bhp and sold for £1,380.

When the Dolomite was announced, the chauvinistic British motoring magazines never mentioned its likeness to any other car, but to any knowledgeable sportsman there could have been little doubt that the engine was almost a straight copy of that fitted to the 8C 2300 Alfa Romeo. The Alfa had been in production for four years, and was just about to be supplanted by a handful of larger-engined, and even more sporting 8C 2600 Monza Alfas. If there had to be a copy of any car's engine this was probably it. From 1931 to 1934 the 8C Alfa had had a particularly impressive competitions record, with wins at Le Mans in 1931, 1932, 1933, 1934, in the Ulster TT in 1932 and 1933, and in the Mille Miglia in 1932, plus a host of wins in other sports-car races. Brian Lewis' car, which Healey bought via Tommy Wisdom, was privately owned, but kept well up-to-date with factory modifications.

The Earl Howe thinking about 'selling a proper sports car with which to beat the world' appears to have permeated Healey's, Holbrook's, and Tommy Wisdom's thinking about the car, but they must surely have realised that they could only hope to sell a few such cars. The car from which the Dolomite's engine was copied, for all its very impressive racing history and Alfa's lengthy sporting reputation, had only sold 188 examples in four years, of which the 'best' year was 1933 when 89 were built. (It is interesting that in 1934, when the straight-eight Dolomite was being designed, production of the 8C Alfa had almost ceased – a mere seven cars were delivered in that year). Alfa, of course, were state-controlled, and as much geared to production of vehicles for military use as to cars for sale to private motorists; their interest in the straight-eight family had already waned, for only a handful of the 2600 Monzas were built. On this evidence, and allowing for the fact that a sports-racing Triumph would not sell on its reputation at first, it must have seemed unlikely to anyone with his commercial feet on the ground that more than a few – 20 a year at best – would be sold. For a company that spent much of the 1930s staggering from financial crisis to financial crisis, the presumption in even attempting the car was astonishing.

Donald Healey's account of the project does not give full details of this potentially exciting car, and it is worth recalling the main features together with comparisons with the Alfa Romeo where appropriate. The ladder-type pressed-steel chassis frame was Triumph's own layout, and was entirely typical of the period, having a beam front axle and a spiral-bevel rear axle suspended on very stiff half-elliptic leaf springs; these had a multitude of leaves intended to promote natural damping friction, and there was further damping in the shape of friction-type shock absorbers. The front axle was further located by forward-facing radius-arms anchored to the chassis behind the

The Olympia Show chassis of the straight-eight Dolomite. The three-gallon oil tank is faired between the dumb irons. The 16-inch diameter brakes were later reduced to 12 inch (Picture: Autocar)

All that remained of Healey's straight-eight Dolomite after it had hit a train on a level-crossing in Denmark while competing in the 1935 Monte Carlo Rally. No-one was hurt but Danish Railways claimed for damage to their train! (Picture: Autocar)

spring pivot, which would have made the potential geometry very interesting indeed if the axle had been allowed to deflect more than a nominal inch or so! *The Autocar's* description of the car stated: 'The frame is not intended to be superlatively rigid, but to be of a carefully graded flexibility, the major stiffness being at the front end where the engine unit adds to the rigidity, and where stiffness ensures good steering and roadholding.' This almost brings to mind Ken Richardson's Le Mans philosophy of screwing up the springs and dampers so far that the chassis had to act as a suspension member too, but it probably stemmed from Healey's experiences with the flat-iron Invictas. In any case, few ladder-chassis frames at the time were really rigid, nor could they be expected to be so as they lacked the depth essential to beam stiffness, and (on the grounds of weight saving) the cross-bracing to ensure torsional stiffness.

When I asked Donald Healey what had happened after the arrival of Brian Lewis' Alfa in Coventry, he said: 'We stripped the engine right out, and I got a man called Swetnam, one of my draughtsmen, to copy and draw up every last detail, down to the nuts and bolts. Our engine was a bit different, of course. I wanted a 2-litre, which meant that we used a smaller cylinder bore, and because we kept the supercharger like the Alfa that automatically meant that our boost was higher. Our compression was a bit higher, too'. To bring the Triumph's capacity just inside the 2-litre limit at 1,990 cc, compared with the Alfa's 2,336 cc, the bore was reduced to 60 mm instead of 65 mm, although the Triumph was equally capable of being bored-out; Donald Healey's 1936 Monte Carlo Rally car was approximately 2.4 litres, probably with a bore of 66 mm, though no-one can remember for certain. (The Alfa, of course, eventually finished up at 3.8 litres by being bored *and* stroked from its original dimensions.) There were twin, four-cylinder, cylinder blocks which sandwiched the twin-overhead-camshaft gear-drive between them. The fully machined crankshaft was supported by no fewer than ten very slim main bearings. The opposed valves included an angle of 90 degrees on the Triumph (easier to arrange for speedy machining), and 100 degrees on the Alfa. A Roots supercharger was used, drawing its mixture through a twin-choke Zenith carburettor which was hurriedly changed for a monster SU instrument because of induction whistle problems that could not be solved. Supercharging boost was 10 psi, and the nominal compression ratio 6.5 to 1; Alfa used 6 psi and a 5.7 compression ratio. No cost was spared in the engine's construction. High Duty Alloys made the intricate block and head castings in RR-Hiduminium alloy, while Triumph made up everything else apart from proprietary items such as carburettors and seals. All lightly stressed components and covers were in electron. A dry-sump oiling system was employed at first, with a three-gallon oil tank mounted in the nose of the car between the dumb-irons and very neatly faired in; this might be thought vulnerable, but surely was no more so than the supercharger and carburettor installation of the earlier 4½-litre 'Blower' Bentleys. While the car was under development, an oil-frothing problem was attributed to the dry-sump system, and the prototypes were converted to conventional wet sumps to the slight detriment of the ground clearance.

Lt-Col Holbrook's budget limitations (Healey said he could no longer remember how much had been allocated, but it could not have been more than £5,000!) put paid to any thoughts of a specially designed manual gearbox, and since Triumph did not possess any gear cutting facilities of their own at that time a complete box had to be bought out. In any case Healey had been impressed by the performance of the pre-selector self-change boxes fitted to such racing cars as the ERAs, a box developed around the Wilson design by Armstrong-Siddeley of Coventry. It was both heavy and bulky, but being built by Armstrong-Siddeley almost guaranteed its reliability, and Healey wanted to be free to develop his engine.

The Dolomite's bodywork, which was closely wrapped around the engine in a fairly standardised sports-car chassis layout, bore some resemblance to the Alfa Romeo 8C. In spite of Donald Healey's insistence that it was styled by Walter Belgrove, I am assured that this is not so, and that it was carefully and lovingly designed by Frank Warner, probably as his last major job at Triumph before he left the company to join the Hillman-Humber combine on the other side of the city. In his many notes to me about the company, Walter Belgrove states: 'You refer to the Dolomite straight-eight as apparently being styled by myself. This is not so, as I had nothing to do with this model. To Warner should go the credit for all the original Gloria and Vitesse saloons, the Gloria and Vitesse tourers, and the Dolomite straight-eight.'

The car as released nevertheless sported a vestigial Alfa-like tail fin between the seats and the spare wheel position, while the general layout of panelling, radiator and door lines was similar. The car first shown – the one driven at Brooklands and prepared for the next Monte Carlo Rally – had cycle-type wings, and originally sported twin aero-screens, which surely could only have been intended for racing. But to confuse matters the cutaway drawings published on announcement day showed twin aero-screens and full-length flared wings, which dipped smartly alongside the doors to fair smartly and completely into streamlined rear wings. The Olympia Show car had flared wings, while the car which did the Monte Carlo Rally also had a conventional folding screen. The car was always intended to be sold with a conventional screen *and* aero screens, along with a hood which could be removed and stowed in a locker behind the seats.

Very little is known about the performance of the developed Dolomite, but Donald Healey told me that he never managed to squeeze the flat-out maximum speed up to the hoped-for 120 mph, and since there was plenty of power present he assumed that the body shape must have been even less aerodynamic than feared. However, continuous testing at speeds in excess of 100 mph was achieved regularly at Brooklands by Healey and Jack Ridley. As mentioned earlier a brief test was carried out by Healey and Brian Twist of *The Autocar* at Brooklands just before Olympia. Twist was no tyro as far as high-performance cars were concerned, as his writings often described runs he had had at Brooklands in other people's racing cars, yet he was undoubtedly most impressed by this Dolomite drive, the car in question being ADU 4, which Healey was to use in the 1935 Monte Carlo Rally. That the project had not been kept entirely secret in the Coventry area is revealed by Twist's comment: 'I was greatly interested to be afforded the opportunity of a fairly extensive run in the latest 'mystery' car – rumours of whose embryo existence have been going round the Midlands all the summer – the eight cylinder 2-litre supercharged Triumph Dolomite.' That the rumours had been well fired with over-statement: 'Some misunderstanding (of the car's purpose) was created by an original announcement that in a secret test at dawn 120 mph had been attained with full equipment.'

The prototype had one very engaging quirk, which reminds us that noise-limitation and refinement is not an invention of the last ten years: 'As soon as we were clear of Coventry the car settled down to an easy cruising gait, and I for my part was immensely intrigued by a delicious whine, not from the supercharger gears, but caused by air rushing in through the twin choke tubes of the carburettor. As we dropped to third for a bend and then accelerated again, the tiny break in that thin whine when top was snicked in seemed immensely satisfying. One must not talk about noise of any kind, however, and as a matter of fact it would be most unfair, since not even Mr Hore-Belisha could object to that noise, as it is not audible outside the car, a fact we proved subsequently.' Sentences were obviously longer in those days, too!

The ride, as suggested by the specification, was

hard and unyielding, though according to Twist: 'The springing with the shock absorbers fairly loose was extremely comfortable, exceptionally so for so fast a machine. When I had been sitting in the passenger's seat, even though we had several times reached about 85 mph, I had rarely been bumped off the cushion.' Either the Coventry-Oxford road was diabolically rough in 1934, or the standards of acceptability have changed somewhat!

Performance at Brooklands, for a first-off prototype, was quite startling. Acceleration was hampered by slipping brake bands in the Siddeley-built gearbox (so all that ERA experience was not quite enough, after all?), and no speedometer was fitted. Acceleration figures, two-up, therefore, were out of the question, so Healey and Twist had to be content with standing-start distances and maximum speeds. These speak for themselves:

Quarter-mile flying maximum speed	102.47 mph
Complete flying lap	98.23 mph
Quarter-mile, from standing start	17.8 sec
Half-mile, from standing start	28.6 sec

All these were two-up, two-way, mean figures.

The best one-way timed speed over a quarter-mile was 104.65 mph, and the highest equivalent 'rev-counter' speed seen was over 106 mph.

Here, then, was a very exciting car indeed, potentially just about the fastest in Britain up to that time if the performance could be repeated on a 'production' basis. Contemporary road tests failed to throw up a single car which could exceed 100 mph unaided, and one had to cast one's mind back to the fabulous 8-litre Bentley for one that could. The contemporary 4½-litre Lagondas could exceed 90 mph, as could the 3½-litre Rolls-Bentleys, but the rest were left way behind; 100 mph was a very exciting speed indeed in the 1930s, to be compared, perhaps, with 150 mph from a production sports car today.

Unhappily for Donald Healey, Earl Howe and most of Britain's sporting enthusiasts, the Dolomite project was to be short-lived. As mentioned in the previous chapter, by the spring of 1935 Lt-Col Holbrook had axed the entire project due to the very serious financial situation which had developed in the group; the accumulated loss of £168,705 by 1933 had been increased by a further £55,761 in 1934. The Board of Directors was revised in November 1934 (just after the Dolomite had been announced) and as they set about a programme of rationalisation and cost reduction the implications for the straight-eight were immediate and obvious. It would be much too expensive, probably difficult to make with average Coventry labour, and not likely to bring profits to the company. The three cars which were made before the axe fell were all prototypes and all slightly different, and having built them, Healey saw no reason why they should not be used to bring publicity and if possible credit to the company. Accordingly he entered ADU 4 for the 1935 Monte Carlo Rally, well-equipped with all-weather equipment, elected to start from Umea in Northern Sweden, and took off to what looked like a near-certain victory. Healey, of course, had already won the rally in the Invicta in 1931 and had finished third overall in a prototype Monte Carlo tourer in 1934. Healey himself remains quite convinced that he would have won easily if he had not arrived at a Danish level crossing at exactly the same time as the train which wiped off the entire front end of the car! The whole of the frontal section and one of the precious engines were written-off, and the occupants were lucky to walk away from it. However, all was not disaster for Triumph on that rally, for Jack Ridley, who also started from Umea, finished in a rousing second place overall, and won the up-to-1,500 cc category outright in a 2-seater sports-bodied version of the 1,232 cc Gloria. The straight-eight car was not used in competitions again for a further twelve months, though Healey himself drove one regularly in and around Coventry. One of the surviving cars was entered for the 1936 Monte Carlo Rally, this time in unsupercharged form, and with the enlarged 2.4-litre engine. Why unsupercharged? Probably because by then Healey had evidence that the narrow crankshaft bearings *were* over-loaded after all, and could not be expected to stand the strain of such a long event without the white metal bearings wilting. (Incidentally, Healey had avoided this problem when building Ridley's successful Gloria in 1935 by arranging for the car to be supercharged only for the tests at Monte Carlo, which meant that the engine only had to withstand super-tuning for about five minutes). Starting from Tallin, in White Russia, the unsupercharged Dolomite battled through awful weather, narrowly missed being involved in a repeat of Healey's level-crossing incident of 1935, and arrived in Monte Carlo unpenalised after a particularly unpleasant journey. After the driving tests had been completed, it was found that the rally had been won by Cristea's monstrous Ford V8 Special with a driving-test time of 1 minute 5 seconds; Healey, with a rather slower car and less practice in the intricate promenade test, clocked 1 minute 9.8 seconds and finished eighth overall, which was also the best performance by a Briton.

But the Monte Carlo Rally performance could not hope to save Triumph's exciting sports car in the face of the company's perilous finances, and the inevitable news was confirmed in the autumn of the same year when a new range of cars appeared carrying the Dolomite name, bearing no relation to the exciting eight-cylinder car, but being an updated variant of the Glorias and Vitesses fitted with Triumph's own pushrod ohv engine.

As he said in his *Motor Sport* article, Donald Healey might well have lost interest in the cars, especially as so much time and effort had been spent on them in 1933 and 1934. However, as he was now Technical Director of the company, there were always other projects to occupy his fertile brain, and the disappointment was soon put aside. In retrospect Healey is still very sorry about the demise of the car, but reckons that it could have been built in small quantities if the backing had been available; on the other hand, he now looks upon the production Dolomite range which ran from 1937 to 1939 as his most important commercial achievement.

But what became of the straight-eight cars? Too often, priceless prototypes like these are broken up and never live to be admired (or reviled) by future enthusiasts and historians, but in this case the cars survived. Donald Healey says he sold the cars to Tony Rolt, who eventually re-sold them to a London company called High Speed Motors. Certainly the cars, and what spare parts were in existence, eventually passed through HSM's hands, where the owners (Giulio Ramponi and Robert Arbuthnot) rebuilt them into very similar cars which they called HSMs. It appears that there were three such HSMs, which had rather different body styles, although the original straight-eight Dolomite radiator shell was retained with a different badge. The engines were all supercharged at that time, and had been converted to SU carburation. The HSM-Dolomite bodywork, constructed by Corsica, was a little more 'up-to-date' than that of the original Triumphs, and consequently the cars had lost some of their racy distinction, although they were better finished and had full all-weather equipment. Two of the HSM owners were Tony Rolt and Duncan Hamilton, two 'characters' who years later were to provide another famous sports

Donald Healey in his native Cornwall in a straight-eight Dolomite, still in racing trim without windscreen or hood mechanism. This is ADU 4, the first car to run

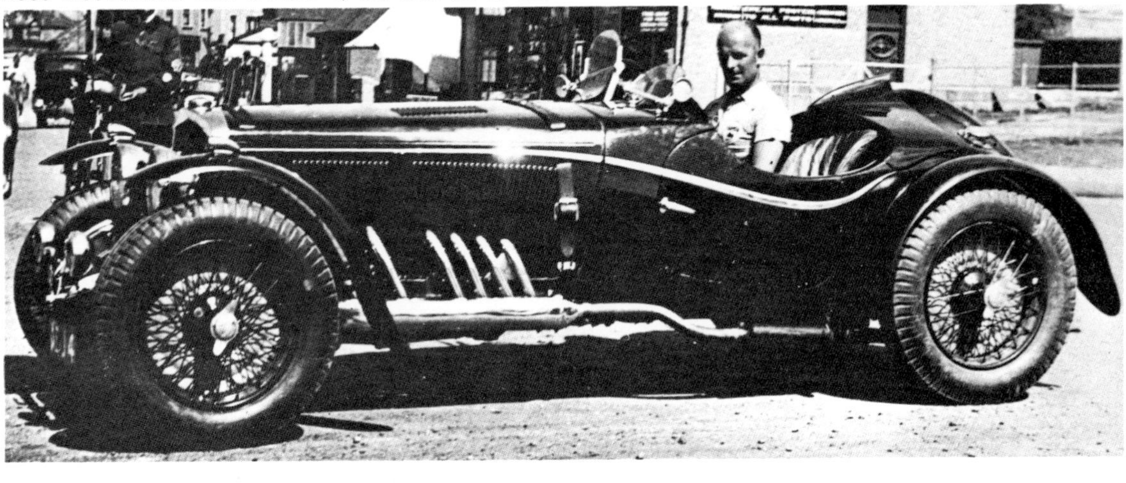

car company – Jaguar – with one of its most famous racing partnerships.

HSMs, or Dolomites, no longer appear in public, and certainly do not attend the Triumph Pre-1940 Owners' Club functions. However, this active little club claims to know the whereabouts of one such car in the Home Counties. When bought in 1958 it had a Jaguar 2½-litre engine (Standard-type) fitted. Later an engine was discovered in a power boat in Scotland, purchased and found to be the original from that car! This car – HYM 224 – still has 16 in brakes, a dry-sump system and Dolomite badges. Incidentally it carries the chassis number DMH 1, which were Donald Healey's initials, and was an appropriate way of identifying a project with its designer.

Asked what had become of the ex-Brian Lewis Alfa Romeo, Donald Healey said that he had rebuilt it following minute examination of the engine, had used it himself for some time, and had then sold it off. It was used as a racing car at Brooklands for a while after that.

For many years, the stories bandied about regarding the failure of the straight-eight Dolomite to go into production have centred around rumours that Alfa-Romeo had threatened legal action against Triumph on the grounds of plagiarism. Donald Healey's story, and subsequent conversation with the author, now makes it abundantly clear that this could not possibly have been so. Indeed, the legal facts of life that existed in the 1930s were very clear. If legal action had been taken by Alfa Romeo against this design any injunctions obtained would also have applied in the same way to the cars subsequently built and sold as HSMs. No-one would have been allowed to sell these cars to any member of the public, let alone race them, without Alfa Romeo stepping in. The fact that solicitor Anthony Blight mentioned legal action in his book about the Roesch Talbots lent fuel to the flames of controversy, but Blight has since said that he has no authenticated evidence. The country's legal records have been carefully sifted by those expert enough to know where to look; no trace of legal action has been found, nor is there any evidence of such proceedings ever being threatened.

All the evidence now points to the decision to cancel the project having been taken purely on good commonsense financial grounds. With the new Board of Directors installed towards the end of 1934, and strong statements being made about costing studies and financial re-organisation, there was clearly to be a period of financial stringency, especially with the purchase of a new factory in the offing. Lt-Col Holbrook was absolutely right (on practical if not on emotional grounds) to refuse to release money for tooling; if he had, Triumph must surely have perished several years earlier than they did, and the subsequent post-war success story might never have taken place. One can also observe that the publicity did Donald Healey's own reputation no harm at all, and indeed may have helped to push him one step further along the road to making his own Healey cars in later years.

CHAPTER 4

Takeover and war

AS THE WAR CLOUDS gathered once again over Europe, the Triumph concern found itself thoroughly destitute. Although most of the staff were retained following the appointment of Howe Graham as receiver, very few cars were actually being made. Whether or not war-material production contracts would have restored the firm to prosperity is neither here nor there (especially as there was to be strict control over 'excess profits' in the next few years), for most of the factories were to be destroyed by bombing anyway. Yet, even in that hot summer of 1939, few people in the motor industry were ready to believe in the approach of another world conflict, and the motoring press and businessmen were more concerned to see what would eventually happen to Triumph. Had not Riley, for instance, been dragged back from the brink of financial extinction by Lord Nuffield less than a year earlier? Had not Lea-Francis been reborn from the moribund ruins of Messrs Lea and Francis? Was not the similar, and neighbouring, concern of SS prospering greatly? Surely some business magnate would be attracted by the good name, the elegant styling, the engineering expertise, or even only by the tax losses to be set against future profits? Would Len Lord or Lord Nuffield come forward? Or Captain John Black or Billy Rootes? Or William Lyons perhaps?

But none of these industry tycoons came forward, perhaps because they knew the magnitude of Triumph's problems, which became even more obvious after the receiver's statements. Triumph's issued capital consisted of £50,000 in £1 Preference shares and £250,000 in 2s (10p... Ordinary shares, which had given the company a quoted stock market rating of only £54,000 before the receiver arrived, and a miserable £3,100 immediately afterwards. The Ordinary shares had dropped like a stone in value from 2s 9d to 1½d (13.9 to 0.6p) on the announcement, though speculators pushed them back up to 6d (2½p) in the next day or so. At the time it was also revealed that the Ordinary shareholders had received no dividend on their interests since 1930, while the luckier Preference shareholders were said to have last seen a return on their money in 1937; this was not strictly true, either, for in the 1937 reconstruction the Preference shareholders had been asked to waive their dividends which had already been in arrears since 1932! Although the factories were valued at £305,200 (a figure which Donald Healey now describes as ludicrously low), Lloyds Bank were still waiting for someone to repay the massive loan and overdraft which had been the cause of the appointment of their nominee, Howe Graham, as receiver. For a time at least, therefore, it looked like curtains for the company, only sixteen years after it had sold its first car.

But a buyer arrived co-incidentally on the very eve of the outbreak of the Second World War. Right at the end of August, Thos W. Ward, a respected engineering and steel-making company based in Sheffield, and a company not previously linked with the motor industry in any way, came up with proposals acceptable to the receiver for a takeover of the assets and debts. Before Hitler and his henchmen put a stop to all normal commercial processes for the next six years, Wards managed to scrape together enough parts and components from existing stocks to deliver perhaps 35 of the rather characterless 12 hp models (though Walter Belgrove thinks about 400 in all were made after the receiver arrived in June), together with a very few Dolomites that were already partly built or actually in stock. Even though the war had started two months earlier, Wards went so far as to issue a statement to the press in November 1939, that they would carry on producing a full product line as long as was practicable, but there is no evidence to suggest that any more Dolomites were built after the takeover.

In fact, most of the staff and work force were dispersed to war work in other Coventry factories, but of the senior staff who were kept on, company secretary J.H. Owen was nominated to remain in control, while Donald Healey was appointed General Manager, to exercise what Wards quaintly called a 'watching brief'. Wards had bought up Triumph with the intention of re-selling it in the most advantageous way, and their immediate policy was to concentrate the available work into as small a factory area as possible, so that the redundant areas and plant could be disposed of to raise cash where practicable. Fortunately for them, the Priory Street premises had already been abandoned by the old company, while the 'new' Gloria Works in Holbrooks Lane was a reasonably self-contained unit which they thought could be sold off without harming the rest of the company. Therefore they decided to concentrate such work as there was on Clay Lane/Briton Road, where the service department, spares, and body erection facilities had been situated for some years. This was logical, and even had a sort of sentimental symmetry about it, for although the address had changed a little this factory embraced the original ex-Dawson Motor Company plant that Siegfried Bettman had first purchased way back in 1921. The company's proudest and latest possession in Coventry, the Gloria Works in Holbrooks Lane (which, one remembers, had once been a Government shell-filling factory, subsequently taken over by White and Poppe in which to make engines for Morris cars, before Triumph had bought it) was to be sold off. All useful spares would be shipped up to the Stoke factory, while plant and machinery would be auctioned off.

Donald Healey's main job under Thos Wards was to find a buyer for the Gloria Works while keeping the car business in the background in preparation for peace-time production again. Healey negotiated with several interested companies, finally selling to the Hobson carburettor company. Laurence Pomeroy Senior (who had been involved with the motor industry for some years in Coventry, notably with the Daimler company) then joined Hobson as their local Chairman and Managing Director, and put down a very elaborate set of testing equipment for developing aircraft carburettors at ground level. Healey was asked to join Hobson to commission this work, did so, and acted as Pomeroy's assistant until he died. It is worth noting that the Claudel-Hobson carburettor was also produced within the grounds of Captain John Black's Standard factories at Canley, and that they had rented a section of the Morgan factory at Malvern Link; all very symbolic no doubt, as it brought Triumph, John Black and Morgan tenuously together again.

Unhappily for Triumph owners, and for those who were looking ahead for the continuity of a well-known make of car, Wards made no bones about their intentions following the takeover. Theirs was to be no Nuffield-style rescue operation – it had always been a purely speculative purchase. These days no doubt we would call it an asset-stripping operation, and condemn it heartily, for Wards were intending to sell off the arms and legs of the corpse, hoping that the body alone would still be worth more than they had paid for it at the end of the day. At the time Wards readily admitted that they never really expected to be able to re-establish car manufacture in any volume after the war, nor even if there had been no war and political events had allowed them to go forward as they wished. However, they were not able to get very far with their plans for dissecting Triumph, especially as the onset of hostilities made one vital difference – Clay Lane/Briton Road was blitzed! Several hundred chassis frames, bodies and engines had been stored in the old factory, and would have been much prized for spares in years to come, but a string of German bombs flattened the place and wrote-off the only physical assets which remained of Triumph cars.

Without the fighting, therefore, it is highly

unlikely that Triumph would have been sold as a going concern, though it seems that Wards were indeed interested in selling the trade-name rights as the final part of the dissection. Without a war, perhaps the company would not have been sold to John Black, and there might not have been any successful rebirth to give any basis for the rest of this book.

As to the assets of the company that remained, after the blitz there was really only the shell of a factory and the 'goodwill' of Triumph's own name with their clientele and distributors. Most of the records and virtually all the spares had been destroyed. Not a single panel, engine component or chassis member was destined to be used for new Triumph cars nor for any other make of car for that manner. Only the unattractively engineered 12 hp saloon, announced in 1939, was to have any major influence on future events, when Standard's stylists used it for inspiration in 1945 in creating the first of the post-war 'Triumph' saloons, the 1800, although Triumph's own 'trade mark' – the dickey seat – was also to be revived for the post-war Triumph 1800 Roadster, probably for rather nebulous marketing reasons than for sentiment. Certainly there might have been more continuity of line if Chief Stylist Walter Belgrove had been responsible for the first cars to be designed following the takeover, but this link was not to be renewed until several months afterwards.

As to the personalities at Triumph when the final collapse came, as we have already noted, Donald Healey, by then a balding but vigorous forty-one-year-old, soon left his watching brief at the moribund Triumph company to join the Hobson carburettor company at the ex-Triumph factory in Holbrooks Lane and undertake vital aircraft carburation experiments. Later he moved across Coventry to join Humber to become involved in armoured-car development. It was at Humber that Healey's desire to make his own car began to mature, though at first he was only spurred on to be the designer of a car which might not carry his name. Like many other motor industry types, who could not actually take part in the fighting, what spare time he had was taken up in planning for the future. Healey enlisted ex-Triumph friends and Humber colleagues to get on with his new designs. The new car's styling reputedly was drawn on the wallpaper of a private house in Coventry, while the general chassis layout was most certainly drawn by a Humber employee, on a Humber drawing board, in Humber's time! Healey appears to have been quite convinced that Wards were interested in putting Triumph back on its feet after the war had been won, and had the intention of offering his designs to them for production as a Triumph car. Since he had been in charge of development for some time, later becoming Technical Director and ultimately General Manager, there was every reason to suppose his plans would be approved.

But Wards were not, apparently, as complaisant. Peter Browning's book *Healeys and Austin-Healeys* (Foulis) quotes one of Healey's co-sponsors, James Watt, an ex-Triumph salesman, as saying:

'Donald and I began to feel that our little team was really getting somewhere and we now felt that we nearly had a good enough design to think about production and that the time had come for us to try and sell our ideas to Triumphs. I had already made two fairly successful approaches to Triumphs, and in February 1944 the opportunity arose for another meeting . . . . . At first things seemed most encouraging and they (Wards in Sheffield) genuinely thought that our scheme and ideas had merit. However, Triumph had had a board meeting recently and I was tremendously downcast to learn that they had decided not to back Healey, mainly for the very simple reason that we were not car manufacturers . . . . . And so we put aside all thoughts of building our car at Triumphs . . . . . . We had begun to call the car "the Triumph" but when we lost the Triumph deal we just called it "the car".'

It is worth pointing out that at that stage 'the car' only existed as a chassis and body design, no engine and transmission having been chosen. Healey obviously was willing to consider the use of Triumph components in the new design, which rather underlines the pre-war impression that the Triumph-designed ohv engine introduced for 1937 was a very fine product. But it is now history that the first production Healeys used Riley engines, gearboxes and rear axles, and that a decision to use Austin engines for a new car in 1952 brought liaison with Sir Leonard Lord, and mushrooming success with large and small sports cars. There were Austin-Healeys until the end of 1970, and a new Jensen-Healey since 1972, while Austin-Healey Sprites (though called MG Midgets) continue to be made in large numbers at Triumph's rival concern in Abingdon. When Kjell Qvale, a rich motor trader from California, bought control of Jensen in 1970, it was at the instigation of Donald Healey, whose products had long been a success on the West Coast; Healey was installed as Chairman of the revamped company, and his son Geoffrey also joined the Board. Healey retired at the end of 1972, to retain only a consultative Board appointment, and to spend more time at his homes in Truro, Cornwall, and the Bahamas.

Maurice Newnham, although finished with Triumph, had by no means finished with life or with business. He had already been decorated for bravery for his work with the Royal Flying Corps in the Great War, and he re-joined the Royal Air Force in 1939. Subsequently he rose to the rank of Group Captain, and was responsible for running the new Parachute Training School at Ringway Airfield, near Manchester, winning something of a reputation for himself by insisting on testing all the new equipment personally before letting loose his recruits on the same gear. In peacetime he returned to several years of active business life with the family motor car distribution group in London before retiring following its takeover to live in Hampshire.

Sir Claude Holbrook, who finally had been Vice-Chairman to the little-known H.A. Reincke in the original Triumph company, re-joined the Army in a staff post, and rose to the rank of Colonel before finally retiring in 1943. Sir Claude also moved to Hampshire, only a few miles from Maurice Newnham and his own brother, Commander Norman Holbrook VC, who was also connected with Triumph in the 1930s. In researching this book I discovered that Sir Claude, by then a remarkably spry 87-year-old, was still very active and was continuing to travel a great deal, as ever.

Walter Belgrove, the Triumph stylist who probably did as much as anyone except Donald Healey to make his name in the industry through his work with the company, was destined to become the only personal link between the Triumph companies. Following the Wards takeover, and when it became obvious that there would be no further car work for the duration, he left Triumph to join the Standard Motor Company, who at that time showed no interest in the bankrupt Triumph concern. At Standard, Belgrove was involved initially in the full-scale drafting of the Airspeed Oxford aircraft, and later transferred to the planning department, where he spent the remainder of the war years working on among other things jig and tool design for the De Havilland Mosquito fighter-bombers (constructed principally from balsa wood) which Standard assembled in great quantities. Captain Black, who became Sir John Black during the war, knew of Belgrove's arrival at Standard, and having admired his pre-war work at Triumph, promised him a design job after the war was over. Indeed, Belgrove's first job for Sir John took place while the war was still in progress, when he was told of the new Vanguard project, and asked to style a body shell for it. Black was convinced that the best-looking car around was the 1942 Plymouth sedan, and commanded Belgrove to style the Vanguard on those lines. The only way this could be achieved in wartime was for sketches to be made of such a car, and since the best place to find them was parked around Grosvenor Square, near the American Embassy, Belgrove was told to take a car and his sketch pad down to London to do the job! Sketching cars from the back seat of his old Standard Eight was simple enough, but in taking the photographic records that he thought were necessary to complete the job, Belgrove confesses to having expected to be arrested as a spy by the American forces who seemed to be everywhere at the time! Later, when the Standard war effort had been wound up, Belgrove was transferred to the engineering department to become Chief Body Engineer. He was to be intimately involved in the re-incarnated Triumph cars for a further decade, missing only the 1800 Roadster and initial work on the 1800 saloon, which had already been completed before the end of 1945.

CHAPTER 5

Under new management

AFTER THE blitz there really wasn't much left of the Triumph company. In Alick Dick's succinct words, it was still 'bust'. With the main Gloria works in Holbrooks Lane already sold off by Wards to the Hobson carburettor manufacturing company, only the bombed-out shell of Clay Lane/Briton Road remained. These, together with the Triumph motor-cycle premises at Priory Street, the city's fine cathedral and much of the city centre, had all been thoroughly flattened in the bombing raids of 1940. Wards had tried to carry on a repairs and maintenance service for the cars as best they could, mainly from the basements which were more or less undamaged. However, the sight of devastation all around, and the fact that they had sold off the most viable factory, must have been discouraging. Even the considerable stock of spares, which would have been invaluable for re-starting production after the war, had been destroyed in the bombing; renewed car manufacture looked to be even less likely than it had in 1939. It was not really in Wards' interests to try to re-establish a car manufacturing company, for this was outside the mainstream of their activities, and no doubt they had tired of their investment, and were ready to sell out.

At this point, fresh from receiving a knighthood conferred upon him by a grateful government for his help in setting up Coventry's shadow factories, Sir John Black at last took an interest. Black had been in sole charge of the Standard Motor Company's affairs since 1934, and had a burning ambition to become the most powerful motor industry tycoon in the Midlands, if not in Britain. Born in Kingston-on-Thames in February 1895, John Black had joined the RNVR early in the Great War, then transferred to the Tank Corps in France. (Here, incidentally, his CO was none other than Clough Williams-Ellis, who later achieved his own lasting fame for the creation of the Italianate village of Portmeirion in North Wales). Demobbed in 1919 with the rank of Captain (which he was to use as a very apt 'handle' for the next twenty years) John Black then joined the Hillman Motor Company in Coventry, where he soon had the undoubted good sense and good taste to marry one of six Hillman daughters.

In 1928 he had been invited to join the administrative side of the Standard Motor Company by R.W. Maudslay, who had become impressed by Black's growing reputation in the close-knit motor industry circle within the city for organisational talent and ruthlessness. Within a year of joining Standard, Black had been promoted to the Board, as Director and General Manager. Maudslay died in 1934, whereupon Captain Black became Managing Director, aged only 39.

Whereas this brusque ex-Army officer was an ardent publicist for his company, he was never a great one for his own glory. After all this time it is still difficult to glean enough about his character, but it seems clear that Black was always difficult to work with, often completely dictatorial, completely outspoken and usually unlikely to accept any modification to plans and schemes he had already decided upon himself. Alick Dick sums him up like this: 'No-one hit it off with John Black really, and this is nothing against him. He was an individualist. You either

Two mavericks of the motor industry who had to do business together. Harry Ferguson (left) whose tractors were made in thousands by Sir John Black (right). Sir John's enterprise and pride brought Triumph into the Standard company in 1945

hated or loved him. I was his assistant or deputy for years, and I alternated between the two fairly often!' The seeds of Black's desire to build proper sports cars probably sprout from the days when Standard were supplying William Lyons' company with special chassis frames, engines and transmissions for the first SS cars. Black and Lyons never 'hit it off' either – probably because both were individualistic, never willing to give best to the other in business – and there is little doubt that Black was always on the look-out for ways to get on terms with SS in the sports car business. This urge strengthened after Black made a takeover offer for SS which Lyons (being the controlling shareholder) had abruptly turned down. Before the Second World War, Standard had neither the money nor the design engineers to branch out into such speculative projects as sports cars, and after all there had never been any such traditions at Standards.

That Black was not only interested in sports cars for their image, and for the profits they would make, is proved by the fact that for a time he was the proud owner of an SS100 sports car himself. He was also one of the first members of the motor industry to support Raymond Mays' BRM project, both in cash and in kind. Fortunately for Mays, he had started commercial links with John Black in the late 1930s when he had decided to make exclusive cars carrying the Raymond Mays name. For an engine he chose the unsuccessful V-8 Standard unit, of which Standard had a large surplus, so Black was delighted to find a new outlet through which to dispose of them. When Mays approached him in 1946, Black was happy to hand over a cheque for £5,000, and a promise to produce the upper and lower crankcase castings and the cylinder-heads for the complex V-16 BRM engine.

Alick Dick sums up what happened when the Coventry 'grapevine' let it be known that the remains of the Triumph company were up for sale, complete with the spares stock and what buildings went with it:

'Just about the end of the war, Triumph itself was bust. John Black wanted another make name beside Standard – just that. As far as I can remember, Sir John sent me out there to the factory with Charles Band, Standard's Chairman. We looked at the place, which wasn't worth a farthing; we bought the firm I think for £20,000, but it may have been £10,000. We sold the factory to the B.O.Morris company for about the same amount, and all we got was the name – for nothing – plus, I suppose, an obligation to supply spares for Triumph cars. But as there were hardly any of them, we really didn't feel any obligation to the old customers.'

Were Standard interested in the pre-war designs? 'Not one tiny bit. We never even gave it a thought. But what you have to remember is that before the war Standard had been supplying parts to SS. Standard had special engine tooling for the six-cylinder engines, and the overhead-valve version of the four-cylinder, of which Lyons took all supplies. Immediately after the war Bill Lyons wanted to buy the tooling – he wanted to make all of his Jaguars in future – and John Black was willing to let him have that so that we could build a competitive car. We kept the four-cylinder tooling, but it just wasn't viable without a new chassis and a new name. So that's why we bought Triumph. Just because Bill Lyons made a sporting saloon, or a sports car, John Black was not going to let him get away with it!'

The place 'not worth a farthing' was the Clay Lane/Briton Road site. B.O.Morris Ltd (who made Morrisflex flexible power-drive equipment) rebuilt it, started production there in 1946, and still occupied the factory more than a quarter of a century later.

The fact that Standard bought Triumph at all was, in hindsight, mere chance. Although Donald Healey's cars had built up a fine reputation during the 1930s there were other worthy names which equally might have qualified for John Black's 'sporting name'. It could, perhaps, have been Lea Francis, another Coventry firm which had survived one bankruptcy in the 1930s, and whose finances were none too strong at the time of the Triumph purchase. There was also a very definite possibility that Lagonda might have come under Standard's control. Indeed, the Staines-based company approached Standard during the war, dangling as bait the splendid reputation held by their Technical Director, W.O. Bentley, and the fine V-12 car which had been produced in the 1930s. Black turned down Lagonda after trying a V-12 car which he described in Bugatti's famous phrase about Bentleys as being 'a very fast lorry'. In any case he was not looking for a going concern, but purely searching for a name.

The British motor industry has always been noted for intrigue, and rival interests often rub up against one another. One startling development that nearly came about was that the revived Triumph company might have been headed by Cecil Kimber, until 1941 Managing Director of the MG Car Company at Abingdon. Kimber had been dismissed (some say quite unfairly) by Miles Thomas (later Lord Thomas of Remenham) in November 1941; Thomas at that time was Vice-Chairman of the Nuffield Organisation, and the dismissal seems to have been due to a clash of personalities, and to Thomas' desire to control Abingdon himself. From MG, Kimber moved on to the Charlesworth coachbuilding concern, then in 1943 to the Specialloid Piston Company in North London. By 1944, however, Kimber seems to have become bored with pistons (as Works Director he had thought it very simple indeed) and knowing of John Black's interest in sports car manufacture he went up to Coventry to have talks with him. Harold Connolly (of MG) stated in Wilson McComb's splendid *The Story of the MG Sports Car* (Dent):

After World War Two Walter Belgrove (left) became chief body engineer at Standard-Triumph. Under discussion with C.W. Walker of Ferguson (later of Chrysler) is the first clay model of the Standard Vanguard (Picture: Walter Belgrove)

'He (Kimber) was going to take me up to see Black for the weekend, to talk about cars and shapes and designs. I felt Black thought Kimber would make a lovely head for Triumph, with the reputation he had, because Black was concentrating on his sports cars then – in spite of the bloody awful thing he was trying to sell, with its coal-scuttle mudguards; it was a dreadful-looking crate. And that's what Kimber said to me, he said you come up with me, we'll talk to Black, we'll get some shape into that Triumph.'

Kimber himself wrote to Harold Hastings (until recently Midland Editor of *Motor*) in January 1945, saying:

'I feel somewhat pessimistic about the future of the real enthusiast's car. Sunbeam-Talbot, Riley and now MG have been or will be wrecked by the soul-deadening hand of the big business interests, and recently I have been staying with John Black who has just bought Triumphs, and what he proposes to do with that old name makes me want to weep. Lea Francis appear to be the only concern left to cater for the real enthusiast, but of course Singers may come into the picture, but I think this is doubtful.'

Kimber was obviously not clear in his own mind what he intended to do after the war ended, and certainly was not completely enamoured by Sir John Black's plans for the Triumph *marque*. What he might finally have decided was never known, for Kimber was killed in a desperately unfortunate low-speed railway accident in a tunnel near Kings Cross station on February 4th 1945.

Connolly's account, in retrospect, is seen to be mildly inaccurate, as at the time Kimber was negotiating with Black Standard were certainly not in production with any type of private car, let alone Triumph sports cars with 'coal-scuttle mudguards'. Standard did not, in fact, secure the final right to make cars bearing the Triumph name until the end of 1945, and Connolly surely must only have been referring to the very first Triumph 1800 Roadster that Black had had made for his own use.

The first public news of the takeover broke on November 9th 1944, when a press statement quoted Black as promising 'After the war Standard's experience and technique gained in the production of aircraft will be applied to the production of Triumph cars of character and distinction.' February 1945 brought a statement from Standards saying: 'With the object of getting back into their production stride as rapidly as possible after the cessation of hostilities the Standard Motor Company Limited has decided to concentrate on two up-to-date models, an Eight of 1,000 cc and a Twelve of 1,600 cc. It is also proposed to produce a 10 hp Triumph of 1,300 cc and a 15 hp model of 1,800 cc.'

Those Treasury Ratings quoted were to remain a very important influence on British car design for a few more years to come. Even though the annual duty to be paid for the privilege of keeping one's car on the road was but a small proportion of overall costs, the horsepower rating did affect insurance premiums, and if unduly high was thought to be a sales deterrent.

Of the new cars promised, a Triumph Ten did not appear at first, and it appears now that Black was already thinking of using up-dated versions of the pre-war Flying Standard Ten engines in a new car although it was to be 1949 before such a car appeared – as the Mulliners-styled Mayflower. The 15 hp car promised in 1945 must have intrigued pre-war Triumph owners, for it could have used an enlarged version of the old 1,767 cc engine or a slightly smaller version of the six-cylinder 1,991 cc unit. Their hopes, however, were soon dashed, and when the Roadster and saloon 1800s appeared in 1946 the 15 hp rating had mysteriously shrunk back to 14 hp!

Among the assets which Standard inherited were the Triumph trade marks, most of which they chose to retain. As now, the Society of Motor Manufacturers and Traders maintained a register of trade marks so that a company could protect its pet names from plagiarism by the opposition. Of the old Triumph names, Gloria, Vitesse and Dolomite are still registered trade marks for Standard-Triumph (or British Leyland as it has now become) although Gloria has yet to be used on a post-war car. The Triumph Vitesse name was re-born in 1962 when it was given to the Herald-based six-cylinder sports saloons which were a reasonable approximation to the type of car (if not a repeat of the quality) that pre-war Vitesses represented. Dolomite, of course, appeared with considerable distinction in 1972 on the first of Triumph's new generation of sports saloons with an overhead-camshaft engine, which has now been joined by the even more exciting Dolomite Sprint. No matter how the old-style enthusiast may squirm and demur, there is little doubt that any of the old Triumph personnel would have been proud of the new Dolomites, even if they cannot be bought with an open top. One name which Standard did not want was Scorpion, which had been used without any distinction on the unsuccessful 12/6 at the turn of the 1930s; purely for interest it is worth recording that Chrysler United Kingdom Limited have now registered Scorpion for use in a car, and Scorpion is also the name of a light military tank which Alvis are making, powered by a Jaguar XK engine! Of Gnat, the old Super Seven Sports name, there is no sign, and who would wonder – it is not the sort of name that one would expect to see today on a respectable four-wheeler device.

Formal handing-over of Triumph's assets, like most legal transactions, took a long time. Negotiated by a Nottingham chartered accountant, Bernard Barnett, the sale included formal assignation of goodwill including 'benefits of orders, contracts, engagements and work in progress' which could not have amounted to much. Completion of the deal took place on the last day of 1945, whereupon the Triumph Motor Company (1945) Ltd came into existence as a wholly-owned subsidiary of Standard.

Commercial and accounting policies now moved into action. Although Standard had sold the six-cylinder SS-Jaguar tooling to William

The first post-war Triumph, the 1800 Roadster, styled by Frank Callaby in 1944. Triple windscreen wipers were unique at that time. Note the wind-up windows and the bench-type seat

Lyons (who had paid for and collected it immediately in case the unpredictable Black should change his mind – which he did!) they had retained the four-cylinder engine tools at Canley. They were to supply only small numbers of engines to Jaguar, for use in their $1\frac{1}{2}$-litre saloon, so there was surplus capacity that would have to be used in new Standard products. Black's first thoughts were to produce a car competitive to the Jaguar so he went ahead immediately with a car for his personal use which, once approved, would go into production. During the war, Standard's Canley factories had been kept busy producing centre-sections for the Mosquito bomber, and had built up considerable expertise in aluminium working, and had accumulated a quantity of rubber press tools suitable for this purpose; with aircraft production running down fast, they were able to make good use of the tools and surplus stocks of sheet aluminium for car manufacture.

Before describing the design and construction methods used for the first post-war Triumph cars, one should recall the facts governing post-war private-car production, restrictions on which were severe, and were to persist until 1951 or 1952. It transpired that the shortage of sheet steel was much more serious than the general shortage of all raw materials, including casting and forging steels. The government therefore decided to ration sheet steel and grant licences and priority to those firms who could guarantee to export the vast majority of their products. The motor industry, the largest consumers of sheet steel in the late 1930s, were obviously going to be hit very hard. A few years earlier the situation would not have been too serious, as vehicle bodywork was usually wood-framed with sheet-steel cladding, but by the middle 1940s the trend had moved to the use of pressed-steel bodywork in its entirety. Casting and forging steel, on the other hand, was not to be subject to licences and rationing, so the industry found itself in an out-of-balance situation not remedied until the large new sheet steel factory at Margam in South Wales came on stream.

With creditable business acumen, Sir John Black decided to make his post-war Triumph cars with aluminium body panels (using the converted Mosquito rubber presses) and tubular-steel chassis as there was no licence problem with tubular steel, either. Even more convenient was the fact that a tubular chassis could easily be made in more than one wheelbase length.

Two new cars – an 1800 Roadster and an 1800 saloon – were to be built, both to be released on the same day early in March 1946. As such they were among the very first truly post-war designs, for other new models which had pre-dated the Triumphs (like the Armstrong-Siddeleys and the Rileys) almost certainly were well on the way as projects during 1939 and 1940.

As has already become obvious from Kimber's and Connolly's remarks, the first Triumph Roadster was styled in 1944, being built originally as a personal car for John Black's own use. His desire to compete directly with the post-war Jaguars might have had more chance of success if he had employed stylists of the calibre of William Lyons (who was personally responsible for the shaping of a Jaguar car), but nevertheless it was hasty of Connolly to dismiss the first Roadster as a dreadful-looking crate with coal-scuttle mudguards; after all, MG carried on with a distinctively pre-war style of sports car for some years in the 1940s, and replaced it with another square-rig layout that few found attractive. However, it would have given Black cause for much thought had he known then that Jaguar were already planning a larger and very much more powerful engine (the twin-cam XK range) which was to give their new cars really high performance, and take them permanently out of the range of Triumph's ambitions.

Nevertheless, for the few designers who were detached from their declining war efforts and set to work on the first series of post-war cars to be produced at Canley the first essential was to settle the styling of the new Roadster, for Black had decided that his own staff were perfectly capable of doing this. Although pre-war Triumph stylist Walter Belgrove was already employed at Standards, and as mentioned previously had been promised the position of Chief Body Engineer when the war was over, he was retained in his planning position until the end of 1945, so could not have a hand in the 1800 Roadster. The young man chosen to style the new car around the chassis and components being laid out by Ray Turner was Frank Callaby, at that time a body designer but later to become the photographic co-ordinator at Triumph. His method of doing the job was thought strange at the time, though such goings-on have become more normal in modern times: 'Sir John Black detached Arthur Ballard and myself towards the end of the war, and set us to work on a car for him. I did the one-eighth scale picture drawings of the new Roadster, which was to be the first of the Standard-built Triumphs. Once we had Sir John's approval, from this drawing Arthur Ballard (now Chief Body Engineer at Triumph) and myself developed all the shapes and made the detail drawings. Arthur worked rearwards from the 'B' post including the folding hood and the dickey seat, and I did everything forward of this, i.e. front wings, radiator, bonnet and facia.'

In body designers' language a 'B' post is the body pillar placed at the rear of the front-door openings; the doors on the Roadster were hinged from this pillar. On a modern car this would be the pillar which supports the upper safety belt anchorages, but in the case of the Roadster it was chopped off at waist level. From what Frank Callaby says, it seems that the car was styled by one man – himself – but that the detail execution was by two individuals. Detroit is often accused of producing a back half for a car which seemingly is unrelated to the front half (and it happened in Britain in 1960 in the case of the first Austin-Healey-based MG Midget!) but here we have an earlier example of which, perhaps, the same might be said. But in fact the two designers worked side-by-side, and were certainly never in any conflict over their aims for the car.

Historians in the Pre-1940 Triumph Owners' Club have drawn comparisons between the post-war Roadster and the last of the pre-war Dolomites, suggesting that Walter Belgrove's pencil was the link. Although this was not so, Standard certainly took over as many of the old drawings and sketches as could be found, and Callaby admits to having been influenced by the older models when shaping the new; some resemblance and a similar general atmosphere, therefore, is logical.

Belgrove, in fact, was always distressed that he took up his post-war position as Chief Body Engineer too late to influence the styling of the 1800 Roadster, as he was none too happy with it. For some reason (and there was no existing

The 1800 Roadster was the last car in the world with a dickey seat. You climbed in over the rear wing, via a foot rest on the bumper's outer edge. The windscreen was surprisingly effective

tooling to influence this) Engineering Director Ted Grinham had decided that the rear track should be much wider than the front, on the basis that a wide rear track would allow more passenger space, and a narrow front track would require less structure between the wheels and might cut down frontal area a little. Belgrove always objected to this crab-track-in-reverse, preferring the more elegant layout where front and rear tracks (as in pre-war Triumphs) were equal, or even that the front track should be slightly wider than that of the rear wheels. The layout on the new 1800s, where there was a five-inch difference in the wrong direction (Belgrove's opinion) made it difficult to produce sweetly tapering lines on any of the post-war cars, and it was not rectified until the Phase III Standard Vanguard was released in 1955.

The 1800 Roadster, once readied for production, was to be made in its entirety in the Standard factory at Canley, with scores of skilled tinsmiths and bodymakers fabricating the body from sheet aluminium, and fitters fabricating the chassis from off-licence steel tubes. The other proposed Triumph product – the 1800 saloon – was to be based on the same general chassis design, but was to have a coachbuilt type of bodyshell which would have to be found from an outside supplier, although final assembly was to be on the same Canley assembly line. Sir John was to have little problem in finding a supplier, as there were several such firms in the Coventry-Birmingham area, all looking avidly for their first post-war contracts; their hey-day had already passed, for during the 1930s there had been an increasing trend for car makers to build their own pressed-steel bodywork. However, it was not for at least another ten years that the last of the independent bodybuilders was taken over by one of the Big Six manufacturers.

As to the styling of the Triumph 1800 saloon, it seems to be generally agreed that it was one of the most elegant of the immediately post-war designs (along with the Riley RM series saloons it was to continue in production until 1955). Its razor-edge lines were by no means a poor relation of anything that Rolls-Royce or Bentley were then showing, and an 1800, or the later re-engined Renown, still looks elegant today. One might assume therefore that the styling was

Proposed revision of the original Callaby-styled Triumph 1800 Roadster, drawn in March 1946 by Belgrove. The car could have been in production in 1947 but Sir John Black would not sanction the re-tooling (Picture: Walter Belgrove)

settled after careful and lengthy consultation with the chosen coachbuilders, was subjected to painstaking modification and refinement, and was only finally committed to production tooling after much thought. The truth, alas, is almost as deflating to a stylist's ego as were the remarks made by rivals about the Roadster. The saloon's styling had not even been started when the Roadster bodywork was completed, because Standard's designers were still mainly committed to war work, and were also heavily involved in the post-war Vanguard project. Black therefore decided to select his bodybuilder first, and to give the firm the job of styling the car into the bargain. He chose Mulliners in Birmingham (not to be confused with H.J. Mulliner – still famous for its work on Rolls-Royce, Bentley and Daimler coachwork) and suggested that they might use the basis of the Standard Flying Twelve/Fourteen for their work. Mulliners set to on this basis, with Leslie Moore trying to achieve razor-edge elegance on an existing shell. But it was uphill work, for the Flying Twelve/Fourteen profile was not easily adaptable to this treatment, and after several weeks of vain sketching, Mulliners were still not able to satisfy Black's own ideas of what was wanted. Leslie Moore went back to designing other Mulliner styles – including a bus, of all things – and later was to be responsible for the styling of the squat little Mayflower, which had much more than a passing resemblance to the 1800 saloon as it eventually appeared.

One morning in 1945, Black, who was tiring of the way in which the saloon's styling had dragged on at Mulliners, suddenly decided that the time had come to show them what he really wanted, so he called up Frank Callaby and, according to Callaby, told him that he required a new body-style based on the Roadster chassis within three hours so that he could show it to the Mulliners management after lunch! In those days, as later, one didn't argue with Sir John, or even point out the difficulties of what was involved, in case he suddenly decided to sack you and start again; Harry Webster says that he was nearly sacked on his first morning as Chief Chassis Engineer in 1948 because he dared to query Black's directive of only three forward speeds for the Mayflower! Therefore Callaby did the only thing possible in the time. He dug out a set of pictures for the Triumph Twelve, released, one remembers, in the spring of 1939, used this Belgrove-styled car as inspiration and started work. By sheer good fortune the Twelve's wheelbase was nine feet, only a few inches different from that of the already-styled Roadster, and although the wheel tracks were a little different this didn't look like being a major headache. Sharpening-up all the rounded corners to produce the razor-edged style seemed to work, and at lunchtime the Managing Director was handed his proposed body-style. Needless to say the seating and all interior body dimensions were virtually the same as for the old 12 hp saloon.

Of such happenings are legends made. Those of us who thought that the so-attractive 1800 saloon, later to become the Vanguard-engined Renown and destined to run for nine years, took weeks of painstaking work to style have been proved wrong. It shows, no doubt, that the 1939 12 hp saloon was a nicely balanced car, and that Frank Callaby had a very sure eye for a line. This rush job is really the single example of the influence of the pre-war designs on the post-war cars. Certainly there wasn't a single item of chassis or hardware carried over from 1939 to 1945, as the bankruptcy sales and the blitz had done a very efficient job of destroying all possible links.

In case pre-war Triumph enthusiasts are asking themselves whether or not the old engines were superior to the SS-Jaguar-engined Standard designs, it is perhaps worth listing the main characteristics of the comparable engines:

1938/39 Triumph 14/65 engine:
13.95 hp Treasury Rating, 4-cyl, ohv, 75 × 100 mm bore and stroke, 1,767 cc, 65 bhp at 4,500 rpm
1938/39 Dolomite 2-litre:
15.72 hp Treasury Rating, 6-cyl, ohv, 65 × 100 mm bore and stroke, 1,991 cc, 70 bhp at 4,500 rpm, later 75 bhp at 4,500 rpm
1938/39 SS-Jaguar 1½-litre:
13.23 hp Treasury Rating, 4-cyl, ohv, 73 × 106 mm bore and stroke, 1,776 cc, 60 bhp at 4,500 rpm
1946 Triumph 1800 engine:
As SS version but 65 bhp at 4,500 rpm

The new car appeared to have gained a few brake horsepower over the pre-war engine built for the SS-Jaguar, but was in exactly the same guise as used by Jaguar in the 1940s.

Designed under the direction of Standard's Ray Turner, the Roadster/1800 chassis was built-up almost entirely from tubes, well braced with cross-members, plus transverse-leaf-spring independent front suspension of the Flying Standard type. The chassis frame underslung the half-elliptic rear suspension, the spiral-bevel axle being controlled by piston-type dampers interconnected by a torsion bar for anti-roll effect. There were two wheelbase lengths – 8ft 4in for the Roadster, which had a rear-wheel track of no less than 4ft 6¾in, and 9ft 0in for the saloon. Main chassis tubes were 3½in diameter, reinforced on their underside to improve beam stiffness. The brakes were hydraulic in the best Triumph tradition, and were self-adjusting.

A four-speed gearbox had synchromesh on the upper three ratios but – horror of horrors – a steering column change! In fairness to Triumph, this was a post-war fashion which spread like wildfire in the British industry during the late 1940s as it was thought the dollar-market customers would appreciate it. The gearbox itself was designed for central control, so the complex linkage required to adapt this can be imagined.

The Roadster's styling, though up-to-date rather than futuristic, was clearly controversial; there was a bench seat to give credence to the fiction of seating three abreast, and a throw-back to the old company by the provision of a dickey seat. This was usually hidden under a metal panel which, when swung forward, doubled as a glass-panelled windscreen, but the seats themselves were hardly practicable for a long journey, and had to be attained by an obstacle climb from a tread-plate on the rear bumper.

The Autocar's 1947 test was as equivocal as

could be expected. The comment on the dickey was: ' . . . occasional passengers can travel comfortably in the rear seats in reasonably fine weather. They have good vision through glass panels in the part of the tail lid which forms a windscreen for them . . .' The report criticised the gearchange as being: ' . . . not quite so clear-cut and positive as is an ordinary gearchange when first and reverse gears are wanted in succession in maneouvring.' They also commented that 'the car is quite noticeably wide, with the result that the bench-type seat really can accommodate three people.' There was no comment on their comfort when so installed, but with a between-doors width of 52 inches they had more chance than most.

The separate headlamps and generally bluff front-end styling did not encourage a high maximum speed, even by 1939 standards, but *The Autocar*'s testers recorded between 73 and 75 mph. The car was relatively heavy at 2,485 lb, so acceleration from rest to 60 mph took 34.4 seconds. The performance of this first test was disappointing, particularly as the car was claimed originally to be capable of up to 84 mph, and especially by comparison with the pre-war Dolomite Roadsters. The post-war Pool petrol could not be blamed for this disappointment, for the Standard-Triumph designers had laid out the post-war engine with the 74-octane mixture in mind. The previous Dolomite Roadster, powered by a 2-litre engine boasting a mere 10 bhp more, was quite significantly faster, recording a timed two-way speed of 78 mph, and reaching 60 mph from rest a full 11.4 seconds earlier; yet it was several hundred pounds heavier, and had the same gearing. All very puzzling, but presumably the post-war car had a built-in headwind that no amount of engine tuning could overcome.

In view of the availability of the rubber-press body tools, and the tubular nature of the chassis construction, the 1800 Roadster never involved the penalty of high tooling costs, and in Alick Dick's words 'was always virtually handbuilt'. Certainly only 2,500 examples were built between announcement in March 1946 and the autumn of 1948, when the only major engineering changes were applied to the car. It would be too easy, at this range, to write-off the Roadster as a commercial failure, but according to the general level of production achieved in British factories in the

The first post-war Triumph saloon – the razor-edge styling of the 1800. Its proportions were sketched round those of the 1939 Triumph 12 by Frank Callaby in a single morning

late 1940s, and because of its low tooling costs, it certainly didn't disappoint John Black or disgrace its original name. Triumph's former Sales and Service Director Lyndon Mills remembers just how much of a stir the car caused when he used the first examples: 'From a sales point of view I can remember it very clearly. I remember my wife and I went off on holiday in one to Lugano, in Italy, and of course new cars were still very rare. Everywhere we stopped crowds of people would collect. There was tremendous interest.'

The Roadster and the 1800 saloon, apart from being the first Standard-Triumph post-war releases, were also among the first new cars to be announced in Britain. The rest of Standard-Triumph's immediate post-war production programme was to be concentrated on pre-war Standard models. The old tooling for the Flying Eight and the Flying Twelve were dug out of store (but not for the intermediate Flying Nine/Ten, which used a different chassis and

Sir John Black posing proudly beside his Triumph Mayflower – an odd little car which combined pre-war Standard 10 performance with 1800/Renown-type styling

enters our story later) as it was considered that an all-new Standard would take too long to appear. In fact the Vanguard was to be delayed even more than had been feared due to Sir John Black, the Government (who owned the Standard-leased Banner Lane shadow factory) and Harry Ferguson, all getting involved in a deal whereby Standard would make the Ferguson tractors and Ferguson would sell them. The tractors had been made in small numbers pre-war by the David Brown organisation, and might have been made by Ford during the war, while the same deal had been offered to Lord Nuffield and Sir Leonard Lord, both of whom turned it down. The Black-Ferguson deal was thrown together rather quickly, reputedly finding its first draft agreement on the back of a menu-card at Claridges' famous London restaurant. The tractor was to dominate Standard-Triumph activities for the next fourteen years, and ultimately was to contribute to the company's takeover by Leyland in 1960/61. Within a very short time, Standard were making more tractors at the Banner Lane plant than cars at Canley, and because there were no selling or support services to provide, the tractor business was profitable and clean of all unwanted wrinkles.

A further benefit of the tractor programme was that it gave a very healthy base for the wide use of the engine which found its way into a whole variety of the car projects; there was also to be a diesel engine which found its way into taxi variants of the Vanguard. The origins of the Vanguard engine have never been described fully, and too many observers have been ready to write it off as 'the tractor engine which made good'. Although no doubt a good story, this was not so, and therefore must now be corrected. When Ted Grinham re-joined Standard as Technical Director at the end of the war he had gone full-circle. He joined the Standard Motor Company in 1929, and had been responsible for the design of all the Standards of the 1930s. He then went to Rootes, where he found that he could not agree with Bernard Winter, and so spent the war years at the De Havilland aircraft company, from whom much of Standard's war-effort was subcontracted. On his return to Standard, Grinham was directed to get on with a new engine design for the post-war cars, and since the Ferguson tractor deal had not been thought of at that time its use in tractors had not originally been considered. Harry Webster says that Grinham's primary influence in the layout of the now-legendary Vanguard engine was the wet-liner Citroen front-wheel-drive engine. The first Ferguson tractors used a Continental petrol engine, on which the Vanguard engine is sometimes said to have been based. Webster's comment was that the Continental engine was specified first because the Vanguard engine was not ready, and any similarities were incidental. The engine became somewhat heavier when it was realised that it would be suitable for fitment in the tractor and would have to be part of the backbone. As to the later diesel engine, there was virtually no similarity. Webster also remembers that Standard-Triumph persuaded Harry Ferguson to offer diesels in his tractors against his will: 'Ferguson is always said to have pressurised Standard into making a diesel engine for him. This is not true. We developed the engine in opposition to Ferguson's insistence that he would *never* want a diesel engine in his tractors. We made some tractors with the new diesel engine in, and proved that it was that much more economical long before Ferguson accepted it. He opposed it!'

Therefore, by the time the Standard Vanguard appeared, the engine intended for it had put on quite a lot of weight to make it suitable for a dual role. The Vanguard was first shown to the public in 1947, when the engine size was 1,849 cc (from a bore and stroke of 80 mm and 92 mm respectively), but by the time it reached production the bore size had been increased to 85 mm, and the capacity to a rather awkward 2,088 cc. There were never any sporting possibilities in the Vanguard, with its short wheelbase, ample ground clearance and bulbous body-style strongly influenced by those 1942 Plymouths which Black had seen so often on his visits to London during the war.

Once the car was in production, and tractors were also flowing out of Banner Lane, Black and Alick Dick (by now his Assistant Managing Director) were able to look around for further rationalisation. Certainly they were influenced in this respect by the unthinking pronouncements of the Chancellor of the Exchequer, Sir Stafford Cripps, who had given his government's edict that car firms ideally should concentrate their attentions on single models aimed at the export market. For this and other good economic reasons Black and Dick were in accord, and during 1948 the pre-war designs – the Flying Eight and the Flying Twelve – were discontinued and the knife-and-fork production methods used in erecting the Roadster and the 1800 saloon came under scrutiny. Fortunately for these two cars, their bodyshells were found to be adaptable to other chassis frames, for there was little doubt that fabrication of the tubular frames was a slow and costly business; in addition the volumes were low, and investment in the pressed-steel Vanguard chassis frame had been very high. The inevitable result was that before the first post-war Earls Court Motor Show, in October 1948, Standard-Triumph announced that the Roadster would in future be manufactured with modified versions of the Vanguard chassis frame, suspension, engine and transmission. Only the bodywork remained unchanged.

The open car then became known as the 2000 Roadster, even though its engine size was 2,088 cc. There were both advances and retrograde steps in the sweeping mechanical changes, which basically made the car less of a sporting tourer than before. The Roadster's wheelbase stayed at 8ft 4in, which was achieved by minor lengthening of the Vanguard's main side-members (the Vanguard wheelbase was then 7ft 10in), but in all other major respects the frames were identical. The main members were pressed box and channel sections, reinforced with similarly pressed cross-members, and the front suspension was by double wishbones and coil springs. Rear suspension was by half-elliptic leaf springs as before, but the axle was now a hypoid-bevel like that of the Vanguard.

The Vanguard engine additionally was rugged and heavy, and though by no means a high-revver it produced 68 bhp at 4,200 rpm from its 2,088 cc, and exhibited an impressive increase in torque over the ex-Jaguar 1,776 cc unit. Unfortunately, the new gearbox was something of a retrograde step. Although it now had very effective synchromesh on all gears there were only three forward ratios, and that awkward right-hand-change steering column control was retained. It was not the fault of the engineers that the car now had three speeds instead of four, but simply that the gearbox was identical with that fitted to the Vanguard, where John Black's dictatorial attitude had specified three gears as being quite enough – in fact he often said that he would like as few gears as possible.

Walter Belgrove was given a free hand to produce a sporting bodyshell on a Vanguard chassis in 1947. The result was this 1950 Roadster

The Autocar testers were not surprised to find an increase in maximum speed of only 2 mph – to 77 mph – but acceleration to 60 mph showed an impressive increase, the time required being down from 34.4 to 27.9 seconds. Fuel consumption was slightly improved, and appeared to offer the prospect of about 26 mpg; on balance, therefore, the new car seemed to be significantly improved. However, the three-speed gearbox can hardly have helped the give-and-take road performance, for the useful second-gear maximum speed was only about 45 mph, or 55 mph if engine noise and revs were ignored! Unhappily for Triumph, however, the really drastic changes wrought to this car did little to improve its sales, and it was withdrawn before the end of 1949, not much more than a year later. By comparison with the 1800 Roadster, sales were higher, but a planned sanction of 2,000 (of which a mere 184 were exported) did not look likely to be repeated, and the car's lack of success in export markets made steel supplies for its future chassis frame production rather difficult to achieve. Standard-Triumph appeared to have lost interest in the car, anyway, and with the Vanguard and the Ferguson tractors selling like hot cakes, the stubby little Mayflower just launched, considerable design activity being concentrated on the next range of Vanguards, and their first thoughts brewing on a new small car, who could blame them?

Sir John Black, however, was not happy to let the car fade away. Had not his business rival, William Lyons, startled the world of motoring with a splendid new engine, and produced a superbly-styled new sports car to accept it? Direct assault from Triumph was now clearly out of the question, for any XK120 would reach 115 mph, and the high-performance version had been timed at more than 130 mph, but Black's sporting (or should one say 'prestige') instincts were not to be denied, and he decided that a new sporting car should be made. It was not, however, a spur-of-the-moment decision, for he had approached Walter Belgrove for a new style as long ago as 1947, when the 1800 Roadster was only one year old. Furthermore, and this must have come as something of a pleasant surprise to Belgrove, there would be no limitations placed on the styling or layout of the car apart from the fact

One ingenious point about the 1950 Roadster was that the bonnet could be opened from either side. The Vanguard engine had twin carburettors for the first time though this was not the engine later used in the TR2

that it was to be based on the Vanguard's 7ft 10in wheelbase chassis and mechanical layout. It was a pleasant surprise because of the constraints under which Belgrove was now regularly placed. In the gentler pre-war days, Belgrove and Donald Healey had struck up a warm and friendly relationship, so that there was never any question of a 'second opinion' being required on a styling job, and Belgrove – being a purist – had blossomed under this trust to produce some elegant shapes and features. In post-war years it was all very different. Ted Grinham, to whom Belgrove, as Chief Body Engineer, reported, was a very strict disciplinarian, and like Sir John Black he liked his own way at all times. Although it would be pleasant to report that there was complete business harmony between the two engineers, the sad truth is that there seemed to be nothing better than an armed truce between them. Grinham had very little knowledge of, nor flair for, styling features, but nevertheless had very decided ideas of what he wanted to see in a car. It was a difficult situation, which incredibly was able to exist for the best part of nine years.

Belgrove's free hand in styling a new Roadster was directed by the first and very simple briefing he received from Sir John Black. In Belgrove's own words, his comments were: 'We want a new Roadster. I have been giving the matter a great deal of thought, and I think we should design and build a thoroughbred sports coupé. I know what you are going to say – that you produced schemes in 1945 and that they are still lying in your drawing cabinets. You were busy with the Renown, Turner was already occupied on the 1800 Roadster, and you were about to start the Vanguard. The war wasn't over, the whole factory was in state of flux, with everyone overlapping each other. Now everybody is organised. I want you to design a Roadster Coupé to replace the 1800; in performance, specification and behaviour I want it to surpass that Dolomite of yours from back in 1938. You've got an open cheque book. Design and build it for yourself – you won't get it of course, but you know what I mean – if you want to power-operate things, do so. You can have the Vanguard chassis and engine, and the wheelbase should be long enough for a two-three seater.' By the standards of the 1970s, this was a very vague product study for a new car, but it was in this way that the Roadster shown at Earls Court in 1950 was started.

My problem is first to give it a name. From time to time it has been called the Roadster 'Cigar', the push-button Roadster, the hydraulic Coupé, the TRX, the TSX, the Silver Bullet, and even the TR1. TR1 is most certainly incorrect – if any car should have that name it was the very first of the TRs, though the designation TR1 never appeared in print either at Triumph or in the press – and as far as all the others are concerned one can take one's pick. TRX is the one which seems to crop up more than other names, though this really only meant TRiumph Xperimental car.

The first approved sketches were dated August 1947, which meant that it then took three whole years for the pencil schemes to be translated into metal. As to the styling itself, there have been many different opinions. Walter Belgrove, on looking back at this project, where he had complete freedom for the only time in his Standard-Triumph career, is still happy with it, though he was always unhappy at the prospect of getting any reasonable shape around a Vanguard chassis which was both too high and too short. Some of its features were considered radical at the time – power-operation for the hood, the seats, and for the headlamp covers, for example. The covers themselves were new to Britain, though the American Cord had tried them in the 1930s.

Walter Belgrove had no doubts about the style. It was a 'stable mate' to the Standard Vanguard, as modern as he could make it, and completely different from the sports cars made by Jaguar, MG, Singer, and others in the 1940s. It didn't have a sporting chassis, as conceived, but that wasn't Belgrove's problem. The wheelbase was short – too short at 7ft 10in for the saloon but acceptable for a two/three seater, even though it would be shorter than any of the old Dolomites or the 1800 Roadster. 'I am satisfied with what I produced, and from hindsight there is little that I would have modified. I think it was a good successor to the 'old lady' of 1938 and 1939. The bodyshell contained no reverse curvature, the line sweeping from nose to tail with the section between the screen pillars having a marked tumble-home.' Nevertheless, the TRX's styling was certainly controversial. It had many features strongly influenced by North American thinking, indeed the whole concept was of a fully equipped convertible rather than a sporting car alone. The lines were influenced by the Vanguard chassis, and particularly by the height of the engine, consequently the whole car was either too high or too narrow, depending on one's viewpoint; several inches of extra width would have helped. The hood was contoured and padded with retraction and erection electro-hydraulically operated, while the body construction was unorthodox. The age-old coachbuilt method of panelling on an ash frame was discarded in favour of double-skin aluminium. There was no dickey seat, but the fully carpeted boot also housed the fuel tank, which lived, full-width, across the tail.

There was nothing special about the Vanguard chassis, and very little work was done on the engine, and this was probably one cause for the car's poor reception. Certainly the Vanguard engine had twin SU carburettors for the first time, but it only produced 71 bhp (compared with 68 bhp), and the car's overall performance was not helped by the all-up weight of 2,716 lb. Readers must make their own decision as to the look of the car, but remember that it was first styled in 1947. Motoring journalist 'Steady' Barker once damned it with faint praise by writing that it was ' . . . a coquettish little glamour wagon, complete with dolly eyelids and a voluptuously feminine air about it. The prototype at Earls Court looked as out of place on the

Dictator and successor. A youthful-looking Alick Dick (standing) and Sir John Black in an early post-war picture

Triumph stand as a tattooed tart at a Garden Party and the motoring Press simply wouldn't have it, not at any price, nor the general public either.' Strange and cynical comments, perhaps, especially as the notoriously outspoken *Motor Sport* magazine said of the same car: 'Triumph appear to have produced a winner for 1951, in the form of the new Roadster. The 2/3 seater body has a very pleasing 'Continental' look and is a light-alloy double stressed skin monocoque with control runs passing between the two skins. Very clean lines render the appearance particularly pleasing . . . The body is up-to-the-minute without being futuristic.'

It was certainly a car that caused controversy. Like Michelotti's first TR3A 'dream car' there were many opinions about the styling, but no-one could take it or leave it. The car had been long delayed from its conception in 1947, one reason being the enormously lengthy period of waiting for the prototypes to be built. Sir John Black first insisted that the cars be built by Helliwells (the Walsall company who had absorbed Swallow Coachbuilding, and were later to make the Swallow Doretti), much to Belgrove's disgust, as he wanted his own Banner Lane craftsmen to tackle the job. Delay followed delay, for Helliwells were more used to dealing with aircraft structures, and eventually it became necessary to return the complete project to Banner Lane.

When the TRX appeared at the Paris Salon and at Earls Court it caused much discussion. It won an IBCAM Gold Medal for coachwork design at Earls Court – the first ever gained by Standard-Triumph – and was selected for exhibition in the Festival of Britain Transport Hall. It caused a stir at the 1951 Geneva Show, too, yet it didn't go into production. Why? Walter Belgrove reckons it was because engine development had not accompanied the body style and as a result the car was plain slow. Lyndon Mills reckons it was because there wasn't sufficient export appeal, and there was still the perennial problem of steel shortages. Harry Webster reckons it was because the car would have been expensive, difficult to build, and slow to sell. The basic problem as far as the buying public was concerned lay with the looks. It was a fashionable car, certainly, but perhaps too fashionable. Its styling has not, in the author's opinion, withstood the passage of time like the 1800 Roadster, the older Dolomite, or any of the TRs. It was certainly a car that aroused emotions. Ted Grinham hated it because Belgrove had been given a free hand in its design. Belgrove never really forgave Grinham for using an uninspired engine under the skin. John Black thought it was ahead of its time, and would go ahead after a delay. Lyndon Mills never liked the look of it.

By the middle of 1951 the car had been 'put on ice', even though Black retained some interest in it until the end of the year. Three cars were built, and two survive in John Ward's hands in the Midlands. The third car was destroyed, the driver at the time being Lyndon Mills, who said: 'My wife and I took one of them down to Bourton-on-the-Water, where one of the electro-hydraulic systems developed a fault and started a fire. We couldn't put out the fire, and that was the end of that one. I can't say I was sorry!' This, then, was the lowest point in Sir John's sporting ambitions for Triumph. His range in 1951 and 1952 consisted of only two models - the razor-edged Renown, and the chunky little Mayflower. Neither sold in large quantities, and neither was in any way sporting. The Managing Director might have been forgiven for abandoning sporting cars altogether, but it was another insult to his pride which sparked off the next project. If ever there was a company which finally pushed Triumph down the road to sports car success it was Morgan, and if ever there was a date which marked the turning point it was Wednesday, October 22nd 1952.

CHAPTER 6

A star is born

IT WOULD probably be true to say that without the Triumph TR2 there would have been no more Triumph sports cars. In terms of commercial importance, the TR2 was as important to Triumph as the Mini was to BMC, the BMW 1500 to BMW, and the VW Beetle to Germany; its arrival was a complete watershed of events.

The decision to make a new, small, lightweight sports car, and the events that led up to it, have been chronicled so often that one might expect the absolute truth and consequences to have emerged by now. Like many other automotive legends, however, many of these accounts have carried a fair amount of supposition and even wishful thinking. It has been said that the decision to make another sports car came out of the blue, and that Sir John Black suddenly presented Ted Grinham with the project, giving him an impossibly short time to build a car; this is not true. It has also been said that Ken Rawlings' well-known Vanguard Special 'Buttercup' had been the spark which lit the fires of sports car development at Canley; this was not true either. The entire TR2 project, it was said, revolved around the choice of a Standard Eight chassis frame as the base; incredibly this last assertion has almost become official history within Standard-Triumph when in fact it is quite untrue. Certainly it would not be true to suggest that the TR sports car came about as a result of long and earnest inter-director discussions over a long period of time. The truth, as often transpires, is rather more mundane, but still extremely interesting. As one of many journalists who have printed part fact, part fiction, I am now more than happy to put everything into its correct perspective.

Sir John Black, as ever, was the germinator of the new project. He had never really forgiven himself, or his colleagues, for the way in which the TRX had had to be abandoned because of the problems connected with costs, production capacity and doubtful sales appeal. In the interim period of 1951 he had talked to many people about this sort of car. One of those who should take some credit is Christopher Jennings (then Editor of *The Motor*) who had gained the impression during regular visits to North America that there was a gaping hole in the market between the MG TDs and the Jaguar XK120s; subsequently he talked about this to Sir John Black, who remained unconvinced. Harry Ferguson's brother, who was running Fergus Motors in New York (Triumph and Morgan dealers) also added his opinions, yet the final push must surely have been when Black's takeover bid for Morgan was rebuffed!

Morgan, of course, was a private company completely under the control of the Morgan family (H.F.S. Morgan, the founder, still being Chairman and Managing Director at the time) and was well-known to Sir John. As early as 1909/1910 John Black had been employed by the patent agents Stanley Popperwell, who just happened to help prepare the original patent drawings for the front suspension of the first Morgan three-wheeler cycle-cars. Later, as Managing Director of Standard, Black had negotiated a deal with Morgan whereby Standard would supply special overhead-valve versions of the 1,267 cc Standard Ten engine for fitment to the Four-Four in place of the Climax engines then in use.

Later, Standards rented two factory departments at Pickersleigh Road during the Second World War for the production of Claudel Hobson aircraft carburettors. Morgan cars had continued to use the special 1,267 cc engine until 1950, when they were able to replace it with the lusty Vanguard design. Incidentally, having obtained their Vanguard engines, Morgan went on to tune them and they raced a twin-SU-carburettor version at Le Mans in 1952 while the TR2 was in process of being designed.

It was, of course, highly unlikely that the Morgan family would want to sell out to 'big business' in the shape of Standard-Triumph, especially as the approach from Standard's chief was typically brusque and to the point. Peter Morgan, who subsequently took charge at Morgan, was kind enough to recall for me what actually took place: 'During the 1951 Motor Show Sir John Black asked to see HFS and myself in his office at Earls Court. Sir John mentioned being impressed by the potential of the Plus-Four and asked my father if he would like to join forces with Standard-Triumph to make the car in larger quantities. Father was obviously flattered at this takeover suggestion, but said he would like to give the offer serious thought and would let Sir John know his answer at a later time. Sir John assured my father that whatever his answer might be, it would not affect the supply of engine units. He also said he had no wish to put my father or I 'out of a job'.

'Subsequent to the interview, I am sure my father and I wished to keep Morgan independent and in two or three weeks' time, after a directors' meeting, a letter was sent to Sir John Black indicating that we did not wish to be absorbed by the Standard Motor Company . . . '

Incidentally, Gregory Houston Bowden's version of this approach puts the date as 1954, which could surely not have been possible, as Black left Standard-Triumph at the very beginning of 1954, as we shall see in a later chapter.

With the takeover offer rebuffed, there was no financial way in which Morgan could come into the Standard-Triumph net, as all Morgan shares were family-owned. Therefore, in spite of his assurances that a decision against a merger would not affect the supply of engines, it certainly seems as if Sir John was determined to harm Morgan as much as possible by starting up on his own

For many years the TR2 was thought to have had a chassis developed from this Standard Eight. But this was not so and . . .

. . . the 1936 Standard Flying Nine is seen to be the TR2's ancestor. Independent front suspension from the Mayflower was grafted on in place of the beam axle and half-elliptic springs of this design

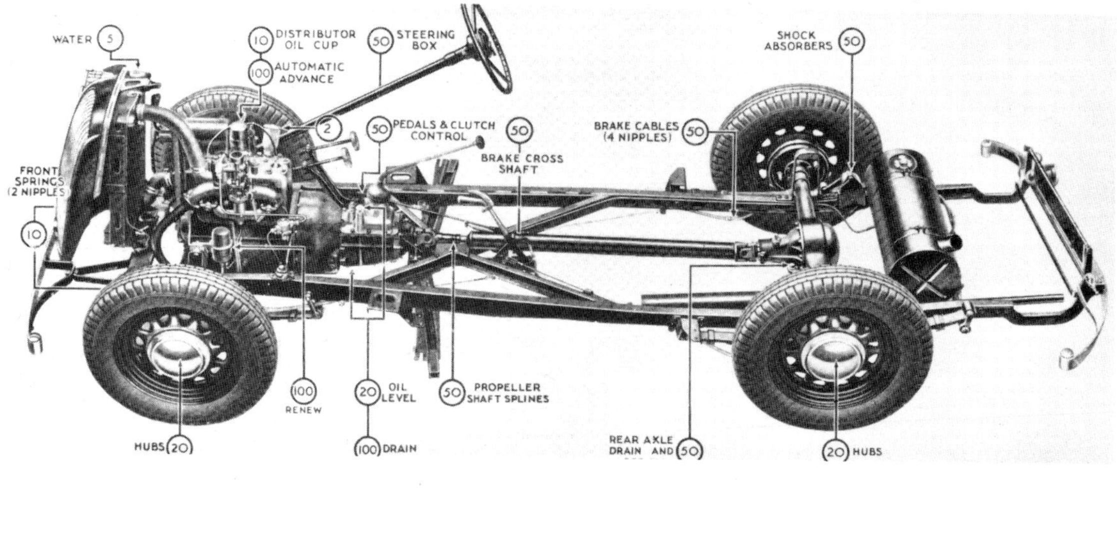

The car that started a revolution – the very first Triumph TR. Note the short tail, the exposed spare wheel and side lamps atop the front wings

accord with the same sort of car; this supposition, incidentally, is confirmed by Alick Dick, who drew a parallel with the circumstances which led to the original 1800 Roadster being produced in the first place.

In the meantime, certain Standard-Triumph engineers continued to be sports car-minded, although this number did not include Ted Grinham. Harry Webster, who had become a power in the department as Chief Chassis Engineer in 1948, was always interested in sports car motoring, and must have known something about the rather successful Vanguard-engined Special which had been built up by Ken Rawlings during 1950, though there is very little evidence to suggest that his TR2 design was later influenced by it.

Nevertheless, it is worth recalling that Rawlings was at that time an employee of P.J. Evans Ltd, of Birmingham, the Standard-Triumph dealers. He decided to build a sporting Special for his own motorsport activities and set about the design, more or less by scouring through the parts bin in the garage and painting the completed car in a particularly delicate shade of yellow, hence its name 'Buttercup'. The basis of the car was a Flying Standard Eight chassis frame, with a Vanguard engine and gearbox, 1938 Standard 12 back axle and Standard Eight independent front suspension and rear leaf springs. The steering box and column was from a Renown, along with a Vanguard-type gearchange. The body was home-made, in single-curvature light-alloy. It must be emphasised that this car, which enjoyed several years of success in rallies, driving tests, sporting trials and the like in Rawlings' hands, was built-up without any help from the factory. However, although there is no indication of factory personnel being influenced by it, the method of grafting components and sub-assemblies from other Standard and Triumph models on to a basic chassis frame was certainly followed by Triumph with their own project in 1952, two years after 'Buttercup' was conceived. Nevertheless Alick Dick is adamant that 'Buttercup' was known neither to him, nor to Sir John Black – and they took the decisions!

Before Webster received the go-ahead for a new sports car project he had already started experiments on crude and simple space-frames. Executive Director of Engineering John Lloyd, then a young man in the engineering department, says that the development work was carried out on a chassis made out of one-inch, 14-gauge angle-iron, all pop-riveted together, as a central backbone, but this was not very successful, particularly in torsional testing. However, the decision to go ahead with a sports car for appearance at the 1952 Motor Show, and production as soon as possible after that, came from Sir John Black early in 1952, not a mere eight weeks before the Show, as has often been suggested, although assembly of the Show car did not begin until then, following a period during which there had been some project design work and the inevitable styling job from Walter Belgrove.

For a historian, one of the fascinating aspects of the Triumph TR2 story is that the origins of its chassis frame have been misquoted, both inside and outside the company, in official or unofficial statements, for more than twenty years! Virtually every reference to the development of the TR2 has stated quite firmly that the chassis frame used to make the prototype was a Flying Eight frame suitably modified to take Mayflower front and rear suspensions. Indeed, this assertion was made several times by top executives of Standard-Triumph whom I interviewed when carrying out research for this book, and it also found its way into several features written about the car around Golden Anniversary time. My discovery that this was not, in fact, the case came when I examined a Flying Standard Eight chassis frame drawing in the spring of 1973. My suspicions were immediately aroused when I found that the Flying Standard Eight, announced in 1938, already had independent front suspension. Why, then, had it been necessary to fit independent front suspension from another car altogether? When I looked at Standard-Triumph's TR2 prototype chassis drawing I found that there was quite obviously no relationship between the TR2 prototype frame and that used on the Flying Standard Eight. There was no cruciform cross-bracing in the old frame, and there was a massive front cross-member to support the transverse-leaf-spring independent front suspension which had disappeared on the TR2 chassis. In side view the main members were completely different as they were kinked up at the front to clear the transverse spring.

I doubt whether I should have solved the mystery had I not, quite by chance, seen a lubrication chart photograph of another Standard chassis frame – that of the Flying Nine/Ten – which bore a remarkable resemblance to that of the first TR2. Further, this frame had the cruciform and the rear damper mountings in the right place, had no kick-up over the front axle line, and did *not* have independent front suspension. Later I was able to discuss this with Harry Webster and John Turnbull (George Turnbull's brother, who was chassis project engineer under Webster on the TR2 in 1952) both of whom confirmed that it was indeed the Flying Nine/Ten frame which was used, and not the Flying Eight. But why had the Nine/Ten frame been chosen, when no such car had been produced since 1939? Why not the Eight frame instead, which had been in production until the end of 1948? The answer came when both Walter Belgrove and Harry Webster remarked that Sir John Black's original requirement was for a cheap sports car, with the very minimum of tooling, which could be sold at a rate of about 500 a year. Looking back, it is difficult to reconcile 500 units a year with a desire to get into the MG TD and Jaguar XK120 market, but it does tie up with an attack on Morgan, who were making about that many cars themselves. Such a production figure was quite impractical if new chassis-frame tooling was involved, so when Harry Webster sat down with John Turnbull to consider their mechanical layout, it must have seemed like a miracle when several hundred Flying Nine/Ten frames were discovered in the Spares Department, and there was no further commitment to hold them in reserve for service and repairs. John Turnbull said that in terms of possible track, wheelbase and structural rigidity it looked about right. As to wheelbase, the TR2 eventually appeared at 7ft 4in, while the Flying Nine/Ten wheelbases were respectively 7ft 1in and 7ft 6in. However, since both front and rear beam axles were specified, the position on their leaf springs would accommodate the difference, and the fact that a completely alien coil spring independent front suspension was added for the TR2 explains the lack of correlation. The Flying Nine car was originally shown before the Olympia Motor Show in the autumn of 1936 (an *Autocar* description carries a photograph of the chassis, TR2-like, as large as life), and production ran on to the outbreak of war in 1939.

Once Grinham and Webster had been told to produce a new sports car in time for the 1952 Motor Show, one that could be retailed to make a good profit at a basic price of £500, they had little time in which to decide on a layout. With such a price target, together with a requirement to make the car exceed 90 mph in maximum speed, and with no more than six months in which to progress from the first rough sketches to

When the crash development programme was complete the TR2 chassis looked very robust. Compare this with the Standard Flying Nine frame (Page 72) from which it was developed

the first completed car, there was no question of a careful project study. An amalgam of existing or recently obsolete Standard-Triumph parts would have to be made around which Walter Belgrove would have to style an acceptable two-seater shell at the lowest possible tooling cost. Once Webster and John Turnbull had settled on the Flying Nine chassis they had to look for modern suspensions. At the rear there was no problem, for half-elliptic leaf springs controlled by piston-type dampers were thought to be adequate, a Mayflower axle (which was in fact almost identical with that of the Vanguard) being chosen with suitably reduced wheel track. At the front, the Mayflower coil-spring independent suspension was chosen, mounted on twin steel towers, braced across the front of the engine (in Harry Webster's words) 'to stop them flapping about'. Front suspension geometry was pure Mayflower, although forged lower wishbones were chosen in place of the pressings used on the original layout. A further improved version of the Vanguard engine, along the same lines as the twin-SU conversion first tried on the TRX, was to provide power, but with sporting categories in mind it was decided to reduce the cylinder bore by 2 mm to 83 mm, thereby lowering the capacity from 2,088 cc to an ideally sized 1,991 cc. The Vanguard's gearbox was to be used, modified so that four ratios (with an un-synchronised bottom gear) were available, and the Laycock overdrive was to be optional. Nine-inch Girling drum brakes were fitted all round, these being thought quite adequate for a car which was due to weigh no more than 1,800 lb and have an engine producing 75 bhp at best.

The proof of the pudding . . . . . TR2 prototype No. 1 in Jabbeke high-speed trim; Ken Richardson achieved more than 124 mph in this car with an unmodified engine. The rear-wheel spats were intended for production at first, but were abandoned

Walter Belgrove had a little more time to produce the body style than has often been thought, but was faced with a very severe limitation on panel complication when Sir John Black suggested that body tooling should be achieved on a mere £16,000. Belgrove was flabbergasted by this, even in view of the stated objective only to make a few cars every week, but the limit affected the whole body style. Reason had at last prevailed over the question of wheel tracks – the reverse crab track of the 1800 and 2000 Roadsters had disappeared, though inevitably the 7ft 4in wheelbase made the TR rather short and stubby looking. All main panels were designed to have as little curvature as possible to simplify tooling arrangements, all hinges were external and visible, while the lights and tail-lamp units were standard Lucas 'off-the-shelf' items. To fit in with the semi-traditional image that Black required (indeed, at first, it had been suggested that an MG TD copy should be attempted!) Belgrove sought to retain an exposed, or at least obviously placed spare wheel. The body's tail swept sharply down from behind the seats, with the spare wheel placed Morgan or MG-fashion in the tail, with the petrol tank filler cap protruding through the very centre of the spare.

By the time enough components were available to build the first car the summer was over, and actual assembly did not begin until the end of August, but by dint of much overtime working, the single car was ready to go on to the Triumph stand at Earls Court, even though it had not even turned a wheel before that day. Harry Webster's engineers were fairly certain that they could achieve the 90 mph maximum speed target, but they had not been able to design the car down to the original £500 price limit; as exhibited, undeveloped and by no means ready for production, it carried a price of £555, or £865 with British purchase tax. Although the little car's reception was kindly, particularly from the newspapers who were looking for all-British cars to boost, the technical press were much more guarded in their praise since they knew that less than eight weeks had elapsed since the prototype build had been started, and that nothing better than an old '60 mph' chassis was hidden under that smooth little skin; additionally, little that was complimentary could be said about the tail of the car, which would obviously have to be redesigned before production began. However there was enough interest particularly from overseas, to indicate that ten cars a week, and a pre-war chassis frame at that, would simply not suffice, so with the Show's doors still open, Harry Webster and Walter Belgrove were both faced with a major re-design. Sir John Black was prepared to allow no more than three months for the transformation scene to be completed, and it is at this point in the car's history that the now well-known figure of Ken Richardson comes on to the scene. Richardson, who had been born and bred at Bourne, Lincolnshire, had been much involved with the BRM project since its inception, not only as a test and development engineer, but also as a test driver of considerable skill; he was quite capable of urging the temperamental V-16 BRM car around any circuit within a few fractions of most racing drivers. Just before the 1952 Motor Show, Ted Grinham, whom he had known for many years, rang up Richardson and asked him to take a test drive in the new sports car that Standard-Triumph were then building. It was hoped that there would be time for a run before the Show opened, but in the event Richardson got his first glimpse of the TR on its stand at Earls Court. Immediately after the Show's doors closed, Sir John Black allowed a few privileged journalists to drive the car at the factory, then urged Richardson to try his hand. He drove it briefly around the factory, up and down the service roads, then drew up in front of Ted Grinham and Sir John Black with a horrified look on his face. When asked for his first impressions, Richardson is reputed to have said something like: 'I think it's the most awful car I've ever driven in my life; it's a death trap!' The TR, it seemed, was just about as terrible as it could have been, the only encouraging thing about it being that presumably it could be expected to improve. Grinham and Black were naturally taken aback at this condemnation of the design, which surprised them because no-one else had yet had the courage to say the same thing. In *The Motor*'s words, published at a later date: 'At this point the Standard company might well have thanked Richardson politely for his expert opinion, but pointed out that questions of production made it impossible to carry out any fundamental alterations to the design. And if they had done so, the TR would have died very soon after its birth.' To their eternal credit, Grinham and Black were impressed by Richardson's candour, and invited him to join Standard-Triumph as the development engineer in charge of the project. Like Harry Webster's team, with whom he would have to work closely, he was given just three months to work the miracle of transformation.

In the many features – and even books – since written about the development of the TR2, Ken Richardson has been hailed as the saviour of the project, the man who changed the ugly duckling into the swan, the man who plucked success from the jaws of disaster, the man who redesigned the whole car. It makes a good story, but while it is true that Ken Richardson's contribution was very important, it would be most unkind to suggest that Standard-Triumph could not have done the job without him. Harry Webster, who was in overall charge of the chassis design and mechanical development of the car, agrees that Richardson was the right man in the right place at the right time: 'He was a very sound development engineer who knew what he wanted to achieve, even if he didn't always know how this was to be done.' Alick Dick was able to tie this contribution down even more closely when he told me: 'We had a chief test driver at that time, and he was getting on a bit, and I don't think he had ever driven a car at more than 80 mph. If he'd gone up to 100 mph he'd have been so concerned at actually doing that speed, he certainly wouldn't have known what was wrong with the car. So Ken Richardson came in. It was entirely wrong to claim that he personally redesigned the car. He certainly contributed a great deal in modifications and suggestions for redesign, but this is very different from redesigning the whole thing. The fundamental layout, the suspensions, the engine and so-on weren't redesigned anyway, just developed. He did manage to turn it into the kind of car which you could then drive at 100 mph continuously. He did work extraordinarily hard on the project, and the development was intensive. I wouldn't like to under-rate Richardson's contribution to the TR, because that was very great, but we mustn't forget the designers who slaved away as well.'

Even before the Earls Court Motor Show was over, Webster had instructed John Turnbull to design a proper chassis, suitable for a 100 mph car, to replace the bare bones of the Flying Nine. Turnbull tackled this by improving on both torsional and beam stiffness. The main side members were deepened and made more rigid, and after that there seemed to be no reason to keep any of the other old metal pressings, so the cruciform was redesigned too. Not a single item in the production frame was common with the 1936 chassis – the general lines remained, including the layout of the main members and the rear damper positions, but that was all. Making sure that front and rear wheels were more related to each other converted the prototype from a lethal wobbler to a rugged, if hard-sprung, little performer.

Improving the 'going' and the 'stopping' was also achieved in double-quick time – and the redesigned car was ready for exhibition at the Geneva Show in March 1953. Bigger front brakes (10 x 1¾in in place of the original 9 x 1¾in) improved the stopping power, even though they quickly gained a reputation for 'grabbing' when British club racing and rally drivers got their hands on the cars – a change of lining coupled with bigger rear brakes sorted that one out. All the engine changes were really a result of the philosophical question: 'How far shall we go, where are we now, and where did we start from?', for Sir John Black's original 90 mph target had already been passed. With a roadworthy chassis and lots of potential still hidden in the engine, Richardson soon persuaded everyone that a guaranteed 100 mph would be a good sales point. The original 75 bhp would not be enough, so a whole series of modifications were carried out to push that figure up to 90 bhp. Even so, it had to be a figure that came with complete reliability. One of the regular sights at the Motor Industry Research Association's proving ground during the early months of 1953 was of Richardson belting round and round the high-speed banked circuit near Nuneaton – sometimes for hours at a time, and always at 100 mph. 'Sometimes we broke the engine – if so we loaded the broken car on a trailer, took it back to Coventry, added another mod, went back to MIRA and belted away until something else broke.' Getting the extra power was a routine job – or would have been if Ted Grinham's engineers had been used to that sort of output. The theory itself was easily understood – get more fuel-air mixture in, burn it well, get it out, and make sure nothing breaks – but the practical achievement takes time. It needed a higher compression ratio (8.5 instead of 7.5 to 1), a higher-lift camshaft, bigger inlet valves and some combustion chamber development to increase the output to 87 bhp and attention to ignition timing and carburettor settings found the other three horsepower without too much trouble. Keeping the engine in one piece at its higher rating took a bit longer, and among other things the cylinder block and the head mounting studs needed attention. One development problem that took ages to solve was one of broken camshafts; everyone knew it was a fatigue problem but no-one could solve it. Thicker camshafts still broke, and reliability was only achieved when some-one suggested making only one end of the shaft thicker. It worked . . .

The most obvious change, of course, was to the styling. Sir John Black didn't really want to change it at all – that was 'losing face' – but there was no doubt that the exposed wheel wasn't popular. Walter Belgrove was asked to re-work the car at the rear and tidy it up generally. In a magazine article in 1973 Ken Richardson suggested that the production car was widened by the simple expedient of cutting it down the middle and adding two inches in the centre (shades of the Issigonis Morris Minor methods) but this does not appear to have been done. At the front of the car the side lamps were moved from atop the wings to the front panel, and the bumper was standardised (it was once intended to be optional), while the windscreen, originally flat and found to suffer in a 100 mph slip-stream, was slightly bowed to counteract this. From the doors back the bodyshell was completely revised, with the spare wheel being moved to a position under the boot floor (accessible through a slot in the tail), the tail being squared up, and a lockable boot being placed behind the fuel tank. The original TR, or TR1 as it became known, no longer exists. The first and only round-tail car was converted rather than replaced, and made its own high-speed name a few months later. In the meantime, Richardson and Lewis Dawtrey in particular continued to put in incredibly long hours on the prototype's development, and Richardson was not satisfied until he could flog the car round and round MIRA's banked track at more than 100 mph without any faults developing. All this high-speed work might have been at the expense of handling development, or work on refinement, but it paid its own dividends. When the production cars won themselves a reputation it was on the twin virtues of high performance and rugged reliability – the TR2 soon became known as the car you could flog and flog and flog, yet nothing would break. Triumph themselves believed there was an engine fatigue problem at just over 5,000 rpm, and didn't like their competition engines to be taken beyond it, but the private owners disbelieved them, and didn't seem to break anything, so eventually even the works rally cars were taken up to 6,000 rpm and beyond.

Slowly, incredibly, a new mood began to develop at Standard-Triumph. The car that few had believed in, the car which was to sell in small quantities and use cast-off components, might just succeed after all. Perhaps here was a real sports car, not a plushy 'boulevard car' like the 1800 or 2000 Roadster, but a real man's car, a 100 mph two-seater Triumph. Could anyone believe it? Would it sell? Would the public be convinced? The engineers were convinced, and so was Ken Richardson. Sir John Black, who never lost his flair for a good publicity stunt, knew that the TR2 needed a real boost to convince the sporting buffs that it was ready for them. An endurance run perhaps or a high-speed demonstration. In typically impetuous manner, Black rang up Ken Richardson one morning and asked him if the new car could beat the speed of just over 120 mph just established by Sheila van Damm in the Rootes Group's new two-seater Sunbeam Alpine on the Jabbeke stretch of the Ostend-Brussels highway in Belgium. Richardson thought it could, subject to a bit of careful tuning, and extra streamlining like the Sunbeam had used (the Alpine had used a modified engine, too). Black then ordered an attempt to be set up without delay, and early one morning in May 1953 the first prototype appeared on the Jabbeke highway. As prepared for the run the TR2 had a full-length metal undershield, a metal tonneau cover, and an aero screen; overdrive was fitted, but the engine was almost completely standard. The rear wheels were covered with spats – at that time thought likely to be options. There were no bumpers, front or rear, though the car had the finalised body shape.

Richardson's first run was quite creditable for a 2-litre car, but at 104.86 mph it was nothing like good enough. All was gloom among the team until Richardson returned to base and laconically suggested that the car might go better if the fourth plug lead was replaced! So the first hundred-plus run had been on 1,500 cc after all. A repeat run in speed trim with all plugs correctly firing produced the sparkling two way result of 124.095 mph over the flying mile (124.889 mph over the flying kilometre). 'Then we all went to breakfast', said Richardson, 'and let the mechanics convert the car from speed trim to normal specification.' After breakfast the same car, stripped of its metal tonneau, and with windscreen, hood and sidescreens in place was taken out again. The figures achieved were perhaps a little super-standard because the metal undershield was still in place – 114.213 mph for the flying mile, 114,89 mph for the flying kilometre, a figure only reduced by six mph when the use of overdrive was cut out on a final run.

Everyone was delighted. Not only had the Sunbeam Alpine's figures been beaten, but Richardson knew that the car was also quicker than Donald Healey's Healey 100. The handling was adequate, the brakes good enough and the fuel consumption figures very promising. With all this performance surely no-one could complain? Sir John Black, who had always been enthusiastic about this car, and Ted Grinham, who had not, were also convinced – the TR2 was to go into production as soon as possible. The fairy tale had come true. Black had his proper sports car at last, after eight years of trying, and it must have given him great pleasure to know that it was as quick as William Lyons' XK120 at lower speeds. The TR story had begun.

CHAPTER 7

Developing a winner

WITH THE sports car prototypes now both developed and reliable, having been rapidly changed from the original ugly duckling to a passable imitation of a swan, Standard-Triumph had to set about getting the car into the showrooms. One could have excused further delays over a sports car that looked likely to sell in relatively small quantities, especially as the company's next bread-and-butter car, the all-new Standard Eight saloon, was just getting to the pre-production stage. But these never occurred, and suitable production facilities at Canley, idle since the withdrawal of the 2000 Roadster and under-used because of the low production rate of the Renown, were quickly re-jigged.

The first track-built TR2 rolled out of the old-fashioned Canley assembly hall in August 1953, only ten months after the just-finished white prototype had been shown at Earls Court, and only about 18 months after Sir John Black had set that two-seater £500 sports car project in front of Ted Grinham. Grinham's design engineers, including Chief Chassis Engineer Harry Webster, had been unable to meet that price target, and following an announcement price of £555 the usual upward creep of costs, plus a very significant improvement in specification, resulted in the car eventually entering production at the still-bargain price of £595 (which the hated purchase tax jacked up to a total of £844). At the time it would be fair to say that almost everyone from the motoring press to dealers, from commercial rivals to customers, found it difficult to treat the TR2 seriously; the word had got around in the very parochial motor industry (which had, and still has, a 'grapevine' second to none in effectiveness) that the original TR had been a pig, that thousands of gallons of midnight oil had been spent on rectifying this, and that almost everything had been substantially modified in the last few months. Richardson, who was proud of the many improvements he (in conjunction with

After a year's production the TR2 had its doors cropped to give more kerb clearance, and the hardtop became optional

Standard-Triumph engineers) had pushed through, did nothing to dispel the knocking talk; as mentioned in the previous chapter his part in the latter development of the TR2 was to be over-staged, and become good Standard-Triumph folk-lore. The fact of the matter was that the TR2 was shaken down into a satisfactory proposition in double-quick time. That this was partly due to Richardson's drive and enthusiasm can never be denied, but it would be completely unfair to other Standard-Triumph engineers to suggest that it would never have happened otherwise. Still, every company needs its legends, and the evolution of the TR2 will always be connected with Ken Richardson's name while Harry Webster and his engineers will be remembered for many other fine cars.

The TR2 also faced the problem of breaking a tradition. Standard had still not established their name as producers of sports cars, in spite of the relative success of the 1800 and 2000 Roadsters. It was, of course, a classic case of the 'chicken and the egg' – the TR2 was the first of the real sports cars, but people were not yet prepared to believe in it because there hadn't been one before it! The TR2, then, for a time looked like building for itself a 'kerbside sports car' reputation. On hindsight, this sort of attitude was quite remarkably obtuse. The facts of power output, weight, and the Jabbeke performances spoke for themselves. The TR2, even in standard form, was certainly capable of more than 100 mph, a maximum speed still rare enough to be remarked upon in 1953, and one that could not be approached by any car of similar price anywhere else in the world. The established sports cars made in Britain were headed by the MG TF and the Jaguar XK120 in terms of numbers built and sold. The TF was MG's (or rather Nuffield's) last attempt to wring profits out of the concept of a 'traditional' sports car. Its 1,250 cc engine was struggling to beat poor aerodynamics, and the British price was perilously close to the TR2 at £550 basic. It was almost as heavy as the TR2, and no less than 33 bhp less powerful. BMC's Press Office never let out a TF for test in Britain, probably because they didn't want its 85 mph maximum speed to look so poor compared with the TR2. MG's attitude to the TR2 is summed up admirably by Wilson McComb in his book *The Story of the MG Sports Car* (Dent):

The TR2's facia in its popular left-hand-drive form. The handbrake remained on the right of the tunnel for right-hand-drive cars

'The announcement at the 1953 Motor Show of two other new models made the situation even worse. One was Triumph's latest two-litre sports car, with a low-revving 90 bhp engine and, originally, a basic price only £5 above that of the TF Midget. Its handling at the limit was more than a little doubtful and it was downright ugly by comparison with the MG, but these faults were forgotten when it proved to be the cheapest 100 mph sports car in the world . . . '

How anyone could call the TR2 ugly when his standard of comparison was the MG TF escapes the impartial observer!

The Jaguar XK120 was an entirely different problem. As far as the British sports car enthusiast was concerned it was both fabulous and unobtainable. Introduced at the end of 1948 mainly as a 'carrier' for a new twin-cam engine intended for the next Jaguar saloon, the XK120 had became a runaway success because of its beautiful styling and high performance. Since 95 per cent went overseas, which meant only about 250 cars a year staying in Britain, not many race and rally types could find one, even if they could afford to pay a total of £1,600 (almost twice that of the TR2) for the open two-seater. In sporting circles the XK120 already had an enviable reputation, both on the race tracks, where Stirling Moss among others had driven works-sponsored cars to victory, and in rallies, where Ian Appleyard in particular had done so much in his own car.

Of course there were other British sports cars with which the TR2 had to contend, but these were either more expensive, like the Sunbeam Alpine (£895 basic), Austin-Healey 100 (£750) or Jowett Jupiter (£725) or were much slower. The only car to match the TR2 on price and performance was the Morgan Plus-Four, which still used the Vanguard engine and was soon to change over to the TR2 engine. But when production was a handful of cars every week (and engine supplies were controlled by Triumph anyway!) there was no commercial threat from that quarter. Once the economic facts of life had begun to sink in, and a growing circle of influential motor traders and pressmen began to realise that the TR2 was a real hairy-chested sports car after all, sales began to grow. Production build-up was very slow at first, particularly because Mulliners' body factory in Birmingham was still struggling to complete the tooling, and a mere 248 cars were delivered before the end of 1953, of which only 50 stayed in Britain. This was nothing like enough to keep Black's shareholders happy, and it needed some sort of instant success, or even a minor miracle, to turn the TR2 into a sales winner. As in all good fairy stories, this transformation duly took place, mainly as a result of one big win – the outright victory in the RAC International Rally in March 1954.

Britain's premier road event in those days was by no means the flat-out special stage event that it subsequently became, and indeed in 1953 it had been a week-long drag that was settled in favour of Ian Appleyard's famous white Jaguar XK120 in the course of ten manoeuvring and regularity tests. But in 1954 the first of a series of toughening-up changes became effective and there were many hours of night navigation in the hills of Wales and Derbyshire. It was sufficiently tough to ensure that only 21 cars from an entry of 240 were unpenalised on the road sections. At the end of it all, at Blackpool, the TR2 had suddenly vindicated itself, not only by winning outright, but by occupying second and fifth overall, taking the Ladies' prize, both start awards and second place in the team award behind the works Fords. Only one of the 14 TR2s entered failed to finish – and there wasn't an MG in the first ten. None of the Triumphs was works entered, or even works prepared; outright victory went to Manchester motor trader Johnny Wallwork, with driving test king Peter Cooper (later to become a Ford dealer in Hampshire) second and Bill Bleakley fifth. Mary Walker's TR2 defeated Sheila van Damm's works Sunbeam Talbot and Nancy Mitchell's works Ford Anglia in the Ladies' contest. The TR2 instantly gained itself a reputation for being rugged and reliable, even if the same could not be

The first TR2 to race at Le Mans was Edgar Wadsworth's car in 1954. Though privately entered, the Coventry registration numbers gives the game away

said for its high-speed handling.

In spite of the intensive development pushed through in 1953, there was little doubt that the TR2 handled in a very singular manner when hard-pressed. There was a lack of wheel movement in both front and rear suspensions, and the ride was none too pliant. The outcome of this was that the TR2 soon won itself a reputation for doubtful handling, and it was only the car's superb torque delivery and strength to withstand the inevitable rally accidents that kept it so popular. Lack of rear-wheel movement, allied to an underslung chassis that obligingly lifted the inside rear wheel clear of the ground under hard cornering, remained a problem until the advent of the TR4A in 1965. More intelligent suspension development (of the TR4, in the early 1960s) plus better radial-ply tyres and a limited-slip differential option eventually improved the car. Vic Elford's comments about his TR4s during the 1963 rallying season were that 'The handling was only mediocre, I suppose, in terms of outright roadholding, but the car was so well-balanced and chuckable that I could make it do anything'.

Early in 1954 Triumph had let out the first cars for road test, and the congratulatory comments must have been satisfying to the engineers who had worked so well. *The Autocar,* testing the TR2 in January 1954, discovered that not only would the car achieve 103.5 mph flat-out, but it would accelerate to 60 mph from rest in 11.9 seconds and to a true 100 mph in just over 50 seconds. The now legendary XK120, by the way, took 12.0 seconds to reach 60 mph from rest when tested by the same magazine in 1950, thereafter pulling well away as its 160 bhp engine got into its stride. More important even than the TR2's outright maximum speed was the rather astonishing overall fuel economy achieved – no less than 32 mpg. This was a combination of light weight, high gearing and a thermally efficient engine, which was to make the TR2 very competitive indeed for the out-and-out fuel economy contests which were so popular in the early 1950s. *The Autocar* gripped its well-known diplomatic manner firmly in both hands and suggested that '. . . the TR2 . . . has a nicely balanced feel which quickly inspires confidence. The suspension is sufficiently soft to provide a comfortable ride, yet at the same time it does not permit excessive body movement, and there is noticeably little roll on corners . . . Roadholding on corners is particularly good, no matter whether they be fast open bends or sharp curves'. There was also a comment that the exhaust system was generally quiet '. . . apart from a healthy but not unpleasing bark over a limited speed range around 2,400 rpm', which did not tie up with the comments of those whose houses lay alongside the rally routes which were soon to receive the TR2's attention. *The Motor,* in their test of the very same car, achieved even more splendid fuel economy, registering 34.5 mpg overall including a long continental trip; probably this was because the car had been fitted with the optional overdrive between tests, and because it was even 'looser' than in January. *The Motor*'s measured maximum was no less than 107.3 mph in overdrive top and 105.3 mph in direct top, though acceleration figures were almost identical. They also commented that this particular car was chassis number 6 with engine number 9 fitted, so too much notice should not be taken of minor deficiencies, and went on to say that the roadholding '. . . shows a consistent but not exaggerated understeer characteristic, so that it is viceless right up to the limit of tyre adhesion'. However, '. . . it is wise to allow for the fact that due to light damping of rear springs an unexpected bump can throw the car off its line to some extent', and 'Unhappily the exhaust system at present in use emits a quite ludicrous amount of noise at engine speeds around 2,400 rpm . . .',

Triumph's first success in the French Alpine Rally was in 1954. Maurice Gatsonides (right) and Robbie Slotemaker won a Coupe des Alpes. This is the Gavia Pass in mid-summer!

Triumph sent a full team of TR2s to Le Mans in 1955. All had prototype disc brakes and all finished, the best at 84 mph

which told more than the opposition's testers had done. *The Motor* were, however, considerably impressed by the car, concluding, by stating, '. . . we nevertheless rate this as not merely the best sports car available at its price, but also as one of the most promising new models which has been introduced in recent years. Not pared down to minimum weight especially with a view to use as a competition car, this model offers a combination of comfort, economy, speed and sheer enjoyment of travel in a responsive open two-seater, which should assure it of very large sales in many parts of the world'.

The TR2, then, was on its way with a couple of adulatory road tests and a big rally win to back up the advertising. As more and more production cars left the lines, exports being three times as numerous as home market deliveries, they began to be used for rallying, racing, and American gymkhanas. Triumph decided that a factory competitions department could no longer be delayed, and set one up around the corner from the Banner Lane engineering department for Ken Richardson to run. From 1954 Richardson's development activities tailed off as competitions grew up, though much of the work and experience gained by the works race and rally cars 'read across' to future production TRs. Richardson himself was not a top-line race or rally driver, but was the sort of driver who could adapt well to the hurly burly of international rallying. His department was nominally answerable to engineering, and staffed by mechanics drawn from those workshops, but Richardson was always a law unto himself who demanded (and usually got) a degree of autonomy not approached again until Stuart Turner's authoritarian reign at Abingdon. Though not blind to the publicity value of long-distance sports car racing, he first decided to concentrate on rallies, where the TR2 looked certain to shine. As far as he was concerned the Mille Miglia was a long-distance rally, too!

The first official Triumph entry in an event was for the 1954 Mille Miglia, where Richardson and Maurice Gatsonides shared a TR2 which eventually finished seventh in its class (behind Ferraris, Maseratis and the like) and 27th overall. Next came the French Alpine Rally, and it was here that the legend of the TR as a mountain goat was born. Even in those days the 'Alpine' was a rally that no private entrant tackled lightly, where the hills were high and the average speeds high. It was on a par for toughness with the Liège-Rome-Liège, and ideally suited to the ruggedness of the TR2. There were three factory cars – for Richardson and Kit Heathcote, Lyndon Mills (later Sales Director) and Jimmy Ray, plus Maurice Gatsonides and Robbie Slotemaker. Unlike a good film script, this first-time entry didn't result in a clean sweep, for the TR2 lost its class to O'Hara-Moore's Frazer-Nash, but Gatsonides won himself a *Coupe des Alpes* for an unpenalised run on the road (one of only 11 to do so) and the Triumphs took the team prize on their first attempt.

Meanwhile, Edgar Wadsworth and Bob Dickson had had a TR2 prepared for them to drive at Le Mans where it was not only the most standard-looking car in the race, but very reliable into the bargain. It finished the race strongly, averaging nearly 75 mph in 15th place compared with Gonzales' winning 4.9 litre sports-racing Ferrari's 105.1 mph in the very wet conditions. Better, however, was to come. No fewer than six TR2s took part in the RAC's Tourist Trophy sports car race held on the Dundrod circuit in Ulster in September, Richardson and Bob Dickson driving one of the factory cars. Not only did all six cars finish, but because they had been formed into two teams they walked away with the first and second team prizes as well! The best individual placing was McCaldin and Maunsell's 19th place, and members of the winning trio were completed by Lund, Blackburn, Dickson and Richardson himself.

By now the TR2 had well and truly arrived, and the sales figures were beginning to reflect the competition successes. In 1954 a total of 4,891 TR2s were made, of which 1,269 stayed in Britain; many of the exported cars went to the USA or to Canada. Changes, however, were planned for the car, and within the past year there had been big changes in the management of Triumph itself. Sir John Black, who as Managing Director had virtually ruled Standards since the middle 1930s, had been involved in an accident in a car which Ken Richardson was driving right outside the gates of the Banner Lane factory, and had received facial injuries and a broken arm. Sir John made a long and painful recovery from this accident, but eventually returned to his office, taking up at the same time the title of Chairman following the death of the much-loved and equally respected Charles Band, who had been connected with the Standard Motor Company since he and Siegfried Bettman had bought themselves financial power in the firm before the Great War. Yet suddenly, on January 4th 1954, Black resigned, putting out this statement: 'As a result of consultations with my doctor today, I have been advised that I am not considered fit enough to return to the enormous responsibilities as Managing Director of our very important company, and I am recommended to go away for an extended period to overcome the effects of the very serious accident which I recently received. My wife and closest friends feel, therefore, with me that I should retire from the Board of Directors and, consequently, from my office as Chairman of the Board'.

At the time, no-one outside the close circle of the Standard-Triumph Board found anything fishy about this statement (although there were many who wondered why Black could not retire to become an Honorary President and keep his Board appointment), and the motoring world at large had nothing but respectful and admiring comments to make about Black's achievements within the firm. Alick Dick moved smoothly up from his position as Deputy Managing Director to become Managing Director, appointing as his new Company Chairman no less a public figure than Marshal of the Royal Air Force Lord Tedder. Nothing further might have come to light after such a clean and swift departure (unless Alick Dick could be persuaded to write his memoirs) had it not been for the publication of

TR2 became TR3 in 1955 by adding five bhp and an 'egg-box' grille

A TR3 'clean-sweep' in the 1956 Alpine Rally, with five Coupes for Tommy Wisdom, Paddy Hopkirk, Maurice Gatsonides, the Kat brothers and Leslie Griffiths

Graham Turner's excellent book about the formation of British Leyland, *The Leyland Papers.* In tracing the development of the Standard-Triumph group during the 1950s, Turner had this to say:

'In 1953 many of the Board were becoming increasingly unhappy with the behaviour of Black himself. He was subject to violent fluctuations of mood, and in the view of one of his closest colleagues had become almost schizophrenic – "he could be the kindest or the cruellest man in the world, the gayest or the most depressed, a heavy drinker or a total abstainer. He lived on a razor's edge and nobody knew which side he might fall". The result, according to Alick Dick, was that "no decisions were taken except by mood". Black was not only a dictator, but an unpredictable one as well.

'He had another habit which was to prove his undoing. He invariably went to the firm's annual Christmas party and, having seen the number of managers present, frequently remarked that there were too many. The next day he named those whom he thought should get the sack. In 1953, his selection included a member of the Standard Board, the engineering director Ted Grinham.

'This provoked a sharp reaction. A substantial majority of the Board decided they would stand Black's behaviour no longer and early in the New Year met at Alick Dick's home at Hill Wootton, near Kenilworth: Black, they decided, must be ousted, though he had only been appointed Chairman (he was already Managing Director) on December 16. Black had had a motor accident a couple of months before, however, and this – they agreed – would be sufficient explanation for his precipitate departure.'

Alick Dick's job was to lead the deputation and make the request, one made doubly difficult because he owed his own eminence within Standard-Triumph to Black's favours. But the result was that Black, faced with what amounted to an ultimatum, realised that he could not possibly prevail, and he eventually signed away his top position. The 58-year-old former Chairman did, indeed, 'go away for an extended period', and might at one time have been tempted to stay in retirement; after all his pay-off had included £30,000 as a separation payment, a Bentley and a Triumph Mayflower, plus the use of a company bungalow in Wales for the next five years. However, Enfield Cables made the motor industry sit up again in December 1954 when they announced that Sir John Black was to join them in the New Year as Deputy Chairman. They could have known little of the reasons for his departure from Coventry, but presumably soon found out as he resigned his position within two months! He then moved into retirement, becoming a farmer at Dol-y-Bebin Farm in Llanbedr, near Harlech. Even there he could not escape completely from the sports cars in his past, for Dol-y-Bebin was only a stone's throw from a well-used club rallying section that became more popular every year. Black finally died, embittered, on Christmas Eve 1965, aged 69. A memorial service was held to pay tribute to his many achievements in Coventry during a 35-year span, which was attended by many hundreds of his old colleagues and ex-employees who had not suffered the sharp end of his tongue.

Fortunately, none of this political manoeuvring became public knowledge at the time, though even if it had it seems doubtful if there would have been any affect on Triumph car sales. One significant and important side-effect of this palace-revolution was that it made the sports cars' future doubly secure. Alick Dick, though no flat-out competition driver himself, was very much in favour of this sort of motoring. In his youth, before World War Two, Dick had competed in works-sponsored Standard cars in the gentle breed of RAC Rally which was so popular at the time, and had come to realise the marketing potential of having a sports car which was successful in its natural habitat of competitions. Whereas Sir John Black was interested in sports cars because they did something for his firm's image, and because he could use them to attack other industry magnates who had come to merit his disfavour, he was no engineer and did not appreciate the finer points of sports-car design. Ted Grinham appears to have stood up well against the difficulties of his Managing Director's methods, but Walter Belgrove could never come to terms with his completely arbitrary methods of new-model policy. Alick Dick, on the other hand, allowed his engineers considerable free rein as far as design was concerned, and there is no doubt that the pedigree of the cars benefited accordingly.

By the end of the TR2's first full year in production, it was beginning to catch on well. The first road tests had been followed by equally glowing reports in other magazines both at home and abroad, and it became more and more clear that similar-priced opposition was not nearly as quick. MG had been forced to substitute their TF's 1250 engine by a bored-out 1500 version, which had done little for the performance because the car's aerodynamics were so poor. The latest Allard Palm Beach (even with a 2.2-litre six-cylinder Ford Zephyr engine) was very much slower and much too expensive, while the Swallow Doretti that used so many TR2 parts was also seen to be slower and more expensive. The Rootes Group had also produced a sports car in the meantime – the two-seater Sunbeam Alpine – but since this was based on the battleship quality of the Sunbeam Talbot 90 saloons (and included chassis members no less than 14 inches deep at one point!) Triumph saw it as no problem to them. The TR2 had a performance and fuel consumption advantage over nearly everything else even remotely in its class, and was to capitalise on this during the next couple of seasons. The interesting technical point is that as the car grew up, both in power and in weight, its performance didn't improve along with it. The TR2 had a big advantage at the time, but by the time the TR3A came along the overall fuel consumption figures appeared to have been eroded from the 32 - 34 mpg bracket to around 26 - 28 mpg, while acceleration figures and maximum speeds stayed more or less unchanged.

On the sales front, all was sweetness and light. Success in the United States had been greater than Triumph had ever dared to expect, especially as this was a new design and Triumph had no sporting reputation on that side of the Atlantic. In Britain the cloth-cap brigade bought just as many as they could lay their hands on, which in those days of car shortages was a miserable 25 cars per week. That first RAC Rally victory was a very good start, but the rallying enthusiasts were even more impressed when Johnny Wallwork took the same car along on the

The first of many – the TR3A after its styling changes, including full-width grille and external door handles, outside Buckingham Palace

London Rally in September, and aided by navigator Willy Cave proceeded to win the event comfortably. The London Rally, by 1954, had become the most difficult night rally in the calendar, for not only did it demand intricate map reading, but many of the roads used were rough or poorly surfaced, and the required average speed was a non-stop 30 mph. It was an event where performance and strength had to be combined, and was one which was thought to reflect accurately the merits of competing cars. The rallying fraternity of the early 1950s, though as keen as ever, had different requirements of their cars from the 'professional amateurs' of more recent times. Not for them a specially tuned, sponsored, serviced and temperamental rally car for use only at weekends, but a car that had to be used for day-to-day transport during the week, had to go rallying or enter driving tests at weekends, and therefore had to be reliable. More than this, there was no time nor little money for regular tune-ups, and it should be easily straightened out if there had been a brush with a wall or a bank during the night's sport.

Once the TR2 had been seen to win the London Rally as well as the RAC Rally, it appeared to fit the bill perfectly, especially when it became clear that the car could get to grips with rallying average speeds so competently. By this it is certainly not suggested that the car could go round corners 'on the rims', but there always seemed to be generous measures of torque and power available, there always seemed to be the right gear at the right time (especially if overdrive was fitted, when one played a seven-gear tune on the two controls) and one never seemed to require the scream of excessively high engine revs to get good results. The trick with the TR2, and with all the subsequent TRs, seemed to be to keep the car rolling along with about 4,000 rpm showing on the rev counter, and changing gear as often as you needed to keep the needle pointing there.

Those early cars certainly had a lot of performance, which was somewhat better than the capability of the brakes and considerably in advance of the handling. Early braking systems led to a certain amount of front-wheel locking when worked really hard, and the handling on rougher roads was only as good as the amount of time the rear wheels were actually on the ground. Such problems were not helped by the rather uncivilised behaviour of the only brand of radial-ply tyre (the Michelin X) then available. The X was remarkable in some respects, mainly in dry-road grip and in the life one could expect from a set, but in its original form it had very abrupt

Maurice Gatsonides and Marcel Becquart with a not-so-immaculate works TR3A after the 1958 Monte. They had pulled up from 58th to sixth on the final mountain circuit

changes in behaviour when pushed towards its limits, particularly on wet roads. Brian Harper, who had an illustrious British rallying career in TRs, Morgans and Austin-Healey Sprites, reckons that he must have had a brushing acquaintance with every difficult corner in Wales, and summed up his TR2 like this: 'My TR2 was a pig on slippery roads, and it didn't go around corners very well either, but it was so quick between bends that I thought it an ideal "point and squirt" machine! I had quite a few minor shunts, sure, but in those days we only had Michelin radials and they were pretty notorious in the wet. We just had to adjust our driving methods to drive a TR properly and stay on the road, but the performance was good enough to win a lot of trophies. The performance was quite enough, we made mincemeat of the MGs, and there were no good XK120 drivers in club rallies at all then. Disc brakes made a lot of difference to the TR, but they were never very fast round corners. My Morgans were no better, but they were even quicker between bends, and even simpler to straighten out after a shunt!'

Back in Coventry, however, the development work put into the early TR2s was still working its way through to the production lines. By the end of that first year the raucous exhaust system had been tamed somewhat (though one would never call a TR2 or a TR3 a quiet car) and the bodywork around the doors had been altered. The first cars had full-depth doors, which had given rise to complaints from people who found getting out of the car awkward when they unwittingly parked close to a reasonably high kerb edge. The solution was simple, if rather costly in re-tooling terms; the bottom edge of the door was lifted a couple of inches and the space below filled-in with a fixed sill. The other important bodywork change was that a snug glass-fibre hardtop became optional – and was very popular among the not-so-young who had grown out of the wind-in-the-hair phase, and among the rally men who liked the idea of a bit of warmth and comfort when going about their nocturnal hobbies. Mechanically, the braking system had already been reworked, with the rear brakes going up to the same size as the fronts and the overall balance being much improved, while the wire-spoke wheels tested by Edgar Wadsworth's

Rough roads, high mountains, and a TR were all symptomatic of 1950s rallying. This was the 1958 Liège-Rome-Liège

Le Mans car and by the works team on the Alpine Rally had also become optional.

Technically, 1955 was a quiet year as far as the buyer was concerned, though there were developments afoot that would eventually prove to be extremely saleable, while in the competitions scene the Le Mans disaster seemed to cast a pall over many other sporting events. In the club rallying field, the TR2 didn't quite repeat its RAC Rally win, though Harold Rumsey's car finished second overall behind another of Richardson's babies – a much-modified Standard Ten which Jimmy Ray rowed into first place. However, Robin McKinney won the Circuit of Ireland, while Jimmy Ray exchanged his Morgan Plus-Four for a TR2 and won the London Rally in his new car. Three names in club rallying that sprung to prominence in TR2s were John Waddington, Fred Snaylam and Ron Gouldbourn (whose principal claim to fame now is that his long-time navigator was a young man called Stuart Turner, who has had a lot to do with the changing face of competitions in the last 20 years or so!). Another sporting performance that rather defied the imagination was a win in the Hants and Berks Motor Club's Mobilgas Economy Run (which was then a no-holds-barred contest) for Dick Bensted-Smith's car, which achieved a quite startling 71.02 mpg! Unable to explain to their customers why a perfectly normal 2-litre sports car should be capable of over 70 miles to every gallon of Mobilgas petrol, the bemused oil company changed the rules, but not before the 1956 event had turned up a similar result – of 64.06 mph by George Heaps' TR2. Bensted-Smith readily confirmed in a feature on his TR2 in *The Motor* that the car had been helped along by a bit of stealth and brave driving. 'We blew the tyres up, used a lot of luck and gravity for 600 miles, and came back with a figure of 71 mpg . . . The Triumph is an inherently economical car, but two factors contributed to this extreme petrol-squeezing; an engine which would pull it up hills in top gear when smaller-capacity cars had to change down and use more revs, and sports car brakes on which one could rely during prolonged coasting. Looking back on our journey, I see that the descent of the Long Mynd involved a 1,000 ft change of altitude with a control at the bottom. Where we coasted all the way with a dead engine, at least one family saloon finished the descent in bottom gear, and then overshot the halt with faded brakes.'

Ken Richardson's works team had less chance than usual to show-off the capabilities of their works cars because of the cancellation of the 1955 Alpine Rally, but three cars were sent to Le Mans with the object of finishing strongly, and additionally to prove (or disprove) a new-fangled invention called disc brakes. The TR2s were all works-built, and little modified mechanically, such that their best speed along the Mulsanne straight was about 120 mph (not as high a figure as that achieved by the prototype at Jabbeke in 1953) but two of the cars carried Girling front-wheel disc brakes, while the third had Dunlop disc brakes on all four wheels. Oversize rear drums were fitted to the Girling-equipped cars, but in all other respects these cars were making a final trial to decide which of the two systems could be adopted for future production. Dunlop discs, of course, had already made their name at Le Mans on the Jaguars which won outright in 1953, while Girlings had been fitted fairly recently on Lotus sports-racing cars. The Triumph kits, however, were the first in 'producible form' and their performance was to be closely watched. It is tragic history, of course, that the 1955 race at the Sarthe circuit was marred by a horrible accident, in which Levegh's Mercedes ploughed into the spectators opposite the pits, killing over 80 and injuring hundreds. Triumph, however, prefer to remember that year as the one in which all three of their cars finished (within a total of only 21 finishers from 60 starters), the best covering 2,026 miles in the 24 hours. Richardson himself drove one of the cars, though Bobbie Dickson and Ninian Sanderson were in the quickest. Dickson shared a car with Ken Richardson in the Tourist Trophy held at Dundrod later in the year, when the Girling brakes were tried out again and where once again they fared well, and TR2s being the best performers among the production cars which started. The rally cars also had their share of glory, including a clean sweep of the 2-litre sports car class on the Liège-Rome-Liège, where Ken Richardson and Kit Heathcote won the class and also finished fifth overall.

However, the life of the TR2 (and many people still talk of all the old-shaped cars as TR2s, no matter how much more recent they are) was coming to a close, by name if not in fact. At the Earls Court Motor Show in October, the Triumph stand was resplendent with publicity for the 'new' TR3. This car, admittedly, was more 'new' in the eyes of the publicity staff than in those of the engineers, for mechanically it had only a slightly more powerful engine (95 bhp gross instead of 90 bhp) helped by a cylinder head with modified porting and larger SU carburettors. Visual changes included an 'egg-box' grille in the mouth of the radiator tunnel pressings, a chrome stoneguard on the front face of the rear wings, and the availability as an option of one of those ludicrously useless occasional rear seats which provided no room for legs or for normal-sized bodies.

The TR2's main sales success was that it gave rise to the TR3. By itself it sold rather less than 9,000 examples in two years. It was still listed as a complementary model after the arrival of the TR3, but this was merely a sales and marketing ploy to ensure that existing showroom stocks of the car were cleared without any financial pain to the dealers. In Britain, a TR3 buyer found that his 5 bhp and the extra styling touches were to cost him an extra £25 basic, or £35 when the imposition of purchase tax was taken into account. However, Standard-Triumph could hardly be blamed for cashing-in somewhat on the success of their two-seaters, which had been launched at considerably lower prices than almost all the opposition, and into which a lot of improvements had been poured in the past couple of years. One reason why there were no more improvements at the time was that the factory were fully occupied in launching the new Phase III Standard Vanguard (the last of Walter Belgrove's styling efforts, one which as usual had been bedevilled by interference from the dictatorial Sir John Black and by the lack of sympathy that existed at that time between Ted Grinham and himself). It was a launch further complicated by the fact that whereas the previous Vanguard had used a separate chassis frame the new car was of monocoque construction and used a body structure from a different construction plant, that of Pressed Steel at Oxford.

More TR3s were made in 1956 than TR2s in 1954 or 1955, although things were not helped by the gathering gloom of a trade depression in Britain, and by the political uncertainties brought on by the Suez crisis and subsequent petrol rationing. If 1956 saw new records broken for the TR3, they also saw an unprecedented rush of competition successes all over the world. In Britain, where TR2s and TR3s seemed to turn up at every rally, hillclimb, driving test and club race meeting, the rallying season was completely dominated by one driver, John Waddington, and his able navigator, Mike Wood, who won no fewer than five national rallies in succession in Waddington's own car. Robin McKinney won the Circuit of Ireland for the second year running and Ron Dalglish's TR2 won the other long-distance event in Britain, the MCC National Rally.

In Europe, Ken Richardson's team was strengthened by the signing of a mercurial young Irishman from Belfast called Paddy Hopkirk, who starred in one of the most astonishing team performances ever achieved on the gruelling French Alpine Rally of July 1956. The Alpine for many years had pitted a mercilessly tough route of mountains and high averages against the best sports cars in the world, and it was in order to honour all those who completed the week-long course unpenalised that the special *Coupes des Alpes* had been awarded. In 1956, the event broke new ground by pushing deep into Jugoslavia, where rough roads and dust were well in evidence, and by the time the tired survivors of this mountain motor race struggled back to the finish at Marseilles only 17 of them remained, including no fewer than five TR2s and TR3s, four of them being works-entered or works-backed. Maurice Gatsonides, Paddy Hopkirk, the Kat brothers and Tommy Wisdom had works cars and Leslie Griffiths won a *Coupe* in his own car. Triumph naturally won their class and swept the board in the team prize. It was with this sort of success that the Richardson legend continued to grow, despite the fact that the cars were rarely other than well-prepared standard models, and that 2-litre sports cars of the TR type were ideally suited to competitions in the late 1950s. Richardson was often a very difficult man to work with, or work for, as some of his drivers found.

The late John Gott, for instance, joined the team during 1955 after several years of success with well-do-do private owner Hal O'Hara-Moore, but by the end of the year he had had enough and moved across to the BMC Competitions Department at Abingdon, where he spent several happy and successful rallying years. There was, also, the unhappy relationship that developed between Richardson and Harry Webster; Webster, of course, was his senior colleague, and directly in control of the competitions activities for some years, whereas Richardson would have liked to run his own little operation without having to refer to anyone else. Both had strong personalities and Richardson was no diplomat; it was inevitable that there should be more and more disagreements, and when the Leyland takeover demanded economy cuts in 1961 one outcome of this was predictable.

Harry Webster, however, was also an extremely busy man in the engineering department. In 1955 he had become Chief Engineer under Ted Grinham, and on Grinham's retirement in 1957 was shortly to become Director of Engineering. Apart from continuing developments on the small saloons and the new Vanguard, Triumph had to find time to maintain the development programme for the TR3, and at the Motor Show in 1956 there was a major sensation when both Triumph and Jensen announced production cars fitted with disc brakes. Since both companies have claimed, from time to time, to have been the first, a bit of explanation about this 'race' is appropriate. The need for disc brakes had been apparent for some time, particularly on cars which were so fast that huge and heavy drum brakes were needed to give them the sort of stopping power to match their high performance. Even after 60 years or more of drum-brake development, fade-free operation was still not easy to achieve (especially as the brakes had become more and more buried inside the wheels and the all-enveloping bodywork of modern cars), and the disc brake became a fashionable talking point. Discs themselves were not very new – like almost every 'modern' invention they had been tried out on the very earliest 'autocars' of the late 19th and early 20th century, while bicycle brakes were really discs operating on a very large disc diameter. Disc brakes of the same basic type as was to be adopted for cars had been used in some fighter aircraft towards the close of the Second World War, but the first successful and widely publicised fitment to a car had been on the factory-prepared Jaguar XK120Cs (or 'C' Types) in 1952 and 1953. Triumph, of course, had raced cars with prototype disc systems in 1955, and other more complex layouts had found their way on to the Lotus sports-racing cars, and the Vanwall Specials and BRMs in the single-seater category.

A famous occasion. Keith Ballisat's 2.2-litre TR3A not only won a Coupe and its class, but beat all the Austin-Healeys on the 1958 Alpine Rally. It is the horrifyingly narrow Gavia again

As far as production cars were concerned, the TR3's disc brakes were announced a few weeks before the Jensen 541 was given its Dunlops, and in terms of quantities there was no doubt about the winner. Jensens, even in the mid-1950s, were made at a rate of perhaps two or three cars every week, while TR3s were now beginning to flow off the production lines at a rate of about 150 to 200 cars a week. The principal disadvantage behind the four-wheel discs fitted to the Jensen – a system almost identical to that adopted on the Jaguar XK150 and subsequent models in 1957 – was that there was no satisfactory handbrake. On the Triumph, however, rear-wheel drums were retained because they made handbrake operation easy and efficient, and – it must be admitted – because they were much cheaper at that time. The interesting little quirk is that although it was Girling who made a flying start in building large quantities, it was Dunlop who held the British master patents. Therefore, although Dunlop production was very much behind Girling at first, they took a very healthy harvest of royalties in the process. Later, of course, Dunlop disc-brake production closed down, with rights and customers being handed over to Girling for future business. All very confusing.

The other TR3 changes for 1957 were relatively minor. The cylinder-head design had finally settled down, after a year of most un-Triumph-style confusion. All the TR2s had had a certain type of cylinder-head, but a modified casting first tried at Le Mans in 1955 was introduced on the TR3. Only months after that, however, a new casting combining the best of both previous designs was introduced, but the change-over did not happen cleanly, so there was a period of a couple of weeks when differing engines were fitted to consecutive cars. The latest head design, named the 'high port' head, was to continue right through to 1967, and gave rather better breathing than the original design. At the same time the rear-axle design was altered – according to publicity from Mayflower to Vanguard type, though in practice this only involved a change to the half-shaft bearings support and other minor details.

It was around this time that the phenomenal success of the TR in America really began to blossom. The TR2, while a very good high-performance car, had not had it all that easy to start with in export territories. Only 3,622 had been exported in 1954, and an extra 1,500 before it became the TR3 in 1955. TR3 exports had started steadily with 4,360 in 1956, but the arrival of disc brakes, the growing competitions record, and the word-of-mouth recommendation that was getting around the sports car fraternity now took a hand. Remembering that the TR3 became the TR3A on the Canley production lines during the late summer of 1957, the statistics show that exports doubled in 1957, from 4,360 to 9,821, nearly doubled again in 1958, to 15,160, and rose to a new high of 20,552 in 1959. There was a slight reaction in 1960 when sales eased to 16,291, but even this was nearly 400 per cent better than three years earlier.

Even more interesting is an analysis of where the TR2s and the TR3s were sold. Whereas Triumph sold less than 9,000 TR2s in all, and no less than 3,115 of them in Britain, the TR3/TR3A by comparison accounted for 57,113 sales in the United States and 4,151 in Canada, compared with 1,490 in France, 1,727 in West Germany and 3,182 in Great Britain. At the height of its successes in 1959 the TR3A went to nearly 80 different countries, including single sales to such unlikely places as Bolivia, Ecuador, Ghana, Vietnam and Cambodia.

Certainly the arrival of a modified TR3 can have had little to do with this sales explosion. The new car first went down the tracks in August 1957, and was shipped in great numbers to the United States at once, but it was not released in Britain until the following January. The latest car had a full-width grille (callously called a 'dollar grin' by its detractors), with external handles to the doors and boot lid. The headlamps were made a little less 'pop-eyed' by pushing them back slightly into the front panel, and there were slight changes to the facia and trim; the basic price in Britain was raised from £680 to £699. Neither was it only Triumph who were benefiting from the sales boost, for Jaguar were finding as much trouble as usual in satisfying their customers, and the MG MGA was selling as well as the Triumph at that time.

More and more enthusiastic owners, certainly, were finding that the TR3 and TR3A was an ideal sporting car, whether for rallies (where it was strong and fast), driving tests (small, manoeuvrable and robust) or circuit racing (cheap to prepare, eminently tunable and easily repaired). The TR3A became everyman's sports car as the MG had been in the 1930s. There were many who knocked it as too common, but many more who stocked up their awards cupboard with its aid. As far as the production car was concerned, it had put on some weight since 1953, with more and better trim, thicker panels, reinforcement here and there and additional fittings, but the power had gone up from 90 bhp to a very solid 100 bhp. Ken Richardson's cars had little success during 1957, partly because a lot of events were cancelled due to the petrol rationing imposed on Europe after Suez. Even so Bernard Consten took third overall in the Liège-Rome-Liège, and an enigmatic young lady called Annie Soisbault won the *Coupe des Dames* in the Tour de France. 1958 saw Richardson's works team take over a set of new cars, delicately painted in apple-green, and rather lighter than standard. This apart, they were never much quicker than a privately owned car; we often thought that this was to encourage the private owners to try to beat the works cars! It was a year where the works cars won things with almost monotonous regularity. Apart from Paddy Hopkirk's outright win in the Circuit of Ireland (his first of several on 'home' ground), Keith Ballisat won a *Coupe des Alpes* in the toughest-ever Alpine (defeating a team of 2.6-litre Austin-Healeys), Ron Gouldbourn and Stuart Turner had a class win in the Tulip, Colonel Crosby in the Liège-Rome-Liège, and Gatsonides in the Monte Carlo Rally. Further, 'Gatso' arrived in Monte Carlo in 58th position after battling through a dreadful snow storm, then pulled up a phenomenal 52 places to take sixth place overall. There was an interesting portent for the future, little publicised at the time, when Ballisat won his class in the Alpine, for his works TR3A was non-standard. The class limit had been extended from 2-litres, which allowed Richardson to enlarge his engines if he could, and with no help from Engineering (there was little love lost between the two departments anyway) an engine was rebuilt with the 87 mm 'tractor' cylinder liners so that its displacement was increased to 2,187 cc. As a conversion it was simplicity itself, requiring no more extra work than fitting the proper TR-type pistons and re-needling the SU carburettors. The result was a deep-lunged engine with considerably more torque if only a little more peak power, a tune that was very valuable indeed for most competitions.

Three years later the TR4 was to appear with a so-called '2.2-litre' engine, which in fact had a displacement of only 2,138 cc, with 86 mm bores; there seems to have been no good reason why the 87 mm bores should not have been chosen instead. The engine started life for the Vanguard with an 80 mm bore, way back in 1947, but no increase in excess of 87 mm was really possible because of the slip-in wet-liner construction. It was one of those unfortunate engines with little built-in 'stretch', not that Standard-Triumph were completely ignorant of this often-rewarding process – the Standard Eight engine started life at 803 cc and progressed to 1,493 cc in 1970, a very creditable 85 per cent increase in capacity which was accompanied by much more than 200 per cent increase in developed power.

The original TR reached the zenith of its success in the late 1950s, both in the showrooms and in competitions. Once the 2.2-litre engine had become available to private tuners as well as the factory, race-engine power outputs reached a peak of between 130 and 150 bhp. So many TRs were raced in Britain that there were special races and championships for them. At one time the rallying scene was so full of TRs that it was seriously proposed that there should be a separate category for them. Everyone who was anyone in British rallying, or who aspired to becoming someone with the least possible effort, bought his TR first. It was only the announcement of the ugly little Austin-Healey Sprite in 1958, and the ubiquitous BMC Mini in 1959, which changed this trend. Even so, the author recalls arriving at the start of his first National British rally in 1959, co-driving a TR3A, and finding that the first 25 starters were all in identical cars. Sid Hurrell made his name as a club racing driver before he started to sell replicas of the speed equipment he had developed for his own car, and there were to be many later famous people (including the late Jim Clark) whose first competition events were entered behind that lusty four-cylinder engine.

Ken Richardson's rallying team were less active in 1959 and 1960 because of his pre-occupation with new racing prototypes (see Chapter 8) and as far as can be ascertained a TR3A never won an International Championship Rally outright. But every one of the major British events fell to a TR at one time or another – Circuit of Ireland, Welsh, Scottish and RAC Rallies, not to mention the London and MCC National events. Richardson found and trained many drivers who later moved on to other teams, not necessarily to better cars but usually to better financial rewards. Their names are legion, and in mentioning some I regret there may be others whom I insult by omission – Tom Gold, Mike Wood, Stuart Turner, Paddy Hopkirk, Willy Cave, David Seigle-Morris, Vic Elford, John Gott, Rob Slotemaker and Tiny Lewis all went on to other teams. Of them all, David-Seigle Morris probably made the greatest initial impression on Richardson, for David's own privately-owned and beautifully-prepared TR3A beat the entire works team of John Wallwork, Rob Slotemaker, Keith Ballisat and Annie Soisbault in the Tulip Rally of 1960, whereupon he was co-opted into the team for the Alpine Rally and beat them all again. After that the rallying team was virtually disbanded, except for selected events, as Richardson now had more important fish to fry. Since 1955 Harry Webster's engine designers had been beavering away at a new power unit, ostensibly merely as an exercise in die-casting techniques, but also as an outlet for Alick Dick's ambitions. Triumph were going back to Le Mans – and this time they were serious.

CHAPTER 8

'Sabrina' and a new TR

THE ORIGINAL TR2 body shape survived for eight years, and was as popular in 1961 as it had been in 1953. Eight years was an awfully long time to keep going with the same styling in the 1950s, especially where the bulk of sales were to fashion-conscious America, but with a cult-car like the TR2 and TR3 this didn't seem to matter. But Triumph were never complacent about the car, and by 1956 or 1957 they were already beginning to worry about future TR developments.

The car needed re-styling, and preferably making a little more up-to-date and comfortable, but for a time it was hoped that the same basic bodyshell would continue. Former Sales Director Lyndon Mills sums up what happened then: 'America was becoming the determining factor in this, in what they wanted, and American dealers suggested that it was time some changes were made. We tried all sorts of things, we tried this and that, and they all looked ghastly – every effort we made. I suppose that proves what a nicely integrated design Walter Belgrove's TR2 really was. Over a period of about two years, I think it was, every now and then we would pick up the design and have yet another go at improving it.'

In the background, however, there were the usual financial worries, for even by then the cost of tooling-up for a completely new bodyshell was very high, and Alick Dick was not inclined to rush headlong into such changes until his sales people demanded it. So it was not until 1958 that the first concrete moves were made to change the car. At about that time, Standard-Triumph had decided to sell-off their tractor-producing interests, which meant that they would immediately raise several million pounds in capital (which Dick wanted to spend on new models) and they would have to move their engineering departments out of the Banner Lane factory, which was being sold to Massey-Harris-Ferguson. One must mention here that tractor production, on behalf of Harry Ferguson, had always been the most profitable side of Standard-Triumph (indeed, there were occasions when even Sir John Black was heard to express embarrassment about the profit margins on tractors, which were high enough for Harry Ferguson to demand, and get, a price cut from Standard-Triumph in the early 1950s) and when tractor production ceased it

'Sabrina', the 2-litre twin-cam racing engine, used at Le Mans from 1959 to 1961. Best power output was nearly 160 bhp

The 'Sabrina' cylinder head layout was a classic of its time, with twin overhead camshafts, large valves and single ignition. Twin-choke SU carburettors were used, though Webers would also have been suitable

The TR3S at Le Mans in 1959 was a longer and wider-shaped glass-fibre version of the TR3A, with the twin-cam engine under the bonnet

changed the whole profit picture such that the eventual sale to another and larger concern became simply a matter of time.

By 1958, Standard-Triumph were well-advanced with a new small car to replace the stubby little Eights and Tens. Called Herald, because Alick Dick's boat was called Herald and he liked the name, the new car was advanced in some respects (such as having independent rear suspension) and a throw-back to the past in others (it was to have a separate chassis frame); it had been styled by Triumph's new consultant designer from Turin, Giovanni Michelotti. He was a mercurial little Italian who had already brought great credit to his past employers (Vignale) and since setting up his own studios had done some automobile work, plus a lot of industrial designs including such deathless products as Expresso coffee machines. Michelotti had been engaged by Standard-Triumph in a rather round-about manner. In 1957 the company was rather desperately looking around for a new styling theme for the new Triumph Herald project, Walter Belgrove having left in 1955 (following that flaming row with Ted Grinham) leaving no suitable person in Coventry in his place. Alick Dick had already been introduced to Michelotti at the Geneva Motor Show in March, but had made no moves to engage him at that time; there was apparently no thought at all about employing an overseas stylist. However, back in Coventry a string of coincidences were to re-introduce Michelotti to Standard-Triumph.

As Harry Webster remembers the sequence of events: 'One day a man called Raymond Flower came to see Martin Tustin; he and his brother were going to make an Egyptian national vehicle, and they were interested in buying engines and axles from us. We started to go over the various technical details, and I asked what sort of car it was meant to be? Flower said they hadn't thought much about that, nor did they have a body style. Flower then said something like "We don't have to worry about that, we can get a body built in two or three months", which made us chuckle, and I said quite bluntly that I didn't believe it. Flower was quite insistent that it was possible, but when I asked him how it could be done he said that was his secret. Furthermore, he insisted that he could get a running motor car in

For 1960 the Le Mans cars were re-bodied to look like 'Zoom' — *see next page*

three months. Instantly I said "Could you do this for us?" and when Flower agreed that it was possible Martin Tustin asked him to have built a sort of "dream car" based on the TR3A chassis, but that we would want to see a selection of styling drawings and sketches first. We still didn't know who Flower's genius was, but about ten days later he came back, laid out five or six sketches and said "Which one would you like?". First of all we had to find out what it would cost, and when he quoted a price for the complete car, inside and outside, for around £3,000, this knocked both Tustin and I right back, not because it was expensive, but because by British standards it was very cheap even for the 1950s! So we agreed to this, it was ready within three months, and it was only when we went to see the nearly completed vehicle in Italy that we discovered it was Michelotti. I was introduced to Michelotti when I went over there, and it didn't take me long to decide that we really ought to sign him up for our future work. One of the cars he had created for Vignale, which Vignale were just starting to make, was that funny little car from Wolverhampton – the Frisky!'

Having been engaged, the next job the little Italian did for Triumph was to re-touch the Vanguard into the Vanguard Vignale, but his first complete styling job for Webster was on the Triumph Herald.

Triumph were in deep trouble over the styling of the Herald (originally a closed two-seater), and it was not until Michelotti quite suddenly suggested that a completely new body shape might look better than modifications to the basic style he had been asked to improve, that the Herald as we know it came into being. The first Herald prototype arrived in the Coventry styling studios on Christmas Eve 1957, and apparently it caused so much happiness among the directors that they all stopped work to go out and get drunk! The Herald, of course, crops up again later in this story, for it was to spawn an entirely new type of Triumph sports car in the 1960s.

With the Ferguson tractor sale completed, a large new assembly hall at Canley was commissioned, and it became clear that there was enough money to finance a completely new TR bodyshell.

Black Beta — the TR3B as it might have been, with a wide-track TR4 chassis under the old body, but with wider wings and a new grille. This was a very impressive car

It was not likely to cost less than £300,000 (which didn't start to compare with the original figure quoted to Belgrove by Sir John Black for the first TR), and there was also the problem of where to build the cars. All the TR3As came from Mulliners in Birmingham, but the TR4 was to be sourced elsewhere. Meanwhile the 'dream car' – VHP 720 (see illustration) – was toted around the firm to let the top executives mull over its style. For the next year or so the car turned up at many public occasions and Triumph Sports Owners Association rallies, attracting a lot of attention by its extravagancies. It was too 'fashionable' ever to succeed; fashionable cars are fine while in vogue, but a production style has to last for years instead of months. The 'dream car' had fashionable wrapped-round windscreen, headlamp hoods, a 'dollar grin' radiator grille and a contoured front bumper, which were all very eye-catching in 1957 and 1958. In any case it all sat on an unmodified TR3A chassis frame, which was certainly in need of modification for the next model.

Woven in and around any new TR sports car project had to be the question of the engine, but it was not until the following year that Standard-Triumph's thoughts in this direction were revealed. Alick Dick made no bones about his liking for a competitions programme, especially if the cars raced or rallied could look like the production car, or a future production car, and by this time he had formed the opinion that the events most likely to give Triumph good publicity were the Alpine Rally and the Le Mans 24-hour race. There had been TR2s at Le Mans in 1954 and 1955, of course, but their best race average speed had been 85 mph. Every year the Le Mans organisers pushed up their qualifying speeds, such that it became difficult for a pushrod-engined TR2 or TR3 to achieve the minimum distance for qualification, even if it ran faultlessly throughout the 24 hours. To get more speed would either mean more power from the existing engine, a brand new, windcheating and therefore non-standard body shape, or a new engine with a lot more power. Alick Dick and Harry Webster both believed in racing a recognisable car, and neither would have sanctioned the construction of special vehicles where the spin-off for publicity purposes was small; neither could understand, incidentally, why BMC should have backed special-bodied Austin-Healeys at Le Mans in the

'Zoom' was a favourite to replace the TR3A when the new car was thought to need a six-inches-longer wheelbase. Behind the screen it is pure TR4. This body shape formed the basis of the 1960/61 Le Mans cars

The TR3A 'dream car' — Michelotti-styled in 1957 — but never intended for production

early 1960s, especially when these were no faster (with the same engine sizes) than the standard-looking Triumph Spitfires. Therefore, after the successful Le Mans performance in 1955, Harry Webster's engineers were set to work on a completely new engine design which, in Alick Dick's own words: '. . . could be basically a racing unit, but I wanted it to be able to get Triumph the team prize at Le Mans, and I wanted it also to be producible, even in quite small numbers, for a top-line version of the new TR; it also had to be a 2-litre engine, of course.' An interesting point here is that the pushrod engines used at Le Mans in the TR2s had never been super-tuned for racing. Ken Richardson's cars were rarely any faster than standard, and never indulged in such legal modifications as high-lift camshafts or the fitment of Weber carburettors. When the competitions department was re-opened in 1962 following Richardson's dismissal, the new staff found to their dismay that all engine-tuning know-how would have to be learned from scratch; the 130 bhp their engines achieved could certainly have been found in the mid-1950s and made the Le Mans cars very much quicker.

Work on the new racing engine took a long time, as it was side-lined from time to time when new mass-production engine work had to be completed, so it was not until 1959 that it was revealed at the Le Mans test days in April. Installed in what looked at a first, superficial, glance like a standard TR3A structure, the new engine was seen to be a purposeful, if rather bulky, twin-cam of altogether conventional design conceived at a time when the best racing engines were Jaguars, Ferraris and Maseratis (except for the eight-cylinder Mercedes-Benz, which was far too complicated for a firm like Triumph to consider something similar), the new engine looked rather like the Ferrari 2-litre Mondial of the period. It was obviously very strong, clearly only at the start of its development, and not nearly as powerful as it might become in the next year or so. The twin-cam cylinder-head accommodated valves opposed at an angle of 73 degrees, and its total weight including all hang-on accessories such as clutch, dynamo and starter was said to be 438 lb, slightly lighter than the normal pushrod engine fitted to all the other TRs. In general construction the TR'S' engine (for that was its name) was clamped together rather like a multi-metal sandwich. From bottom to top there was the large cast sump, the lower crankcase casting,

The designer of many fine Triumphs between 1957 and 1968, Harry Webster became Director of Engineering at British Leyland's Austin-Morris division. The model is an early study for the Triumph 1300 (1965)

the upper crankcase, the separate cylinder block and the aluminium cylinder-head. All auxiliary drives were grouped together at the front of the engine – camshafts, distributor, water and oil pumps – and there was provision for fan blades on the nose of the crankshaft pulley. Like most new projects being developed in a car factory, the TR'S' engine soon acquired a nickname: one of the supporting characters in a popular Arthur Askey TV series at the time was a young lady with an extremely well-developed figure called Sabrina, and a look at the profile of the overhead camshaft timing gear covers at the front of the engine will immediately show why the workshop fitters plumped for 'Sabrina' as their engine's nickname. It was a name which stuck.

If for no other reason, Sabrina was historically important, for it was the first overhead-cam engine of any nature that had carried a Triumph label since Donald Healey's ill-fated straight-eight Dolomite engine of 1934. Twenty-five years later, here was a modern design with approximately the same capacity, half the number of cylinders, no supercharger, yet giving more horsepower in a relatively undeveloped and completely reliable form. Cylinder dimensions were fashionably over-square, with a bore of 90 mm and a stroke of 78 mm adding up to a capacity of 1,985 cc. At first the compression ratio was a modest 9.25 to 1, and with the twin-choke SU carburettors fitted the power output was in excess of 150 bhp at about 6,500 rpm. The cylinder-head layout was conventional Jaguar-type, or Ferrari-type, with large inlet valves and single offset ignition. Laid out initially by Dick Astbury, who later was to join Ricardo, Sabrina was clearly a very promising design, and capable of more development; indeed, a target of at least 200 bhp (100 bhp per litre – still a very competitive figure at the time) had been set for the engine in its final form, while at the other extreme it was thought that a softly-tuned production version with single-choke carburettors might be marketed with 120 bhp. One criticism that was made at the time concerned the engine's size and weight. Because of the auxiliary drive layout and the generally stiffer construction, Sabrina was $3\frac{3}{4}$ in longer than the TR3 engine, measuring $26\frac{1}{4}$ in in all.

It was the sheer size of this interesting new engine which caused a fair amount of confusion in the ranks over the new TR projects. Without too much investigation ever being made, it was thought that the extra length of Sabrina could only truly be accommodated in a car with a longer wheelbase than that of the TR3A. In view of the fact that Triumph eventually managed to squeeze the long six-cylinder engine into the TR5 with very little change to radiator layouts and none at all to the front suspension, it is now really surprising to note that in 1959 it was thought necessary for no less than six inches to be added to the wheelbase of the Le Mans prototypes. This six inches found its way into several of the TR4 projects (or TR3B as they were known internally) because everyone from Alick Dick downwards was quite convinced that the twin-cam engine would eventually be offered as a high-price option. Such a wheelbase (7ft 10in) never reached the production stage, and the remarkable thing about this six inches of costly red herring is that when a twin-cam engine was eventually fitted to a proper TR4 in 1962, it slipped in to the normal production body and chassis without any fuss apart from the moving around of cooling systems and auxiliaries!

At the time, however, the intention was that any new TR chassis frame would be endowed

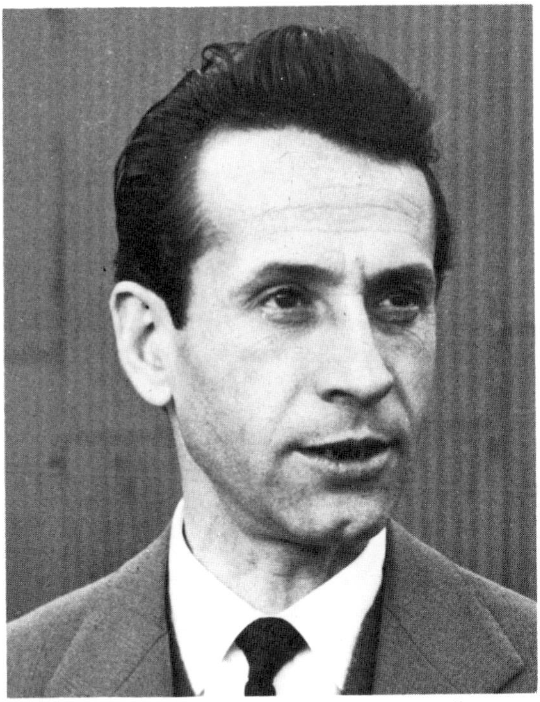

Giovanni Michelotti, the brilliant Italian stylist responsible for all Triumph body styles between 1957 and 1970 apart from the TR6

with the longer wheelbase, with wider front and rear tracks, and with the adoption of rack-and-pinion steering in place of the existing cam-and-lever layout. The long wheelbase was purely to accommodate the twin-cam engine and to give Michelotti's styles more chance to have an imposing nose; it was not intended to give any extra space in the passenger compartment. The widened tracks were to be achieved by building out the chassis frame structure and the spring towers, while the rear-track increase was merely by lengthening the tubes between the differential casing and the brake drums. There was to be no change to the location of the main structural members, and the rear-spring base was maintained. Unhappily, there was also to be no change to the run of the chassis members under the rear axle tube, which meant that the new cars would still lift rear wheels when they ran out of axle movement and there would be little improvement in the ride.

There was, however, one instant piece of redesign conceived by the engineering department when they decided to build-up some TR3As with the standard chassis frame, but with wider tracks and the new steering layout. These, of course, would have looked completely ungainly because of wheels sticking out at the sides of the wings, so it was then necessary to have sets of more bulbous wings added to an otherwise unchanged TR3A bodyshell. The resulting prototypes – TR3Bs or 'Betas' as they were Triumph-coded – were generally liked, and were really very nice cars and gave much more of an improvement over TR3A behaviour than these minor changes would suggest. Beta was a viable project for some time, particularly as it would involve only minimal tooling expense, and it was suggested that it might continue alongside a newly styled TR4 to

Vignale made a small quantity of this car, the Triumph Italia, which used a completely standard TR3A chassis. It was very expensive, but contained several Michelotti ideas for the future

The true forerunner of the TR4, based on an unwidened TR3A chassis and using a Herald Coupé roof. Michelotti then amalgamated the best of this and the Zoom styles to come up with . . . . .

give American dealers the best of both worlds. There was one particular experimental car, painted and trimmed black and bearing the obvious nickname of 'Black Beta' which performed and handled like no TR had ever done before, for it had the 2.2-litre engine and a variety of extra touches.

For Le Mans in 1959, however, bulk and brawn won the day. The race cars, which looked rather like race-prepared TR3As, hid the Sabrina engine in the longer-wheelbase chassis with the wide tracks plus rack-and-pinion steering. The extra wheelbase was accommodated by modifying the front-wing profiles, while the body shells were built up of glass-fibre. It would have been logical to expect cars for the billiard-table surfaces of Le Mans to be lightened, so no-one is now prepared to admit to the reasons for these Le Mans cars being very heavy – at 2,025 lb so heavy that only a handful of GT Ferraris in the race were weightier! Certainly there was no good reason why the glass-fibre shells should be so thick and rigid, nor why the chassis frames should have full-length channel-section stiffeners running the length of the main members.

No-one ever found out how aerodynamic or otherwise the TR3 or TR3S body shape was, nor how to improve it without making the cars look completely non-standard, but there was no doubt that the Sabrina engine's extra 50 bhp didn't produce the dramatic increase in maximum speed hoped for. The old TR2s had reached about 120 mph down the Mulsanne straight in 1955, but it seems doubtful if the TR3S cars achieved more than about 135 mph (or 140 mph if they were really pressed). The weight didn't help, either, though lap speeds were much improved. 1959 was Triumph's first race with the twin-cam engine, and not a happy one. Richardson's decision had been to run with fans on the engines (who needs fans at 135 mph at Le Mans with a front-engined car?); minor out-of-balance problems led to two of the cars retiring when a broken fan blade ploughed through the radiator shells, draining out all the water and seizing the engines. Before it retired, Ninian Sanderson's car achieved a lap in 4 minutes 46 seconds (105.3 mph) though it was the last of the cars to retire (driven by Peter Jopp and Dickie Stoop) that was so desperately unlucky. Their car had already had its fan blades removed, and was pressing on well in a very creditable seventh place when, after 22 hours, the car had to be withdrawn with an oil-pump drive failure.

The twin-cams didn't appear again until the 1960 Le Mans, but in the meantime the search for a new body style for the TR was hotting up. After the Michelotti 'dream car' had been as-

. . . the finished article. The 1961 TR4; note the 'power bulge' necessary to clear the carburettors

sessed fully, it seemed to be agreed that a basically similar full-width appearance should be authorised; the little Italian stylist was therefore set to work under a typically terse, if poetic, Triumph project code of 'Zoom'. The first Zoom prototype (see illustration) looked promising enough, and perhaps even sufficiently slippery for it to be used at Le Mans. Alick Dick was not averse to entering non-standard-looking TRs if they would eventually turn into production shapes; that way, it was reasoned, Triumph could 'do an MGA' by racing Le Mans cars that would subsequently be revealed to have been prototype try-outs for a new generation of cars. Therefore, while development of Zooms continued, it was decided that the 1960 Le Mans cars should also look like that. A quartet of thick and rigid – and therefore heavy – glass-fibre bodies were built up, and grafted on to the existing race car chassis.

Well before the 1960 Le Mans race, however, there had been second thoughts about the merits of Zoom for a new car. The several factors involved in this change of direction included the looks of Zoom, that continuous uncertainty over the longer wheelbase, and the fact that the irrepressible Michelotti had built-up yet another different prototype! This one had been styled around the confines of the original TR3A tracks and wheelbase, and while undeniably narrow and looking a bit high (see illustration) it had certain points, notably in its frontal treatment, which was most attractive. Harry Webster then decided to let Michelotti combine all the merits of this prototype, and the Zooms, on a standard wheelbase with wider tracks (as already used on the Black Beta. Yet another Triumph project code – 'Zest' – was born, and it was this style which eventually came to be chosen for production as the new TR4.

Zest is one of those motor industry compromises which has turned out much better than it had any right to expect, for broadly speaking the frontal treatment (as far back as the windscreen) was the restyled TR3A on the wider tracks, while the rest of the car was almost pure Zoom. The new car had hooded headlamps, and a recognisable relation to the TR3A radiator grille, with a bonnet panel low enough to need a faired 'power bulge' over the tips of the twin SU carburettors. Publicity-wise it was not at all like the Le Mans cars, but since they would be seen before the TR4 was announced it was not thought that this would present too much of a publicity somersault when the time came.

Once the styling had been settled, the twin decisions of where to make the body shells and how much to alter the mechanical components had to be made. Finding a source for bodies proved to be easier than at first feared, for Triumph had purchased several small metal-pressings companies in view of their need to build the Heralds, Meccano-fashion, from several body sub-assemblies. One such purchase was Hall Engineering in Liverpool, just up the road from Speke airport, which was building Triumph Herald bonnet assemblies and office furniture, the company's original line. Stopping the office furniture lines, re-hashing the available space, and streamlining the whole production process gave enough space for TR4 bodyshells to be made, and with very little publicity Standard-Triumph became in 1961 the first major motor company to arrive on Merseyside, blazing a trail subsequently followed by Ford and Vauxhall. From then on, people on the Liverpool - Coventry roads have become very used to seeing long and high transporters, perhaps with a dozen TR bodyshells stacked on their side, on their way to Coventry for final assembly. The bodies were pressed, assembled, painted and trimmed before leaving Liverpool, mechanical assembly being carried out at Coventry.

Mechanically neither Dick nor Webster could see much need to make big changes. The four-cylinder engine had already cultivated its own legend, and in spite of some work on a six-cylinder car (using the Vanguard Six 2-litre engine) it was decided to stay with the big-four. The 86 mm bore version, giving 2,138 cc, which had been an optional since 1958, was to become standard, with the older 1,991 cc engine remaining as an option on the new car. The only other major change was to be to the gearbox, where a new casing was needed to accommodate an all-synchromesh cluster. Synchromesh on all forward gears was yet another Triumph sports car 'first', because MG and Austin-Healey, not to mention Jaguar and Sunbeam, were still struggling along with their crash bottom gears. The launch was planned for the autumn of 1961, hopefully after a series of good performances by the Le Mans cars, and in time to announce a range topped off by a de-tuned version of the Le Mans Sabrina engine.

Triumph went back to Le Mans in 1960 hoping for better things. Their new bodies caused quite a stir, though few journalists actually realised that they might be indicative of the new shapes then brewing in Coventry. There had not been time, nor – it seemed – much point in putting the new cars into a wind tunnel for checks on aerodynamic drag and cooling, so it was not known whether or not the Zoom shape was more slippery than the TR3A shape had been. Reason had prevailed in the engine development departments, however, where it had now been agreed that fan blades were not needed, so there should be no fear of a repeat of the 1959 failures. Comparisons between the two bodies were difficult to make with any certainty, for the Le Mans organisers in their infinite wisdom had imposed a regulation calling for full-width ten-inch deep windscreens in place of the much lower screens people had used in 1959. Naturally this jacked up the frontal areas significantly, and made it impossible to assess other changes with accuracy. For Triumph, however, the 1960 event was much happier than 1959 had been, for all three cars finished, taking second, third and fourth places in the 2-litre class just behind Ted Lund's very rapid 1800 MGA, which ran with a non-standard coupé body. The best of the cars, driven by Keith Ballisat and Marcel Becquart, covered 2,149 miles at an average speed of 89.56 mph. What must have been a disappointment to all concerned was that the fastest race lap was 4 minutes 55.2 seconds (102.0 mph), which was 10 seconds slower than in 1959, with no circuit changes and virtually no engine specification differences between the years. One reason was that the cars, incredibly, were even heavier than before, with the best of them weighing in at no less than 2,180 lb (155 lb more than in the previous year), but it was also significant that their best flat-out speed recorded by the radar speed checks on the Mulsanne straight was 128.6 mph. The biggest disappointment, however, must have been with the behaviour of the engines, which, in spite of a full year's development, let the team down 'on the day' when the valve inserts, which had been reduced in hardness on the advice of the valve-seat suppliers, were hammered down so much that nearly all valve clearance was lost and power much reduced. Harry Mundy, then Technical Editor of *The Autocar*, summed up Triumph's feelings in his post-race round-up by commenting: 'It must have been a great disappointment to those behind the Triumph team – the only one to be running at the end of the 24 hours – that they did not qualify on distance. For a considerable part of the race they ran consistently if not spectacularly. They were handicapped by a dry weight of nearly 20 hundredweight – more than that of a production TR3A. As the race proceeded the valve stems of the experimental twin-overhead-camshaft 2-litre engines stretched, clearance was lost and power dropped off. In many hours of bench-testing at full power that failure had not come to light, and this demonstrates the value of road racing as part of the proving programme of a new design which may be used eventually in a production car'. When those words were written, immediately after the race, the real reason for the engine problem was not certain, though the effect of a complete loss of clearance was the same.

The breast-beatings and recriminations which followed the 1960 race can well be imagined, especially as the company was now fast approaching a state where mounting losses were calling for economies to be made on all sides. The competitions programme was cut right back for the following year, though Alick Dick was long-sighted enough to allow the team of Sabrinas to be pitted against the Le Mans marathon for a third year. 1961 was, thankfully, a complete vindication of all that the Sabrina's engine designers had ever hoped for, though there was many a sour voice raised against the great weight and ponderous appearance of the cars themselves. With the best of the engines now pulling at least 155 bhp before the race (and notably, slightly more than that afterwards!) and no further attention given to the streamlining, the best lap times were reduced by at least eight seconds, and the best race average rose dramatically to 98.91 mph, with a distance covered of 2,373 miles. Better than that, all three cars finished, two strongly and one not so strongly, in ninth, eleventh and fifteenth places, and the coveted team prize was won at last. Keith Ballisat and Peter Bolton shared the fastest car, which was also the best British car to finish. *The Autocar's* comment, via Harry Mundy, was more charitable on this occasion: 'The only team to finish the race intact was Triumph – an achievement indeed, and some recompense for last year's disappointment when, again having finished intact, the cars were disqualified for having failed to complete the required distance in the 24 hours. Again this year they were handicapped by a dry weight of nearly 20 hundredweight – the weights of the three cars being approximately the same as last year – yet the race average of their fastest car showed an improvement of the order of 10 mph. Their success earned them the Georges Durand Prize'.

This time there was every reason to shout very loudly about the cars' performance, especially as it came at a time when the company's fortunes were at a low ebb, and the takeover by Leyland had just become a reality. Before the engines were stripped, Triumph went so far as to hand out one of the cars – the Ballisat-Bolton example which

A 'Zoom'-shaped TR3S at speed at Le Mans, 1960. Note the engine oil cooler faired into the nose under the water radiator

had finished ninth – to Edward Eves of *The Autocar* to try on the local Warwickshire roads; this was a signal honour for the magazine, for no other publication appears to have tried the car at all. Eves, who was by nature more of a rallying person than a demon driver, had no chance to try the car on a circuit, but spent an afternoon on the public highway, with the car still plastered with huge racing numbers (No. 27) and scrutineers' seals. The engine had always been remarkably docile, and this was proven as the car was first driven through Coventry's traffic: 'As I drove through Coventry, feeling horribly conscious of the racing numbers which still adorned the sides of the car, my only concern was to keep moving to prevent the engine from overheating. After the previous troubles, no fan is now fitted; only a carefully designed duct takes air through the radiator. Actually the water temperature did not at any time rise above 75 deg C. I was duly thankful that there was no tendency to oil a plug at low engine speeds, for at 3,500 rpm torque and noise come in together with embarrassing *éclat*. Although not recommended, it was quite possible to dawdle at 2,800 rpm in top.

'But this is no treatment for such a car. Once the road was derestricted a change down into second sent the revs rocketing to 6,500 almost before I could stop them; 6,500 in second corresponds to 76 mph and it took just six seconds from the 30 mph limit. A change up into third, and 100 was reached in 17 seconds from the derestriction sign. I make a special point of accelerations from 30 mph, because this is a Le Mans car, rather inclined to stagger away from a standing start. . . .'

But this was the swansong of the TR'S', so that the Conrero-developed car with its space-frame chassis and special streamlined body that had been under consideration for 1962 was never finished, and never seen in public. During the winter of 1960/61, Alick Dick had at last found the buyer for his company whom he had seeked for so long; after several years of talking to other motor industry competitors as diverse as Harry Ferguson and the Rootes Group, Rover and Massey-Harris, the Leyland Group – master-minded by Sir Henry Spurrier and pushed on in their expansion plans by Sales Director Donald Stokes – came on the scene as suitors. But with losses caused partly by the credit-squeeze which then bit hard in Britain, economies had to be made. In such circumstances a freeze on recruitment is obvious, quickly to be followed by the axeing of promotional departments. It can have been little of a shock to Ken Richardson, particularly in view of the limited nature of his competitions activities, and the often difficult relations between his little department at the Radford factory and Harry Webster's engineers at Fletchamstead, to be told at very short notice that his department was to close, and in a very short time indeed he left.

As the department was closed and the staff dispersed, the cars were reassembled and put away in a corner while it was decided what to do with them. All the expertise of their operation was not to be lost, however, for in the final year at least they had been maintained by the Engineering department, where Ray Henderson was very much *au fait* with the project.

Ken Richardson himself left Triumph a very bitter man. Hired by Ted Grinham in 1952 to help turn the ugly duckling of a TR1 into the very saleable TR2, his personal legend had grown up around this work and the splendid reputation earned by his works rally and racing cars all over the world. With very few exceptions his cars were neither super-fast nor super-light, but their sheer rugged reliability and appearance in the right place at the right time in rallying gave birth to a rallying reputation not held by many other cars. His drivers, particularly the discoveries like Paddy Hopkirk and Tiny Lewis, seemed to be groomed in order to leave and find their fortune with other teams, and it must have been a source of much regret that there was never any more money to spare to pay the very best to drive his cars. From Triumph, Richardson moved on to the small Lancashire firm of TVR, where he mounted a low-key competitions programme with the BMC-engined glass-fibre-bodied sports cars, but within a couple of years he had left the motor industry for good. He has now returned to his home town of Bourne, where he never sold his original house, to work alongside Raymond Mays, just like old times.

The twin-cam race cars seem to have disappeared. During the autumn of 1961 and winter of 1962 they were re-assembled, and eventually shipped over to the New York premises of Standard-Triumph, where it was intended to use them for a motor racing programme. That never seems to have materialised, and what remains of the unique twin-cam cars is mouldering at the back of a garage somewhere in North America. Towards the close of 1961, Martin Tustin, then Triumph's chief executive of the American subsidiary, disclosed to the press that the factory was still considering marketing a twin-cam version of the newly-announced TR4, but this is now seen as a kite-flying venture to assess the interest there. The interest was strong enough, but by then Leyland had decided that small-volume sales were not for them. Sabrina was buried, before her full potential and power could be discovered. Leyland were not, however, completely blind to the merits of the sports car, and authorised the completion of tooling on the TR4. But more important things were already brewing within the Engineering departments, and because they were centred around a much smaller and cheaper car the sales possibilities were higher. Someone had lit the fuse under 'Bomb'.

CHAPTER 9

Alick Dick's last Triumph

WITH LEYLAND now in control of Standard-Triumph, and the company still making a loss, everyone was expecting to see rapid and far-reaching corporate surgery; surely a lot of heads would roll, surely departments would disappear and surely the new model programme would suffer? The big surprise was that this didn't happen at once. Leyland personnel joined the Standard-Triumph Board of Directors, but outwardly there were few changes. The revamped and much-improved Herald 1200 was launched in the spring, Leyland management made encouraging noises, and the motoring press recovered its composure. Within the company, however, the changes were already taking place. Fringe activities were axed (including competitions, which to hard-headed Northerners like Leyland were definitely a luxury), and a lot of management cars were withdrawn. The new model programme was scrutinized, sifted, examined, but didn't seem to suffer. Indeed, the two important projects that Alick Dick's management hadn't felt able to approve – the new small sports car and the replacement for the Vanguard – went ahead with all speed.

It was in September 1961 that the sensational departure of almost all of the original Standard-Triumph Board took place. Henry Spurrier (Chairman of Leyland) finally fired of the financial losses that were still piling up, and this was coupled with his impatience of the Alick Dick method of management. Let extracts from Leyland's own statement to the press tell it all:

'Mr A.S. Dick is to resign from the company, and Mr S. Markland is appointed Managing Director of Standard-Triumph International. Further, we have asked Messrs K. Aspland, E. Brimelow, M.T. Tustin, H.S. Weale, M. Whitfield and L.A. Woodall to retire from the Board of STI, some of whom will be retained in an executive capacity.' In fact the only three directors who were not sacked were Donald Stokes and S. Baybutt (a Leyland financial expert), along with Frank Dixon, who was Deputy Managing Director, and who had owned Hall Engineering at Liverpool before Standard-Triumph bought it. In big business such a wholesale change of management could only bring alarming rumours in its train; in this case they varied from stories of blazing rows between the Leyland and Standard-Triumph management (which was true up to a point), to rumours of an impending close-down of car production altogether in favour of expansion into a new line of commercial vehicles (which was not even considered). The rumours spread, were increased by mere hearsay, had tall stories added to them, and began to damage Leyland's stock market standing. Leyland were sufficiently worried to raise the veil of their corporate operations a little. Sir Henry Spurrier was persuaded to make yet another statement, in which he commented that: 'It was expected that conditions in the car industry would improve rapidly in the spring of 1961, and that Standard-Triumph International would have been operating at a substantial profit during that period. Unfortunately, losses continued to be made during those months, and it became clear to me and my colleagues of the Leyland Board that it was essential to bring in drastic economies without delay . . . Mr Stanley Markland, Deputy Managing Director Leyland Motors Ltd, and now appointed Managing Director of STI, will introduce immediate measures designed to effect substantial economies in all overhead expenditure . . . We think it desirable to state categorically for the benefit of our many distributors and dealer friends that it is the intention of the company to stay prominently in the car business. New models will be announced in due course . . . . '

Even such a bald statement of intent did not quell the dealers' unrest completely, and it needed a further stiff letter to all of them, listing what the new management had in mind for the future, to restore anything approaching peace in the chain.

Although the first new model to be announced after the upheaval was conceived, designed, developed and put into production under Alick Dick's direction, there is little doubt that Stanley Markland would have approved of it. Markland was a died-in-the-wool Northerner, a rare example of an engineer who had risen even above his own department to take an increasing share of management responsibility in the ever-expanding Leyland Group. At the time of his appointment to Standard-Triumph, Markland was already Managing Director of Albion Motors Ltd (who made trucks in Scotland) and was Works Director of the main truck plant at Leyland, so it seemed clear that there must be an un-announced ally at Coventry to hold the fort and make many decisions when Markland was away. This ally was already in residence – Donald Stokes, already Sales Director of Standard-Triumph in addition to a similar post with Leyland. Although Markland left the group a few years later, he can be credited with many of the gritty decisions which led to a rapid and rather unexpected financial turn-round at Standard-Triumph. His successor was Donald Stokes, later to become Lord Stokes and Chief Executive of the entire British Leyland complex. What had looked like

A line full of TR4As. Live axle and independent rear suspension chassis are intermingled

REQUEST FOR SEASON TICKET

BRITISH RAIL

It would be most helpful if you would complete and hand this form to the Ticket Clerk at least 24 hours before ticket is required.

This will provide the essential information necessary for preparing your ticket in advance, and avoid delays at peak periods.

In the event of the ticket being "lost and found", the address given will enable us to return it to you quickly.

Surnames (Please use CAPITAL LETTERS) Mr./Mrs./Miss	
Christian or Forenames	
Address	
From	Via
To	
Class	Period
Commencing Date	Expiry Date

Present Ticket
No.
Expiry Date

For Office Use Only
New Ticket No.
Rate

BR.25616

being a huge loss in 1961-62 was reduced to £1½ millions, still frightening enough, but one that could be absorbed in relation to Leyland's own burgeoning profits. Recovery after that was swift, with the company returning profits in 1962-63, and improving their position annually after that. The staff redundancies – there were 700 in total – did not affect the new-model programme, and Leyland had good news for the motoring press when they revealed their new sports car in September, the TR4.

The waggish newsmen instantly christened this car 'Alick Dick's last Triumph' which, in a way, it was. It was the last model he had seen through to production, and one that looked to have built-in success written all over it. To the dealers and, it was hoped, the customer it looked like a whole lot of car, but Leyland were canny enough not to put all their efforts behind the new car, and continued to make the existing TR3A in modified form alongside it for several months. This revised TR3A came rather confusingly into the act in the winter of 1961/62, for in America (where it was sold exclusively) it was called the TR3B, yet it had no direct relation to the TR3Bs or Betas that Engineering had played with during the previous couple of years. These interim cars had neither the wider-track chassis nor the rack-and-pinion steering of the true Betas, but were merely TR3As fitted with the TR4's 2.2-litre engine and the new all-synchromesh gearbox. The wider tracks and improved steering were never sold under the old body.

But after announcement, what would the world think of the new TR4? Although there was much of the very successful TR3A under the skin, the new body style was different enough from anything that had gone before. After all, said the doubters, it had full-width body sides, and an almost uncontoured wing sweep; the MGA, the Austin-Healey 3000 and the Jaguars all had more contouring than this so would the TR4 be accepted? Surprisingly enough, in view of the reputation all the TRs still hold, there was even a suggestion that the TR had gone 'soft' – an adjective of scorn as far as a proper sports car was concerned. These often-muted sneers must have been one of the reasons for a revival of interest in factory-sponsored rallying during 1962, for the public needed convincing that the 'old wine in new bottles' cocktail was still to their taste.

Visually, then, the looks of the TR4 were controversial at the time, even if the engineering they concealed was well-known. The three years of Le Mans racing and piecemeal development of TR3Bs, Zooms, 'dream cars' and Zests, had been brought together into a very harmonious product. Mechanically the TR4 had little new. The bare bones of the TR2/3/3A chassis remained, with important though structurally minor changes at the front end to support the rack-and-pinion steering, and the 3½ inches increase in wheel track. Like the fabled story of the centuries-old axe (which was still original, although it had had three new heads and two new handles) there was always to be something carried over from one model to the next. In the case of the TR4, almost all the chassis was familiar, while the new body shell had been designed to fit in with it. Along with the new steering, a Triumph Herald type of collapsible steering column was also specified; collapsible, that is, not at will, nor for adjustment, but when subjected to abnormal loads in an accident. A head-on collision in a TR3A had always carried the possibility of the steering column being forced into the passenger compartment; with the TR4's more sophisticated arrangement this was no longer possible.

As to the bodywork and its fittings, it had not just been a whim of Michelotti to make it that way. Alick Dick's regular sales tours in America had convinced him of several fallacies that existed in sports car marketing, one of which being the theory that sports cars were sold to young men. Soon after the TR2, and later the TR3, became cult-cars in the United States, it became clear that a high proportion of sales were not to young men who thought no further than the next rally or driving test meeting, but to men (and women) who might politely be described as being of a mature age! The bulk of sales were going not to the young, but to the young-at-heart or the would-be young. Dick saw them as wanting to recapture their youth, a youth which they had probably missed because of the American depression and the rigours of the Second World War. Recapturing a missed youth was fine and laudable, but as many of them were already through their first ulcer and working on their first

Detail comparison of the two TR4A suspensions. Above is the independent rear, based on the Triumph 2000 layout. Only minor changes were needed for the live-axle version. The main chassis members are unchanged and the damper position retained

divorce it would not be possible to sell them a car where draughts, a lot of noise, and wind in the hair were main attractions. The next car would have to be more civilised; more than this, it would have to be civilised without losing out on sports car characteristics altogether. In other words, said Dick: '. . . we had to flatter a chap into thinking he was still young, while making sure that the car really suited him as he really was!' Dick also said that on a trip across America with his wife: '. . . it became very evident to me that we had to improve on the TR3 specification with things like winding windows, and we had to have space to carry sets of golf clubs in the car: this we did, but it was also obvious that we would create a gap in our model line-up, and that was one of the reasons why the Spitfire came along . . . . . The TR2 went out to America, and sold like hell, and no-one knew why it was selling. It wasn't for quite a time after this that we found that in fact the average age of the buyer was 48! They drove these cars down the freeways at 65 mph, which is all they were allowed to do, in some discomfort, and taking on the sporting image of the few people who drove round and round Le Mans, and on the Alpines rallies'.

Apart from catering for these customers, by standardising fitments that had not previously been offered in the TR3A, the TR4 was also different in many basic respects from the TR3A. At the front of the car, although the front wings were still bolted rather than welded to the main structure, the full-width bonnet panel was now arranged to hinge from the front. Apart from being an additional safeguard in case the catch gave way, it also allowed superlative access for service to the battery, hydraulic systems and engine ancillaries, all of which were grouped towards the rear of the engine bay. Although the petrol tank was still positioned behind the seats, high up between the wheel arches, the boot itself was very much larger and of a more convenient shape. Alick Dick's 'two sets of golf clubs' could finally be accommodated, though they would have to be ditched if the spare wheel was needed, as this was stored in the boot floor and had to be extracted through the boot rather than out of a post-box slot like in the TR3A. Michelotti's styling, and the search for more passenger comfort, had led to the elimination of cutaway doors, one of the reasons for this being that wind-down glasses could be fitted in place of the bolt-on canvas and clear plastic side screens that all sports cars had used until then; it was yet another of Triumph's minor 'firsts' in Britain, as the MGB, the revised Austin-Healey 3000 and Midgets and eventually the Spitfire itself were all to follow the lead. An interesting point about these drop windows is that they were actually cheaper than the side screens which they replaced; at the height of the cost-cutting and blood-letting carried out by Leyland during 1961 it was suggested that the TR4 should revert to side-screens, a move that was only forestalled when a careful costing analysis produced the evidence that there would then be a cost increase to the door assembly!

Inside the car there had been a wholesale revision. The seats themselves, the distribution and type of instruments, plus the still-awkward siting of the handbrake lever, were all recognisable TR3A features, but the facia layout and general package were all new. The full-width facia incorporated face-level ventilation – connected to the outside world by ducting from the scoop at the base of the windscreen – and heater controls which looked as if they had been designed in rather than thought about afterwards. There were carpets on the floor, and a carpeted space behind the seats which made no pretence of being other than a useful space to stow soft bags. The average man who likes his face-level ventilation would probably credit the 1964/65 Ford Cortina with being the first British car to have such niceties, but Triumph were probably the first to provide such things in 1961. It was not as comprehensive, nor perhaps as flexible as the later systems, but a ready blast of cold air could be guaranteed. The flow could be turned off or graduated, and made to squirt air in most directions. The vents also had the rather endearing ability to pass through bugs and small leaves that had remained unfiltered by the gauze in the screen inlets! These inlets, incidentally, were placed in what might at first have been thought to be a low-pressure area (one where the air would have seemed likely to be sucked away rather than blown in), but such are the quirks of vehicle aerodynamics that there was enough deflective action in the raised flap to ensure a good blast.

Naturally there was to be a hardtop option, but once again an attempt had been made to provide something different. Urged on by the sales side of the company, who had argued that many would be happy to face open-air motoring on condition that their hair would stay reasonably in place, the engineers had come up with a novel two-piece hardtop where the top panel alone could be removed if required, or the whole hardtop could be taken away as normal. Removal of the top panel meant open-air motoring with reasonably good aerodynamics, for the rear portion of the top used a large glass window in a cast aluminium surround, which doubled both as a hardtop structural member and a roll-over bar for crash protection. The removable top panel could be substituted by a simple frame and a rectangle of hood material, which was immediately christened a 'Surrey' top, after a particular type of coachbuilding feature that had enjoyed a vogue on horse-drawn carriages a century earlier.

Strangely enough, the concept of the two-piece hardtop and the Surrey top were never really popular. Thousands of hardtops were bought and used but few seemed to appreciate the half-way house provision. It was fairly costly to make (mostly because of the use of the aluminium rear window surround), and it was abandoned for the TR6. Sales Director Lyndon Mills remains puzzled about this, being firmly convinced that it was several years ahead of its time (like many Triumph features) when it appeared in 1961. 'In 1973 it would be considered fashionable, and very safe. The rear window had that cast-aluminium member for roll-over protection, and the removable top panel meant that you could enjoy 'Targa' motoring if you wished. The Surrey top was a rather whimsical little name for the frivolous little hood panel you could use in that space on the top. You left your metal roof panel at home in the summer, and took along the folding Surrey top for it if it rained. Very practical and not expensive.' However, most people who bought the hardtop version of the TR4 never bothered to remove the roof panel, or never even discovered from their handbooks that it could be done, so the marketing advantage was lost. 'Now if we re-introduced this on the latest TR6, I bet we would really have something to sell!'

The 2.2-litre engine was almost identical to the 2-litre from the TR3A, apart from the 86 mm-bore wet liners compared with the 83mm liners of the 2-litre version. No-one now seems to know why the TR4's engine capacity was 2,138 cc and the bore 86 mm, when the Vanguard had been 2,088 cc and 85 mm bore for many years, while the tractors (from which Ken Richardson had obtained his first 2.2-litre, 2,187 cc, conversions) used the 87 mm bore. Its carburation was still by courtesy of twin $1\frac{3}{4}$ inch SUs, which contributed the height of their damping piston bodies to the natural rock of the engine under torque to make essential the provision of a bulge in the bonnet panel. This 'power bulge' was on the right-hand side of the engine cover, and acted as an extra 'aiming marker' on right-hand-drive cars; conversely it was well out of the way on the left-hand-drive models which made up to majority of production. With competitions activities in mind, particularly SCCA racing in America and rallying in Europe, the original 2-litre engine was still on offer as a no-cost option. Very few cars were ever built like that, however; owners who wanted to convert back to 2-litres from 2.2-litres found it very easy merely by using spare stocks of TR3A liners and pistons.

The all-synchromesh gearbox was a great advance, and was to form the basis for the Triumph 2000 box, and later that of the Stag. Addition of synchromesh to bottom gear is by no means the simple operation that it might seem, and necessitated a completely new gearbox case and many new internals. The change was 'notchier' than before, but the efficiency of the synchromesh was never in doubt. The Laycock overdrive option remained, operating as before on top, third and second gears. Those in the know quickly found a way of tricking the linkage to allow overdrive first gear as well, but since the overdrive manufacturers didn't approve because of excessive torque, and because this meant that one could get overdrive reverse with rather drastic effects, such a trick was rarely used on racing or competition cars.

By 1961 Borg-Warner had put their new medium-sized Type 35 automatic transmission into production, and it was beginning to gain custom and acceptance on the smaller-engined models for which it was designed. The author was employed at Standard-Triumph at the time the first automatics of this type were fitted to the cars, and remembers how much thought went into the question of specifying such a system for the sports cars. On the TR3A, of course, there had been neither the availability nor the desire to offer an automatic option, but on the TR4, with its more mature image, perhaps there ought to be one. While the sales, marketing, and dealer liaison staff were pondering on this very interesting problem, John Lloyd's mechanics set about grafting a Borg-Warner Type 35 box into the TR4. Mechanically the marriage was quite successful; an automatic likes to be in partnership with an engine that develops lusty low-speed torque, and does not need to be revved hard for good performance; this, of course, the TR4 could guarantee. The principal problem in shoe-horning the much bulkier transmission into the car was that the chassis frame had to be cut about. More seriously, though, the torque converter housing was considerably bulkier than the clutch housing it was to replace, and the gearbox tunnel needed to be widened so far as to encroach seriously on the passenger foot wells. Even though there was adequate space to accommodate the two pedals still required, there wasn't enough left over for floor-mounted dip-switches, footrests and feet to distribute themselves around what was left.

If the sales people had eventually wanted an automtic TR4 there would certainly have been a lot of reshuffling needed in those footwells, but fortunately they discovered that what most buyers of TRs liked was the fact that one couldn't drive it the easy way, that there *was* no automatic transmission option, and that the car had to be driven every inch of the way. The project was therefore shelved, and there appear to have been no regrets that an automatic option was never available on a TR. However, fashions inevitably change and, when MG came to offer a similar installation in their MGB from 1967, they found enough response to make it worthwhile, so when Triumph began to market the Stag they found that over half of all their sales had the optional automatic transmission. Is there a moral to be drawn? Only that the sports car enthusiast seems to be getting less enthusiastic, and that future sports cars from British Leyland will certainly have a two-pedal version; the latest four-speed

Spot the differences? The TR4A had a new grille and chrome side-stripes for identification

Borg-Warner and Automotive Products boxes are both smaller and lighter than the early designs, which should make them easier to squeeze in, and more acceptable in operation.

Even without an automatic option, however, the TR4 was a success. It had a friendly greeting from the world's press, and a very encouraging start in the United States. It also gave Triumph an excuse to get back into competitions (see Chapter 11) and the cars began to flow out of Canley's new assembly hall in ever-increasing numbers. Though Triumph were never again to approach the level of their huge TR3A sales of 1958 and 1959, the TR4 did much to bring the volumes back into that area. In 1962, more than 19,000 TRs were built, over 3,000 of them being the TR3B 'interim' car designed to keep the Americans happy while supplies of the new car built up; only 1959 had beaten that total. Back in Britain, what might at first look like the derisory total of 964 cars were sold, but the dealers were clamouring for more. Exports took priority, as ever, and in any case that sales figure was higher than in any year since 1955, when the export drive was still getting into its stride. A year later sales had dropped a little. There were two reasons for this, one being that the Americans were at last beginning to tire somewhat of the same old mechanical formula, now in its tenth year with very little change, and the other very important one being that Triumph were now preoccupied with building up sales of its incredibly popular new Spitfire. Total sports car sales in 1963 were a new company record at over 30,000 in the year, or about 600 every week, which equalled the MG production rate for the first time. A year later sports car sales had risen yet again, for the TR4 was still selling strongly, particularly in America's sports-car orientated West Coast. Leyland-Triumph, as the Coventry factory was now known colloquially, was booming as never before, and when it became clear that the new medium-size saloon, the Triumph 2000, would also justify the confidence put into its conception, it seemed as if the new management could do no wrong.

Design and development goes in cycles in any modern car-manufacturing concern. There are only so many designers and development engineers, and only so much tooling capability to go around. After the TR4, Triumph had had the Spitfire to contend with, followed by the 2000. The Vitesse (the six-cylinder version of the Herald 1200) had been fitted in during 1962, and work on the all-new small car was going ahead slowly. Harry Webster's engineers, who were happily throwing many of their efforts behind the Spitfire Le Mans project, were now encouraged to have another look at the TR series.

The pattern with the re-juvenation of the TR now became apparent. When the TR3A became the TR4, almost all the changes had been to the body, its appearance, styling and comfort. For the next version, there was no question of changing the body style, but there was now every incentive to make mechanical changes. All the improvements made to the TRs in more than 20 years have been done with an eye to interchangeability; a new gearbox had to take the place of the old one without disturbing its surroundings, the TR4 bodyshell had to drop on to the old chassis virtually undisturbed, and for the latest car the chassis changes envisaged would have to be accommodated under the TR4 pressed-steel bodyshell with the minimum of disturbance.

There had been growing pressure on Triumph to make radical changes to the TR4's chassis. Dimensionally similar to the bare bones of the 1936 Standard Flying Nine, and hampered for so long by an underslung frame member at the rear, the TR2/3/4 chassis and suspension had never been renowned for ride and refinement. In the good old days of hairy-chested sports cars this had not seemed to matter, but once the refinements and creature comforts of the TR4 body arrived, more critical eyes were cast on the ride and handling. Press reports which had been friendly and complimentary about the TR2 and TR3 began to snipe at the TR4. There was criticism about the lack of rear-wheel movement, the hard ride, and the bump-steer on rough roads. That the rallying team found that works cars with even harder suspension could be put round corners at surprising speeds was no answer; these cars spent some of their time with the rear wheels off the ground, had very brave drivers, and the inestimable advantage of using radial-ply tyres which were still not standard on the production car. The Abingdon rivals were also making an impression on public and press opinion. Although the Austin-Healey 3000 which (like the TR) dated from 1952 had nothing to boast about, Sid Enever's new MGB, launched late in 1962, used its Austin-based suspension and mechanical components to great purpose. The MGB's ride and handling was undoubtedly better than that of the TR4, even if the car was neither as fast, roomy, nor as well-equipped. 'There was a gradual build-up of criticism of the roadholding of the TR4, especially on bumpy surfaces,' said John Lloyd, 'but it was all from Europe. From America, where nearly all the TR4s were sold, there were no complaints. Likewise there were never any complaints about the Spitfire, either.'

Chronologically, the Spitfire – with its simple swing-axle independent rear suspension – had already been in production for some time, and when it was decided to go for a new chassis and independent rear suspension for the latest TR it was at first feared that such a layout might be chosen for the bigger car. However, a much more significant car had been the Triumph 2000, announced in the autumn of 1963, which brought a much more sophisticated type of independence to the Coventry production lines. Since the weight, wheel size and power to be transmitted was broadly similar between the two cars, it was a relatively easy decision to opt for the same sort of suspension for a new TR.

The TR5's engine produced 150 bhp (gross) at first. The metering unit was behind the distributor and driven from its shaft

If the new car was to have independent rear suspension of the semi-trailing-arm type, this would mean a completely revised chassis frame. But the car would still look rather like the TR4, so it couldn't have a completely new model name. Therefore, TR4A was chosen, and actually applied to the car's publicity, whereas TR3A is a name applied to the car by its buyers and not formalised by the factory in badging or publicity. At first, however, the engineers were worried about the possible space problems that might follow from using coil-spring suspension like that of the 2000 saloon, which would inevitably mean strong chassis members above them, and probably alterations to the bodyshell. One way of keeping the springing medium compact would be to use torsion bars, tucking them well out of the way alongside a central backbone, and absorbing loads from the semi-trailing arms through simple bell-crank linkages. This was a very compact little scheme that would not, however, allow as much design similarity as was required. In addition the old bogey of cost came into the equation, for torsion bars always tended to pile on the pennies due to the spline machining required at each end. A more detailed look at the Triumph 2000 showed that although its suspension could not be accommodated under an unmodified TR4 body shell, a modified version might be, so the torsion bar proposals were abandoned.

The new rear suspension's geometry was to become very much a 'European standard' in the next few years. Massive cast-alloy semi-trailing arms embraced the wheel hubs, had the outboard drum brakes attached to them, and were attached to the new chassis frame by large rubber-bushed pivots. Some observers liked to call this a semi-swing-axle layout, since it was neither swing-axle nor trailing arm. Its major advantage was that it was simple, and that the resulting wheel geometry, while not perfect, gave very controlled wheel-camber changes. With a pure trailing-arm layout the rear wheels would roll with the car, thus reducing the tyres' cornering power at exactly the time when it was most needed; with a pure swing-axle system the roll-centre would have been too high, camber changes excessive, and cornering behaviour rather unpredictable. The semi-trailing layout produced camber changes such that under roll the outer wheel took up a slightly negative camber, which was thought to be highly desirable. The pivot axes of the trailing arms were parallel to the ground, crossing each other at the centre-line of the car at a point several inches ahead of the rear-axle axis.

Although superficially the TR4A and 2000 suspensions looked alike, there were several important differences. The TR's track was several inches narrower than that of the 2000, and the need to accommodate everything under the existing bodyshell meant that lever-type dampers were fitted in place of the telescopic dampers used in the saloon; the dampers were supported on a strong chassis bridge-piece behind the rear-wheel axis, which also served to support the rear-axle casing. As on the 2000, the articulating drive-shafts included a splined joint part way along their length to accommodate the plunge which takes place as the wheels rise and fall; at first these splines tended to stick and jam when under full torque in a lower gear, and it needed a very special and well-tested grease to cure this problem. Locking was obviously most undesirable, as it would effectively prevent the suspension from moving any further – in other words a classic example of infinite roll-stiffness!

Apart from conferring yet another first on the TR in the sales stakes (exploited by putting a bold 'IRS' in chrome script on the boot lid) the new suspension did away with the old bogey of the underslung rear axle. Gone at one stroke was the problem of having limited rear-wheel movement. To support this new rear suspension a new chassis frame was needed. This was tackled logically enough by leaving the wheelbase and front track in their existing positions relative to the front wheels and starting from there. Since the height of the rear roll centre had fallen from 9.88 to 4.35 inches, this meant that the roll axis had also flattened considerably, but thus encouraged Triumph decided to go further along this development theme by redesigning the front suspension to cut down understeer yet further. This was done by relatively minor repositioning of the inboard pivots, and the net result was a front roll centre raised from 0.75 in to 7.81 in above ground. The new chassis frame bore no resemblance to the old design, being bell-shaped in plan view, and laid out to give completely different stress paths. Main frame sections, and torsional stiffness, were much increased, as was the rigidity at the rear. The suspension load-carrying part of the chassis ended at the rear bridge piece, but hefty rearward extensions were specified as before. Why? Because the Americans, who had originally shown great interest in the new independent rear suspension, backed down when they learned of the cost penalty that went with it. Since they had no particular complaint against the TR4 and its live-axle, they therefore insisted on there being provision for a conventional axle, and half-elliptic leaf springs. At first there was great reluctance within the factory to sanction this, but eventually there was a clever compromise which retained the new chassis frame almost completely, except for the deletion of the bridge-piece supporting the coil springs and the

Styling, engineering and tooling for the TR6 body was completed in a mere 14 months by Karmann. The chassis and main structure remained unchanged. The TR6 is the only non-Michelotti style seen from Triumph over a period of 15 years

nose of the axle. The half-elliptic springs were mounted to the outswept portion of the new frame, and shackled to the rear of the chassis extensions, the sole purpose of which on the IRS car was to hold up the back of the bodyshell. Even the position of the lever-arm dampers was retained. The chassis also contained several features that were not at that time obvious, nor publicised. There was space for an automatic transmission to be fitted if the fickle Americans should once again change their views, and there was also provision for the longer six-cylinder Triumph 2000 engine which Webster was convinced would one day be needed. Little was done to alter the engine and transmission, which had been trouble-free in the TR4. The 2,138 cc engine continued, with an extra four advertised bhp, and used Zenith-Stromberg carburettors which had first been fitted during the life of the TR4. External recognition points were limited to badging, plus a chrome flash along the side of the front wing, which also housed the front flashing indicators.

Triumph owners who now treasure the refinement of their six-cylinder cars should reflect on their good fortune, for at one time the TR4A looked like inheriting a new version of the old four-cylinder unit that would have had to run for some years to pay for itself. With requests for more and more performance becoming rather insistent, Triumph engineers had had a look at their old Vanguard-based design during 1963 and 1964. There was a proposal to increase the cubic capacity of the related diesel engines at the same time, and for a period it looked as if the 2,138 cc engine would be enlarged, by over-boring, to nearer $2\frac{1}{2}$-litres. This could not, of course, be done by substituting bigger 'wet' liners, and therefore it was proposed to convert the engine to 'dry' liners, which allowed more freedom for a larger, 92 mm, bore. Prototypes produced a gratifying increase in torque, some improvement in horsepower, but a horrifying loss of engine refinement, and almost everyone breathed a sigh of relief when the project was scrapped; if not, the TR4A would have had the biggest, roughest four-lunger since the Austin-Healey 100s of nearly a decade earlier.

There was an unavoidable weight increase due to the new chassis frame and the independent suspension (in fact the live-axle variant of this car was 29 pounds lighter than its more sophisticated running mate, yet about 63 pounds heavier than the less-strongly built TR4), and in spite of the increased power output there was very little improvement in performance. Maximum speeds appeared to be slightly up – some test figures gave 109 to 110 mph in overdrive top – and fuel economy appeared to be slightly improved. The press reports were all very happy with the new rear suspension, one typical report commenting that: 'The greatest improvement in this TR undoubtedly comes from the new rear suspension. This is very similar to that used on the Triumph 2000. Because there is much less unsprung weight to control, and the springs are no longer the locating members for the axle, the suspension is much softer and better able to cope with rough roads. Longer front springs give more suspension travel, and consequently the ride characteristics have changed out of all recognition. Before, one could never forget the live rear axle, which pattered and thumped about, especially if disturbed in a corner taken under power. Now the TR can be driven deliberately fast at obstacles it would have shied from before . . . . . Cornering is transformed, and there is now a steady degree of understeer with quite a lot of body roll. If power is applied early in a bend, eventually the tail will slide out, but this doesn't happen until well beyond normal speeds.'

Praise from the press was all very well, but would the public buy it? We have already seen that the Americans wanted a choice between the old and the new type of suspensions, and unfortunately I have not been able to ascertain in what proportion they were supplied; in 1965, however, the year in which the TR4A was released, at least 3,000 more cars were shipped than in 1964 when only the TR4 was produced, so the rejuvenation appears to have worked. At home, too, all was well and Triumph were able to release rather more cars to British buyers than before; TR4A sales exceeded 1,000 in each of the years 1965, 1966 and 1967 – the first time that three consecutive 'four-figure' sales years had been achieved. However, as far as Harry Webster's engineers were concerned, they had lost interest in the 'old' TRs, especially as Ralph Nader's attacks on the safety and digestion of motor cars was making itself felt. The mid-1960s seemed to be occupied by a lengthy debate about these topics, and it was with little surprise that European manufacturers learned of the regulations which they would be required to meet in the 1968 season. Changes would be required to the TR engine, and this time their release date was to be tied to a legislation date rather than a marketing opportunity.

Pollution laws and anti-emission legislation are subjects that will for ever be burned on the hearts of engine-development engineers on both sides of the Atlantic. Meeting the requirements, which have progressively tightened every year since 1968, has taken up much time that ought to have been spent on increasing power outputs or improving fuel economy. Who knows how many new engine developments have been delayed by years, or even cancelled altogether, by these new laws? In 1966 and 1967, when the work necessary to meet the first set of limits had to be carried out, few people in Britain knew the first thing about emissions-limitation, and all had to start virtually from scratch. However, even at that stage of the game it became obvious that the old TR engine could not be made to comply, and that a new power unit would be required; it was a happy coincidence that the marketing appeal of the old engine was beginning to flag at last, and that the sales staff would have required a new engine even if the emission laws had not intervened. Harry Webster and Ray Bates therefore dusted off one of the various contingency plans for the TR range which they had been refining through the years – the fitment of a six-cylinder, Triumph 2000-type engine. This had already been around for some time – it was originally a six-cylinder version of the Standard 10/Herald unit, and was machined on many of the same transfer-line tools – and had been fitted into saloon cars since 1960. The little 'mini-E-Type' GT6 coupé was also due to have the same engine, and the Vitesse was scheduled to be upgraded to 2-litres at the same time.

The very first TRs with six-cylinder engines had been built in the days when there was a desperate search for a TR3A replacement; those engines had been of the pre-2000 variety, not very powerful, and certainly with no sports-car character. Fitting the engines into the TR4A chassis was going to be no sweat as provision had been made for it, and the transmission was well up to the task of dealing with the torque. However, since the TR4A boasted of 104 bhp, and the best of the 2000 units only produced 95 bhp, something drastic would have to be done. Up to then, tuning 2000 engines had never been a very rewarding business, unless radical solutions like triple double-choke Weber carburettors and wild camshaft timing had been specified. The works rallying 2000s of 1964/65 could call up a very noisy and extrovert 150 bhp at 6,000 rpm, but had an idle rather reminiscent of a Leyland bus and fuel consumption in the super-tax-payer's class. Bill Bradley's Group 5 racing 2000 progressed to prototype Lucas fuel injection, and a new cylinder-head, and this, with very little development once it had been made to stay in one piece, produced no less than 175 bhp.

In the meantime, however, another branch of the engine design team had been looking at ways of increasing the swept volume of the four-cylinder derivative of this unit, both for a four-wheel-drive light commercial vehicle to be based on the Triumph 1300 installation, and for further developments of that car. Their conclusions were that while there was absolutely no chance of increasing the cylinder bores yet again (they had started life at 58 mm, and were now out to 73.7 mm) there was quite a lot to be gained by an increase in stroke. One remembers at this stage that the one immovable dimension on the 803, 948, 1,147, and 1,296 cc fours, plus the 1,596 and 1,998 cc sixes had been the same 76 mm stroke. This was partly due to the fact that the original engine, conceived at the end of the 1940s, had been very 'under-square', becoming progressively nearer 'square' as the cylinder bore was increased, and partly because that particular aspect of production tooling in the Canley engine shops would have been very expensive to alter!

But if a longer stroke was the only way to get more capacity, this was the way that Webster would go and having taken such a big decision he then allowed *two* new strokes to be commissioned. The four-cylinder engine became 1,493 cc (by a stroke change to 87.5 mm), while the six-cylinder engine was pushed up all the way to 2,498 cc by a hefty stroke increase from 76 mm to 95 mm. This meant an increase in crank throw of 9.5 mm (0.374 in), which also meant that connecting rods and pistons would have to be redesigned, though the depth of the cylinder block would have to remain unchanged. The ratio between crankshaft throw and connecting rod length was still considered acceptable when the design layout was complete, and it next became apparent that the cylinder block would have to be widened to allow for the radius of the extra throw. A major casting change was therefore needed to allow for this – one which has now been commonised on the other six-cylinder engines. Things began to look brighter for the new TR – at first called TR4B before later radical engine changes made the new TR5 name justified – now that a deep-breathing 2.5-litre was to be used. Even so, merely enlarging the swept volume was hardly likely to be enough. The sales staff, especially those having to sell the car in Europe where out-and-out performance was required to suit the fast new motorways, wanted more performance and lots of it. At last, it seemed, they had awakened to the fact that the TR's performance had stagnated for far too long, and the new car would have to make up for the delay in one fell swoop.

At first the job of uprating the performance went ahead in a conventional way. There was the advantage of a new cylinder-head (called the 'full-width head' in the department) which combined simpler mechanical construction with much improved porting and therefore power possibilities. The first TS (or Touring Sport) version of the 1,998 cc engine had been pushed up to about 105 bhp with the aid of a more ambitiously designed camshaft and the new head, but was not considered flexible enough for the average buyer. When enlarged to 2½-litres, the power output could be considerably higher but still with unacceptable idle and traffic behaviour, and by the time it had been tamed to behave in the proper manner peak power was back to not much more than 110 bhp. It was at about this time that salvation appeared in the guise of the Joseph Lucas fuel injection system, even though its use had not, at first, been intended for pure power-improvement purposes.

Fuel injection first crept into Triumph because of the emission-limitation problem. When the new regulations were published requiring a limit on the presence of hydrocarbons and carbon monoxide in the exhaust gasesmany designers were in despair. By comparison with the much more stringent limits which now exist, and the ludicrously tight requirements still posted for the coming years, one wonders just what they were worried about. However, as Harry Webster points out, at that time no-one knew anything about emissions and it all looked very serious. At first it was thought that the only way to beat the limits was to work with such expensive hang-on devices as after-burners and catalysts, which Lucas could supply, having had much experience of this sort of thing in the aviation-engine business. Work was started in a not very successful manner, and it was apparently some months before Triumphs and Lucas between them decided that they really ought to be tackling the problem from the other end, making sure that the mixture that went in to the engine was more perfectly constituted rather than trying to clean up the mess that came out. The answer to correct mixture, perfectly distributed, seemed to be fuel injection, and since Lucas had just decided to 'get their feet wet' in producing such systems Triumph started development on this basis. Early systems had been horribly expensive, of course, so Triumph were most pleasantly surprised to learn that they were not going to have to pay through the nose after all. Much later, of course, it was found that adequate control of distribution and mixture could be achieved by careful setting of the revised Zenith-Stromberg carburettors, but this was not known until it became quite clear that the injection system could not be made to cope unless extra environmental controls (including temperature and altitude sensitivity) were built in. Once fuel injection had been thrown out of the emissions-control arena, it needed little encouragement for Harry Webster and John Lloyd to get their heads together to find ways of marrying injection to a much increased output for the rest of the world. Fuel injection, they knew, could be relied upon to give very good distribution and precise metering at all speeds. Was it not a distribution and flexibility problem which existed on tuned versions of the $2\frac{1}{2}$-litre engine? Furthermore, an injection system might be expected to tame the wilder camshaft timing more effectively than could carburettors. Engines were built quickly, and proved these points beyond all doubt. The first production engines used an ex-rally-car camshaft giving no less than 70 degrees of valve overlap, pushed up developed horsepower to 150 bhp (gross) at 5,500 rpm, and maintained a lumpy, if reasonably acceptable idle condition.

With such a system, the TRs performance was transformed, and it did not need much persuasion to show management that the large increase in horsepower was worth the substantial cost increase they would have to accept. What probably tipped the balance was the thought that

Karmann's modified tail treatment was a successful way of giving the TR6 a distinctive appearance as well as providing practical advantages

suitably modified engines of the same type could be dropped into the Triumph 2000 with rather electrifying results. The idea of a 2000TS, which had been the original cause for six-cylinder engine development, soon changed to the 2.5 PI project. The first cars built used super-tuned TR5 engines, and were entered for the RAC Rally of 1967 – one to be driven by racing driver Denis Hulme and the author. The event itself was cancelled, but works experience of the cars confirmed that for the saloon the engines would have to behave in a much more civilised manner. The 2.5 PI, released a year behind the TR5 in the autumn of 1968, had the same basic engine developing 132 bhp, and was an immediate success; when the performance was matched by a more up-to-date style, particularly in the passenger compartment and on the facia, it became a best-seller. It was, of course, the basis of the successful British Leyland assault on the 16,000-mile World Cup Rally in 1970.

Once the decision to 'go injected' with the TR5 had been made, little time was left before the car's announcement in the autumn of 1967, and the body styling was left alone. This conformed with the now normal Triumph pattern of changing things on the TRs; the bodyshell had been changed first in 1961, the chassis had followed in 1965, and now the engine had been replaced in 1967. As far as the American market was concerned (and this market alone was due to take more than three-quarters of the revised car's production) they could not have the benefit of fuel injection; their car was to be called the TR250 instead, have the same 2,498 cc engine, but fitted with twin Zenith-Stromberg carburettors of the carefully set-up emission-controlled type. There was nothing like as much power, either, for the 'federal' version disposed of a mere 105 bhp, virtually the same output as that of the old Vanguard-based design. It was perhaps inevitable, therefore, that their response should be muted, and American demand for TRs fell really substantially for the first time since 1961. On the other hand, this meant that more cars could be made available in Britain; every TR250 not built meant that there was space on the production lines for another British or European TR5. British sales in 1968 totalled 1,136, the fourth consecutive four-figure total, and the highest since 1955.

There was very little to distinguish the TR5 externally from the TR4A (although the TR250 customer was presented with speed stripes – a North American fad – *across* the nose) except that there was a new front grille, new badging proclaiming the inclusion of 'PI' to passers-by, and the addition of dreadfully pseudo wheel covers which gave the impression of cast-alloy wheels being fitted, and were in fact dummies. Even dummy wheel nuts were fitted to the covers! Chassis changes were limited only to the standardisation of radial-ply tyres at last, bigger front brakes, and the beefing-up of the chassis-mounted final-drive unit and drive-shafts; incidentally, the American customer no longer had the choice of independent rear suspension or a live axle, as the 'old' design of live axle had been withdrawn. Inside the car, the facia's surface had turned from polished wood to a matt finish, and the original design of fresh-air ventilation had given place to the standard type of adjustable 'eyeballs'. There were rocker switches in place of the old toggles, and the steering wheel spokes were padded to placate the American authorities.

The fuel-injection system was not without teething troubles at first, especially because of the high under-bonnet temperatures generated, and there was a particularly annoying whine from the high-pressure fuel pump, which eventually was tucked away in the boot as far from the driver's ears as possible. The Lucas system was, and remains, a simple one, lacking some environmental controls that would have made it more refined (and obviously more expensive); starting was often a problem, and in the early days there was more than one case of an under-bonnet fire. This happened to a close friend of mine, whose car (a 2.5 PI saloon) caught fire in the middle of Coventry; after calling the Fire Brigade, whose appliances were only a couple of hundred yards away, he watched the car burn itself to scrap and went home by bus! Yet in spite of the often over-publicised difficulties with such brand-new equipment, there was no gainsaying the dramatic improvements in performance. Whereas a TR4A might perhaps reach between 106 and 110 mph, a TR5 could reach a full 120 mph. Two seconds were clipped off the standing-start quarter-mile sprint, and a full 20 seconds off the time required to reach 100 mph from rest (down from around 48 seconds to 28 seconds). Acceleration from rest to 60 mph was down from about 11.4 seconds to less than nine seconds, and to pay for all this the fuel consumption usually fell to around 20 mpg. The car itself was slightly lighter, mainly because the engine itself was lighter than the old 'four-lunger'. The improvement was completely out of the ordinary; every motor manufacturer likes to sell a new model which beats the old one by a measurable amount, but these differences turned the TR5 into an entirely different class of sports car. It was as quick, if not quicker than the Austin-Healey 3000, which was dying, and quite a lot quicker than the unsuccessful MGC which was to be announced at the same Earls Court Show. All this performance had to be paid for, of course, and the British basic price leapt from £800 for the TR4A to £985 for the TR5 (a total with purchase tax of £1,212).

However, even before the TR5 was ready for release, Triumph management had realised that time was running-out for the original Michelotti body style. The British Leyland merger was as yet no more than a gleam in Lord Stokes' eye, and he was still committed to supporting a running battle against MG and Austin-Healey. The search for a new style began during 1965 and 1966, although Michelotti's first designs required a completely new shell and chassis. This car, which looked distinctly like a grown-up and restyled Spitfire, was coded 'Fury' at Triumph, and included MacPherson strut coil-spring suspension at front *and* rear (the rear suspension being blooded on the race track in Bill Bradley's successful racing Spitfire) and a smooth frontal aspect which incorporated Lotus Elan-type flip-up headlamps. The only car built used a Triumph 2000 engine in its first 'TS' tune, for the 2½-litre engine did not then exist, but the project was soon dropped when it was decided that a new body and chassis components could not be entertained in addition to all the engine changes. However, for once the prototype was not scrapped without ceremony, but instead was sold off. Early in 1973 it surfaced again for sale in a motoring magazine, being offered for not less than £3,000. A buyer would certainly have a unique car in his possession, but would have found chassis and body spares very hard indeed to find!

The TR6's 1973 facia layout, still using the same group of instruments as the TR2, but with all the latest safety fittings and ventilation

Eventually it became clear that even a new bodyshell on the fairly new all-independent chassis would represent too much investment, and that the best which could be done was to face-lift the TR4A shell. Completely new shapes were, in any case, not easy to find, for by the time existing 15 inch wheels, legal requirements, lengthy six-cylinder engines and the existing passenger box were laid out there didn't seem to be a lot of room for manoeuvre. Normally Michelotti would again have been invited to make proposals for the face-lift, but at that particular time – 1967 – he was heavily committed to other work, for Mazda and Daf with new saloon cars and for Leyland on new commercial vehicle cabs. For the first time since 1957 Triumph would have to look elsewhere for their styling advice, and there was the additional in-house problem of a lack of tooling capacity and time. Although nothing could stop the release of the TR5, the revised shape was needed urgently. One of the motor industry's little coincidences then turned up in the shape of a chance conversation between Harry Webster and a German motoring writer called Bernard Hopfinger, who happened to know that the German coachbuilding company of Karmann were in the process of expansion and were looking round for work. Webster therefore contacted Karmann, set them what he thought was a near-impossible target both in terms of time and capital limits, and awaited results. Karmann soon produced a clay mock-up of a revised TR4A, where the main panels were left intact, including the scuttle, floor and doors, but with major changes to front and rear styling. Not only was Karmann's style pleasing, and accepted without modification for the TR6, but they could also promise completion of tooling design and tooling manufacture in a rather miraculous 14 months; similar facilities in Britain could promise no better than 24 months.

The TR6 style, therefore, was under way at the time the TR5 appeared, and progressed so well that the TR6 could be released in January 1969, only 15 months later. The TR6, though based on the TR5 shell, was very noticeably different. The frontal aspect, with headlamps pushed right out to the edges of the new grille, and a long smooth bonnet panel that had at last dispensed with the TR4's 'power-bulge' (there were no longer any tall carburettors whose dashpots had to be cleared), looked much smoother, while at the rear a near-relation to the Stag/GT6/2000 Mk 2 styles had been evolved. Lyndon Mills' old favourite Surrey top two-piece hardtop had been abandoned, and in its place Triumph styled their own one-piece hardtop with quarter-windows behind the door glasses, and no roll-over hoop protection.

Chassis-wise, there had also been a few changes. With the unexpected and rapid enaction of the British Leyland merger, Harry Webster was promoted to become Technical Director of the Austin-Morris division (which was the original BMC design department), and in his place to Triumph came Spencer King from Rover. King had already made his name along with Peter Wilks in connection with such cars as the Rover 2000, the turbine cars, and – not least – the mid-engined Rover P6BS prototype coupé. Along with the late Derrick White, the racing car designer who had finally quit the Lola-Honda camp to join Triumph as a chassis design executive, King evolved changes to the TR chassis that it had needed for some time. The independent rear suspension first introduced for the TR4A had been partially successful in conferring the longer wheel movements and softer ride which were sorely needed, but had not cured the strong understeer altogether. The final changes made in time for the TR6 included an increase in wheel-rim width, from $4\frac{1}{2}$ inches to $5\frac{1}{2}$ inches, and the provision of a $\frac{5}{8}$ in diameter front anti-roll bar. The inclusion of an anti-roll bar could only encourage understeer, but this was to be traded against an improved ride, and the wider wheels would speed up the response, especially with the wider-section tyres. That it did not succeed entirely is instanced by *Autocar's* comments in their road test: ' On the MIRA road circuit we eventually understeered (the TR6) almost straight ahead after applying full power in second gear on the apex of a dry corner. Unless traction is broken at the rear wheels (impossible in the dry) the tail stays in line, and even on wet surfaces there are no real problems in having so much power on tap.' Very interesting indeed were the comments about the ride in the same test, which indicated just how much the standards of behaviour required of sports cars had been modified in recent years: 'Even on the smoothest surfaces the TR6 feels taught and joggly; on rough roads it thumps along and patters round corners with lots of action but little insulation for the occupants.' How times had changed; from being roundly condemned for having a hard ride in 1962 with the old rigid rear axle, the TR had been praised for a great advance when it adopted an independent rear suspension in 1965, only to be condemned again because this was thought too hard in 1969. Truly, it seemed, the age of the hairy-chested sports cars was coming to an end.

As far as the American market was concerned, their TR250 became a TR6 (or TR6 Carb, as it is known within Triumph), complete with the new body style and all the latest safety-features. So they missed out on a TR5 as such altogether.

After the TR6 was released in 1969, very little further development was lavished on it, and a casual observer would be excused for thinking that British Leyland had lost interest in it. Yet every year sales were to go ahead at much the same rate as before – British sales, slightly down in the 'build-up' year of 1969, were up to 1,308 in 1970, and 1,288 in 1971 – and the car has continued to benefit from progressive improvements to meet the burgeoning American safety regulations. For America, the engine changes have been gradual, and power output had been slightly reduced by 1973 (along with nearly everyone else's) while with the fuel-injection version Triumph had at last succumbed to dealer pressure to make the engine rather more tractable by specifying a new version of their camshaft, with only 36 degrees of overlap. In 1972 the engine power claims were re-calibrated to bring them in line with new European practice, and the 150 bhp (gross) has been reduced to 125 bhp (DIN), where each and every one of those 125 horses is available at the clutch to give high performance. In February 1973 minor cosmetic changes were made, which included new fire-resistant seating materials, and revised brightwork. There was a new 'bib-spoiler' under the front bumper which was claimed to improve high-speed stability by killing the lift caused by air rushing underneath the car. The one mechanical improvement was that the latest 'J' Type of Laycock overdrive was fitted, though this could not now be operated on second gear.

The TR series have now had a very long run of more than 20 years in production – their 21st birthday came on the opening day of the Earls Court Motor Show in 1973. The plush, rapid and still-good-value TR6 PI is a completely different car from the first Standard Nine-based TR prototype that graced Earls Court before it had even been driven. Between those two dates at least 220,000 TRs were built, and not a single one of them could be called dull. Whatever future plans British Leyland have for the TRs – and they do have plans, make no mistake – they will surely want to retain the character that the TRs built up. The TR, like almost any car made these days, 'grew up' as it aged, with the result that it tended to leave behind the true sports car enthusiasts who could afford little more for their sport; Triumph were not oblivious to this threat, but were not able to plug the gap until the early 1960s. A new smaller car, destined to sell in even greater numbers than the TRs, had been in Alick Dick's mind since the mid-1950s; in 1961 when he left the prototype existed, but it was the new Leyland management which eventually put it into production. If the 1950s had been the decade for the TR, the 1960s certainly belonged to the Spitfire.

'Bomb' or the first Spitfire prototype, made by Michelotti in 1959/60. Only the facia layout and the door profiles were changed for production cars

CHAPTER 10

Leyland and the Spitfire

THE STORY of Standard-Triumph's search for a business partner throughout the 1950s has already been told; Alick Dick's almost constant pre-occupation in turning a medium-sized car firm into a large sized one by merger is well documented in Graham Turner's book, *The Leyland Papers*. It is sufficient here to recall that Standard-Triumph prospered for many years due to the profits derived from tractor production on behalf of Harry Ferguson, and that soon after the tractor interests were sold off to Massey-Harris the financial fortunes of Standard-Triumph went into a traumatic decline.

Sir John Black had started the ball rolling by talking to Harry Ferguson himself in 1953, and after Alick Dick became Managing Director he had merger talks with Rover, Rootes, Massey Ferguson, Rover again, and finally – Leyland Motors. During the autumn of 1960 and early 1961, Standard-Triumph's financial situation had become dramatically worse. In Britain there was a credit squeeze, which raised the cost of financing car purchases and caused many prospective buyers to put off their new-car decision. With the vast majority of TR3A production destined for overseas and principally dollar markets, the sports car side remained healthy. Home sales of TR3As were 638 in 1959, 640 in 1960, but a shatteringly low 63 in 1961. The company began to lose money fast, and it was clear that without a partner, and one not dependent on the vicissitudes of private car sales, there would probably not be a Standard-Triumph group for much longer. Merger talks with Sir Henry Spurrier of Leyland began on November 14th 1960, and the merger (really a takeover by Leyland of Standard-Triumph) became public knowledge on December 5th. Leyland were to offer two Leyland shares for every 15 Standard-Triumph shares, which put a value on the company of around £18 millions.

The Leyland takeover came only just in time, for it needed every effort to turn Standard-Triumph into a profitable company, an effort which was helped somewhat by an upturn in the British market during 1961 and especially 1962.

In March 1961 Sir Henry Spurrier took over the Chairmanship of Standard-Triumph which Alick Dick had only held for three months and began to exert the Leyland influence. That spring of 1961 is still remembered in Coventry as a very grim time for the company. Apart from the obvious economies (which were to include closing down the Competitions Department as soon as decently possible after Le Mans) many managers lost their company-owned cars, and there was a recruitment freeze. Indeed, the author claimed a minor sort of record by joining Standard-Triumph in May 1961, probably the first staff appointment to be authorised after the original staff freeze applied by Leyland!

As far as the company's products were concerned, Leyland's first idea was to carry out a frenzied engine-swopping exercise, which included such ludicrous combinations as the Herald 1200 engine in a Vanguard bodyshell, but more importantly included approval of the Vitesse programme, in which the Herald was endowed with the lengthy six-cylinder Vanguard engine in 1,596 cc form, an engine that was to find an application in the sports cars before very long. The new TR4, or 'Zest' as it was code-named

This show-finished Spitfire chassis shows off the backbone construction and the transverse leaf independent rear suspension

within Engineering, was well on the way to being tooled, and since the original TR2/3/3A series were entering their ninth year of existence a replacement was obviously going to be needed before long; what happened to the TR4, and how it developed over the years, was chronicled in the previous chapter. Apart from approving production of the Vitesse, Leyland also approved a start to the 'Barb' programme, which was the code-name for a new large-medium saloon car to replace the Vanguard, and was to be released in 1963 as the Triumph 2000. Studies were also put in hand for the next small saloon car to be announced, originally thought to be the Herald replacement, but the 'Ajax' project would have to wait until the 2000 was established, and eventually appeared late in 1965 as the Triumph 1300.

There was always a space problem at Canley, and it is really not surprising that for a whole decade the TR2 and its successors were the only sports cars to be made by Standard-Triumph. Until the vast new assembly hall was completed (using capital realised by the sale of the Ferguson tractor rights in 1959) there was only room for one sports-car production line, especially when that sports car used different components from every other car in the range. Unhappily for the world's sports enthusiasts, it has usually been the case that sports cars never sell in sufficient quantities to make special facilities worthwhile; with a limited amount of factory floor space, the larger-production bread-and-butter saloons must take priority. Only a small specialist factory like MG at Abingdon can concentrate on sports cars – and there have been suggestions that even Abingdon's days are numbered as British Leyland's rationalisation programme gathers pace.

The next Triumph sports car, when it came after the TR4, would have to be broadly based on bits and pieces used in quantity-production saloons. Logically, too, the new car would have to be smaller than the TR2/TR3 cars, which meant that it would have to be based on power trains lifted from the smallest Standards. During the 1950s Standard-Triumph had been building the dumpy little Standard Eight and Ten, which could never have been accused of being a sports saloon, in spite of Jimmy Ray's RAC International Rally victory in one in 1955. The cars were short, high, and by no means advanced in design.

More Spitfires have been sold than any other Triumph sports car. 412 VC was one of the first, eventually becoming a Competitions Department development car

The engine, though, which was originally 803 cc when announced in 1953, had already been bored out to 948 cc and was proving to be both tunable and robust. It was not until 1956/57, when the TR3 was established as a world-wide success, that the new small sports car was seriously discussed, though its very conception was part of a chain of circumstances that Standard-Triumph could not have foreseen at that time. With the Standard Eight and Ten due for imminent replacement, it was hoped to substitute the existing bodyshell with a new unit-construction body of more up-to-date design. The existing car had been tooled and manufactured by Fisher and Ludlow in Birmingham, who though independent at the time (1952 onwards) had since been swallowed by the BMC combine. Sir Leonard Lord told Alick Dick quite bluntly that BMC were not interested in providing facilities within their empire for Standard to make a new car that would presumably compete with some of their Austins or Morrises, so the only viable alternative was the still-independent Pressed Steel Company at Cowley; Standard were already established customers at Pressed Steel, having placed tooling and production orders for the Vanguard Phase III saloon in that direction. Unfortunately for Standard-Triumph, due to a quite unprecedented rush of new models from other customers, Pressed Steel were quite unable to promise priority either for tooling or for production assembly by 1959.

Not being the owners of a unit-construction body-building plant of their own (the TR3A, for instance, was made by Mulliners) Standard-Triumph were in a real quandary, particularly as it seemed that the old model was beginning to die on its feet and a replacement could not be long delayed. The solution, when made public, appeared ingenious, and by the standard of the day rather anachronistic. The design team, now led by Chief Engineer Harry Webster, elected to go for a separate self-supporting chassis, with a body to be built-up 'Meccano-fashion' of several smaller-than-usual sections. The sales team were delighted to see that this allowed alternative body styles to be fitted without vast extra tooling costs, while the savings to be made by replacing only parts of the body after a major accident was something that the publicity staffs trumpeted assidiously during the car's launch. Alick Dick, meanwhile, had managed to take over several smallish pressed-steel manufacturing companies – including the Forward Radiator Company in Birmingham and a firm of office-equipment manufacturers in Liverpool called Hall Engineering; sections of the new car's bodyshell were to be made out, and the whole bolted together in Coventry. The new car became a Triumph instead of a Standard, as mentioned earlier was dubbed Herald after Alick Dick's own boat, and spelt out the beginning of the end for the Standard name, even though the new car's motive power was the Standard Ten's 948 cc engine. The front suspension was new and conventional, though blessed with phenomenal swivelling ability that conferred a very small tuning circle of 25 feet to the car. The rear suspension was independent, itself a novelty for British cars, but to save costs was a very simple sort of swing-axle, in which the springing medium was a transverse leaf spring clamped at its centre above the differential casing. Production of the Herald began in January 1959, and the car was announced in May.

Paradoxically, therefore, it was the company's failure to find a builder for an up-to-date saloon car body that eventually ensured the birth of the new small sports car, coupled with the engagement by Alick Dick of Giovanni Michelotti as the firm's styling consultant. Michelotti had already retouched the Vanguard – to make it the Vanguard Vignale – and was given the Herald as his first major project for Standard-Triumph. Michelotti was always a very prolific artist, eating and sleeping car design in addition to his normal working hours, and struck it off very quickly with the Standard-Triumph management. As Alick Dick says: 'Michelotti was a great influence on the company, he was a wonderful character and still is, and he has got this ability of interpreting one's ideas on paper. When we came to start talking about new sports cars, I knew exactly the car I wanted but I had no power of drawing it – certainly I can't draw at all, can't even hum God Save the Queen! I remember sitting with him at the Motor Show, at Earls Court, trying to agree on a design for the TR4; he could design cars in about five minutes, you see, but at the time he would insist on designing feminine cars. I called him an unhelpful old so-and-so, and insisted that the TR4 should be a masculine car. He's the only stylist I have ever known who would design cars to one's own ideas, not his own. However, as far as I know the Spitfire was Michelotti's own styling idea. I had been to America, and as soon as I came back and I saw this car I was convinced. Michelotti was always reeling off designs, you couldn't stop him. If you took him out to dinner he'd get practically every menu in the restaurant and design a car and hand one out to each waiter! As soon as I had looked at the car I liked it, I knew Harry Webster did, and Martin Tustin too, and it was obvious that it was going to meet the gap that would open up when the TR4 moved further up the market.'

Michelotti had indeeed produced his own sports car prototype, by shortening the wheelbase of a Herald chassis and going on from there, and the first car, nicknamed 'Bomb' as soon as it got back to Coventry, used as many Herald components as possible. That first car would have been voted pretty by any standard, but in comparison with the existing 'frog-eye' Austin-Healey Sprite it was quite mouth-wateringly attractive, and obviously offered remarkable commercial prospects. That first car, however, was delivered to Coventry from Michelotti's Turin studios when the company's finances were at their lowest ebb, and it was speedily stowed away in a corner of the experimental workshops as a potential lost cause. Fortunately for the hundreds of thousands of Spitfire owners in the world, who would otherwise have had no such car to buy, Leyland recognised a good thing when they saw one, and almost immediately approved production of the new car. The 'Bomb' project sprang back into life, the Michelotti prototype was dragged out of its dusty corner, and development re-started.

There were minor styling changes between the prototype and production car. Externally the only change was to lift the top of the door pressings very slightly to allow full-depth side windows to be fitted (and allow them to retract fully when wound down), while the Michelotti facia was rejected in favour of the familiar central instrument cluster. Facilities for production of body panels proved easier to find than in the case of the Herald, with the Forward Radiator Company, now owned by Standard-Triumph, being allocated the work. One reason why tooling was completed so speedily (the car was announced only 18 months after re-activation, a whole year earlier than the Triumph 2000 which started at the same time) was that Forward Radiator cut corners in manufacturing the tooling as it was expected that the Spitfire would sell at a similar rate to the TR4. That Triumph's own forecasts were proved wrong is now well-known, and

Triumph's ingenious way of taming the GT6's rear suspension. The lower wishbone converted the suspension to 'double wishbone' geometry, and the half-shaft 'doughnut' accommodated the plunge (Picture: Autocar)

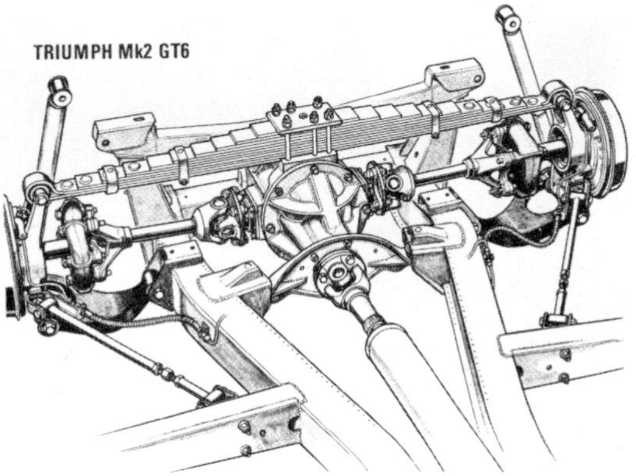

The GT6 Mk 3 had re-styled nose and tail sections and was first produced in November 1970

although the accountants were very grateful, Forward Radiator were soon faced with the task of making some of their 'temporary tooling' a lot more permanent and long-lasting. For no very good reason the new car was to be called 'Spitfire' – it certainly didn't have any Triumph relations which were named after other aeroplanes, but one presumes that ex-Chairman Lord Tedder had liked the name and added it to Triumph's list of registered trade marks. Previous Triumph names, where names had been preferred to numbers, had been related to ships and both Renown and Mayflower had been Sir John Black's ideas. Some wag in the factory suggested that the unsuccessful 1950 Roadster (the 'hydraulic coupé') should be called the Marie Celeste because no-one wanted to stay aboard!

Though there was quite a lot of Herald thinking and parentage in the Spitfire, it would be completely wrong to think of the car as modified-Herald. Like so many such projects before or since, the differences multiplied as development proceeded. The first Michelotti prototype had used 948 cc Herald Coupé mechanicals throughout, including a cut-and-shut Herald chassis, but in the meantime the Herald was growing up with a much-modified 1,147 cc engine and higher gearing. The bigger engines were adopted for the Spitfire, with sports tuning to lift the advertised horsepower to 63 bhp at 5,750 rpm. Herald front and rear suspensions were also used, with minor changes to rates and damper settings, together with the rack-and-pinion steering along with a collapsible steering column which was a safety feature years before legislation was to demand it. The chassis, though similar to the Herald in concept, was very different in detail. In principle it was a backbone design, as was that of the Herald, but in conjunction with changes to body construction the outriggers and bracing members had been deleted. The new chassis was designed around a wheelbase $8\frac{1}{2}$ inches shorter than that of the Herald, and the only common parts were suspension mountings and supports. Allied to this new approach in chassis frames was the layout of the bodyshell. Triumph had had considerable quality problems in building the Herald, mainly due to the sometimes difficult task of matching together the various body sections without allowing water to leak through the gaps. To obviate this on the Spitfire the new open two-seater shell had been designed in one piece apart from the swing-forward bonnet, and incorporated strong sills to take the place of the outrigger chassis and box-section pressings behind the seats to act as pick-up points for the forward-facing rear-suspension radius arms. The windscreen was removable in the same way as that of the TR4.

Because of the Spitfire's Herald ancestry, little major development work was needed, which was probably a good thing as the correct pre-production bodyshells were rather late arriving from the Forward Radiator Company. A part of the early development work was done using a completely disreputable and down-at-heel-looking short-wheelbase Herald convertible, which factory tester Gordon Birtwistle still swears was the best-handling swing-axle car ever to come out of the Fletchamstead experimental shop. Commercially, the arrival of the Spitfire could not have been more welcome to Standard-Triumph, particularly as the deadly rivals down the road had now converted the ugly Mark 1 Austin-Healey Sprite into a reasonably acceptable Mark 11 along with a bit of shameless badge-engineering to bring about the re-birth of an MG Midget. In the United States more than anywhere, the new Spitfire fell into a price bracket challenged only by the Sprites and Midgets, and it only needed a friendly welcome from the press to ensure a good start in life. Though the styling of the Triumph and the small Abingdon products were very different, this took a few months to become obvious. The author remembers vividly taking an early pre-production Spitfire as a service support car to the Triumph team in the 1962 RAC Rally, to assess how useful the Spitfire would eventually be to competitions, and having it mistaken for the rival product. Hurrying through the night in wildest Wales to get to the far side of some windswept and benighted mountain, the Spitfire was suddenly stopped by a couple of country policemen who were firmly convinced that they had caught red-handed a desperado who had been reported as driving around in a stolen Austin-Healey Sprite! It took several minutes of careful explanation, and detail examination of the badges, not to mention a look at the rally service plates and the spares being carried, before the law was convinced that this car was indeed not a BMC product.

The press were quick to make comparisons between the Coventry and Abingdon products, mostly concluding that although the Spitfire cost about £62 more than a Sprite (the Spitfire retailed at £730 at the time) this extra could be justified by such refinements as wind-up windows, much easier accessibility to the engine compartment for service, nicer styling, and a higher degree of creature comforts. In addition the Spitfire was undeniably much more roomy in the two-seater cockpit, being several inches wider across the shoulders and having more leg room and more stowage space, and it was adjudged to give a softer, more 'modern' ride. The performance of early Spitfires and the current 1100 Sprites was remarkably similar, so it was quite clear that a titanic sales battle would be joined in many markets. Soon after announcement, the British government bestowed a hefty cut in purchase tax on new cars, which instantly jacked up demand for everyone's products. Following these cuts, the Spitfire found itself selling at £641 total (or £530 before tax); this compared with £587 for the more sparsely-equipped Sprite, £599 for the MG Midget, and £659 for the Morgan Four-Four which had a 1,340 cc Ford Classic engine.

In behaviour the Spitfire could not have been more unlike the TR4, its big brother. The new car was altogether more delicate, rode softer, was more responsive and had an almost 'feminine' character in many respects. The performance was clearly more than adequate for an 1,147 cc car. Maximum speed was around 92 or 93 mph, general fuel consumption something over 30 mpg, with acceleration to 60 mph of about 17 seconds. Creature comforts were often praised in the magazine tests which appeared during the winter of 1962/63, along with the car's general controllability. There was, however, one area of disagreement – that of the rear suspension's behaviour. The Spitfire, it will be remembered, used a simple transverse-leaf-spring swing-axle system, geometrically identical to that of the Herald saloon apart from the revised settings, and slightly decambered into the bargain. To fit a swing-axle suspension had been a major policy decision made in the late 1950s by Harry Webster, as being one of the cheapest ways to provide IRS. A swing axle's predeliction for adopting peculiar wheel angles under cornering stress was well-known, and had been documented for many years, but the official way of taming this was to put much of the developed cornering power through the front wheels, and to give the rear suspension as little roll stiffness as was feasible. In addition, it was desirable to ensure minimum wheel-camber change on corners, which could be helped by ensuring that the laden car adopted negative camber angles in the first place. Even after 11 years, the main market for the car, the United States, has remained basically happy with the swing-axles, but there was an instant and growing dislike of its behaviour in Europe. There was little doubt that, when pressed, a Spitfire on normal cross-ply tyres could be made to change quickly from steady understeer to strong final oversteer, a characteristic fortunately well-signalled in advance, and controllable by the excellent and direct rack-and-pinion steering. It was also true that the camber of rear springs as received from the suppliers could vary by several degrees, and that cars built with top-limit springs handled less well than they should have done. The situation was not helped by the use of road wheels having rims only 3½ inches wide and 5.20 x 13 in tyres – though this was an exact parallel of BMC practice. The author's Spitfire was lucky in having a lowish rear suspension, but progressive improvement by the addition of, first, wider wheel rims, and latterly, radial-ply tyres transformed the handling. Webster's engineers were fully aware of their problems in this area, and pushed on with the development of a modified system, but were always discouraged by very firm statements from the sales division that the car was perfectly acceptable.

And acceptable it most certainly was. While the TR4 continued to sell well, the Spitfire rapidly built up its own following. The car really got into full production during December 1962, and by the end of the following summer had been made

The GT6's tail, once rounded like an 'E' Type Jaguar, later shared a cut-off style with all other sporting Triumphs. This is the 'federal' version with side-repeaters and other extra equipment

more desirable by the additional optional hard-top, and by the offer of overdrive as an option. The overdrive was like that fitted to the Vitesse, was electrically operated, and worked only on top and third gears. It did nothing for the performance, but under certain conditions worked wonders for the fuel economy. Strangely enough, although the Competitions Department considered overdrives almost essential in their TR4s, they never used them in the Spitfires used from 1964 onwards; by that time there was a big choice of available rear-axle ratios and outright maximum speed was only required at Le Mans and in the Tour de France, for which there was a suitably high ratio. Triumph rarely needed to advertise their Spitfires in Britain, but when they did they were able to use one very creditable fact – that the Spitfire's turning circle was even smaller than that of the Herald; the wheel lock was identical but the shorter wheelbase made all the difference.

When the Spitfire was announced, it was badged 'Spitfire 4', whereupon many know-alls sat back and exclaimed 'Just wait for the Spitfire 6!' At the time a Spitfire 6 could not have been further from anyone's mind, even though it might have been a gleam in Harry Webster's eye, as the Canley factories were flat-out with work. There was, of course, no good reason why a Spitfire 6 or something like it should not eventually be developed, particularly as the relationship between the four-cylinder Herald and the six-cylinder Vitesse was obvious. Anyway, putting bigger engins into smaller cars was not always a simple task – the author remembers with horror the antics of a privately converted Herald on the race tracks, into which had been inserted no less than a 3.4-litre Jaguar engine! At the time – 1962 and 1963 – Triumph were simply not interested in making any more variations on the Herald/Vitesse/Spitfire theme. The busiest assembly track at Canley could be seen any day accommodating Herald saloons, coupés, convertibles and estate cars, Vitesse saloons and convertibles, and Spitfires. The Spitfire was not badged as a Spitfire 4 in anticipation of a six-cylinder version, but to eliminate confusion in America, where the Vitesse was sold as the Sports 6; the two names were simply made as different as possible.

With the Spitfire beginning to sell at a rate of

500 every week – a figure which would have been exceeded if more space could have been found down that production line – Triumph became Britain's biggest sports car producer in volume terms. There was time to look around at later developments of the Spitfire, and a widening of the range, too. A six-cylinder version of the car was being talked about in a gentle way, but Webster first gave Michelotti his head in the production of a fastback body style on the car. This was completed during the winter of 1963/64, originally using a normal Spitfire chassis and mechanical components. It soon became clear that the added weight would not make it a very attractive proposition on the Spitfire as it stood, and for a time it was used as 'executive transport' for senior engineers. The styling exercise, even if it had not been followed up, soon proved both its worth and its aerodynamic qualities when the Competitions Department decided they needed a full-length top for the 1964 Spitfire Le Mans cars. Glass-fibre hardtops were moulded direct from the Spitfire fastback, and were later adopted by the rallying team as well.

With so many Spitfires being sold there was little need to make engineering changes, but it was after only two and a half years that the Spitfire Mk 2 was released. Nearly 46,000 Mk 1 cars had been made, of which 9,104 stayed in Britain. The Mk 2 was little changed, especially in looks where the only recognition point was a slightly different front radiator grille. The engine was boosted to 67 bhp at 6,000 rpm, mainly thanks to a revised camshaft profile, and a fabricated four-branch exhaust manifold (not the same as used on the tuned rally or race cars, but introduced as a result of it). A diaphragm clutch was fitted for the first time, and wire wheels appeared as an optional fitting. The price crept up a little, to £666. Inside, all was luxury, for the new seats looked squashy and inviting and the floor was carpeted.

Once the Spitfire Mk 2 was rolling, and looked likely to sell equally as well as its predecessor, the Leyland-Triumph management could concentrate on more radical changes. In 1965 Britain's economy, though fragile, appeared to be reasonably healthy, and there was no way that anyone could have predicted the savage credit squeeze which was to hit the motor industry very hard in the middle of the following year. In the industry itself, the ever-active 'grapevine' had telegraphed the news that MG were planning to release a smart GT version of their MGB, and at the time they were thought to be doing enterprising things with the small sports cars based on the Mini-Cooper S engine. The Canley production lines could also be persuaded to accept yet another variation on the Herald family track, so the concept of a Spitfire 6 was revived. The ever-enterprising Syd Hurrell made up a Spitfire 6 of his own to show at the 1966 Racing Car Show, but as this car was expected to transmit about 100 bhp through a normal Spitfire axle (something the factory Competitions Department had found quite impossible) it was not thought to be a serious project. Triumph's Sales Department were asked about a six-cylinder car, and decided that for marketing reasons it would have to be as different as possible from the Spitfire 4. Accordingly, it was decided that there would never be a fastback version of the Spitfire, nor would there be an open version of the six-cylinder car.

Once again, development of the six-cylinder car was fairly swift, especially as it went ahead in parallel with the development of a revised Vitesse range. Triumph were, and still are, very attached to the practice of giving all their projects code-names, so it is very surprising that the six-cylinder car, or GT6 as it was soon to be named, never had one. As the original Spitfire had been 'Bomb', and the Vitesse had been 'Atom', it was suggested that the amalgam might appropriately be called 'Atom Bomb', but no-one thought it very funny at the time. If the Vitesse had not been due for enlargement from 1,596 to 1,998 cc, it is likely that the GT6 would have been given a 1600 engine, but since this smallest version of Standard-Triumph's six-cylinder engine looked doomed the GT6 automatically inherited the 2-litre, in almost the same form as used in the Triumph 2000. The Vitesse was also due for a stronger, all-synchromesh gearbox, also used in the GT6. Prototypes of the all-synchromesh gearbox were around as early as 1964, and were used in several race and rally Spitfires (including Le Mans 1965) before fitted to a production car. There is also a suspicion that they were fitted to competition cars when the rules said they should not have been, but it is always easy to fake a 'crash' bottom gear if a scrutineer is suspicious, and in any case it did nothing for the performance . . . . What it did do was to allow the peaky competitions engines free rein as bottom gear was so much easier to find in a hurry. The six-cylinder engine didn't rev anything like as freely as did the Spitfire, so a much higher axle ratio was needed. The Competitions Department had always been told that a 3.89 ratio was the highest possible within a Spitfire casing, and so it was, so a new case and stronger half-shafts were needed when the 3.27-to-1 GT6 ratio came along.

The GT6's fixtures and fittings, of even more importance now that the public had a standard of comparison in the MGB GT, had to be good, and for a start it was decided to re-design the facia. The main instruments were re-located in front of the driver's eyes, and new switches and dials installed in the centre. As with the Jaguar 'E' Type fixed-head car, there was no division between passenger seats and the luggage area. There was a large upward-opening rear window, through which luggage was also stowed, and the luggage floor was carpetted; the spare wheel and bigger fuel tank lived under this floor. Fortunately there was no attempt to provide even 'occasional' seats behind the front seats, though there were cubby holes where valuables could be hidden.

As far as the suspension was concerned, only minor changes had been made, and even before road test cars were given to them the motoring press were asking whether a simple swing-axle would be able to deal with the extra torque and horsepower of the 2-litre engine, especially as the new car's weight distribution was so very different. Added to the uncertainty of the comparison, Triumph had taken it upon themselves to 'soften' the car to make it more appealing to American tastes. Spring and damper settings were as supple as possible, and there was therefore more wheel deflection than normally expected on a Spitfire. British readers might ask whether there was justification in Triumph being so interested in satisfying their American customers perhaps at the expense of other markets. Triumph's answer to this would always be that that was where the majority of sales were made. Of all the sports cars made up to the announcement of the GT6, since Standard-Triumph had come into being at the end of 1945, 91 per cent had been exported, the vast majority of these going either to the United States or to Canada; British home sales alone could not support a sports car industry like this, and American tastes had to prevail.

This, however, did not prevail on the judgments of British road testers, who by now had broken free of the diplomatic bonds which made earlier tests so very difficult to understand. *Autocar* picked up its GT6 test car in the summer of 1967 and had this to say about its handling:

'The car is decidedly sensitive to all this power and the bonnet can be seen heaving up and down in proportion to the throttle opening. This characteristic naturally affects the rear swing-axles, which change track and wheel camber as the suspension goes up and down. . . . Lifting off in a corner caused the back of the car to rise as the weight transfers forwards and the rear wheels then take on positive camber with a narrow track between them. This reduced their cornering power considerably and the tail swings out immediately . . . . We feel it is a pity that the limitations from the continued use of swing-axles should detract so much from what is basically such a good car, and we urge Standard-Triumph to make improvements without delay.' This, of course, was shattering criticism, and summed up what most of the British press thought about the car. Although the GT6 was, indeed, a very good car, there was no doubt that something would have to be done about the rear suspension.

In the meantime the extremely popular Spitfire had come in for some attention. The Spitfire Mk 2 only lasted for a couple of years, but nearly 40,000 cars were built. The Spitfire Mk 3 was designed to be faster, more comfortable, better-braked, and better-equipped. As far as looks were concerned you recognised a Mk 3 because it had a 'bone in its teeth' – that, at least, was the nickname it soon gained. Triumph had lifted the bumper to meet a proposed American safety requirement that never materialised, and it now sat squarely across the mouth of the grille. Under the skin the engine was much improved, with the 1,296 cc engine first used in prototype form in the 1965 Alpine Rally, and a production version of the racing four-port head (so competitions *does*

The Spitfire in Mk IV form. Nose, tail and hardtop styling were all new for 1971

improve the breed, after all!). An output of 75 bhp was claimed for the bigger engine, and the car could just about reach 100 mph in favourable conditions. The folding hood was new (it replaced the 'build it yourself' variety fitted to earlier Spitfires), along with bigger brakes. The Mk 3 was the most popular of the Spitfires in Britain so far, but few British drivers can have much idea of the popularity of this car (and the GT6) because so very many of them are exported. The 100,000th car was built in the autumn of 1967, which meant that Forward Radiator's over-worked body-building factories had been turning out at least 400 sports car bodies every week for the past five years.

Whatever the British buyer might have thought of the first GT6, the export market looked healthy enough. About 8,000 GT6 coupés were built in the first year – probably as many as Triumph could make, as every one had to be squeezed into the already overcrowded Herald/Spitfire/Vitesse production line. But the criticism had hurt, and hurt badly. Improvements to the rear suspension had been mooted for some time (in fact this was almost a perennial project in Coventry) but the final solution to the problem had all the marks of a typical Webster solution. It killed the evils of the swing-axle camber change and jacking-up problem, provided very good wheel geometry indeed, yet retained just about everything which would have been costly to alter. The new rear suspension was released on the GT6 only (the Spitfire was still thought to be acceptable) in the autumn of 1968. In place of the swing-axles, there was a 'wishbone' system, where the transverse leaf spring located the top of the hub carrier, and a reversed cast lower wishbone located its bottom pivot. The half-shaft found itself with a large rubber 'doughnut' to accommodate plunge and twist, and the radius arms were moved in toward the middle of the car. At the same time the Mk 2 GT6 was given a more powerful engine (104 bhp with a TR5 cylinder head and a new camshaft profile identical to that of the latest Spitfire), the 'bone in teeth' front bumper from the Spitfire, air extractors in the rear quarters to help the ventilation, and a new facia including a matt wood finish and TR5-type rocker switches. All in all, the GT6 Mk 2 was a much-improved car, which fully justified its price increase in Britain from £1,024 to £1,125. Press reports were very friendly to the new car – *Car* magazine suggested that the GT6 had a 'sanitary' rear suspension at last!

Triumph then settled down to churning out as many of the Spitfire Mk 3s and GT6 Mk 2s as they could – the rate now being up to more than 23,000 cars every year – while the engineers and sales staff decided what they should do next. Work had been going on in Engineering for some time towards a successor for the cars. Indeed, one project dear to Harry Webster's heart was a new design – coded 'Lynx' – which was to be a front-wheel-drive car, though this was soon killed off when it was decided that the Triumph 1300/1500 would be the only front-wheel-drive car ever to be built by Triumph. Someone, somewhere, had got their sums wrong at the costing stage; although the Triumph 1300 when first designed looked remarkably cheap to build, later experience showed this to be unfounded. It was significant just how much more expensive the Triumph 1500 became when it replaced the 1300 in 1970. Michelotti was therefore given the job of restyling the Spitfire and GT6, though not completely. Triumph's rear-end theme for the early 1970s was going to be based on the Stag style – with a cut-off tail and horizontal tail-lights. Getting that on to a new version of the GT6 and Spitfire was easy enough, but it led to wholesale panel changes as far forward as the doors. Michelotti, however, still liked the look of his original cars, and didn't want to alter too much. Superficially there might not appear to be much change, though just about every skin panel is different. At the front of the car, Michelotti and the Triumph styling studio slaved away for months on a variety of schemes, with an Opel GT or Lotus Elan smooth-bonnet style with pop-up headlamps the favourite. However, the same worries over North American legislation that were to affect Stag killed off the hidden headlamps, and Michelotti contented himself with a smoother version of the original where the raised seams on top of the wings were removed, and panel joints made along the sides of the wings instead. Inside the car was a revised facia yet again, and for the first time the Spitfire inherited speedometer and rev counter dials in front of the driver.

Of more importance on the Spitfire was a revised type of rear suspension – though not the 'bottom-wishbone' scheme used on the GT6. The Spitfire received a variation on the simple swing-axle layout where the transverse leaf spring was allowed to pivot on the top of the axle casing; this, of course, gave much reduced roll stiffness compared with single bump stiffness, and kept camber changes to a minimum. It was a great improvement over the old layout; unconfirmed stories in Coventry suggest that Engineering Director Spencer King once turned one over when exploring the absolute limits of adhesion. Of equal importance to the Spitfire was its all-synchromesh gearbox, like that of the GT6 but with wider internal ratios, and the standardisation of wider ($4\frac{1}{2}$-in) wheel rims.

It is an interesting comment both on cost-inflation in Britain, and on the improvements made to the cars' specifications over the years, to compare prices of the new cars with those of their first derivatives. The GT6 had first been released in 1966 at a price of £800 basic (the same as that of the TR4A), while the 1970/71 Mk 3 car weighed in at £970. The Spitfire had started in 1962 at £530, reached £550 when the GT6 was released, and had risen to £735 for the Mk 4 car. Fortunately for Triumph, and in the face of those who suggested that the restyle was not obvious enough to be worth doing, sales continued to increase. In 1971 over 25,000 of the Spitfires and GT6s were delivered, and there was a happy occasion at the end of the year when the 200,000th car was built.

No-one would ever question the success of the Spitfire, with over 200,000 built, and probably more cars being made in 1973 than ever before, but how should the historian judge the GT6? In isolation sales of around 5,000 cars a year would not be enough to justify the car's existence in the volume-conscious 1970s. Triumph with the GT6, however, have been much cleverer than were MG with the MGC, for the vast majority of the mechanical items are shared with other models, assembly is by 'Meccano methods' and only the coupé body shell is unique. If the GT6 had a drawback once the rear suspension had been changed, it was that it was physically a very small car. The impression of 'mini 'E' Type' which it always gives is also true of the interior passenger space. The GT6 is purely a two-seater with a lot of room for luggage, and once one becomes accustomed to this its purpose falls into perspective.

On the North American market the GT6 and the Spitfire have become completely different animals from the versions we know in Britain. The GT6 Plus, for instance, was never a car known in Britain, being the 'federal' version of the GT6 Mk 2, where the progressively stiffer emission limitation laws began to take their toll. Whereas the GT6 in Britain boasts 95 bhp (DIN) at 5,250 rpm (recalibrated from the 104 bhp of the 1969 models, though without actual engine change) the 'federal' car can only muster 79 bhp if it is to keep its exhausts clean. As far as the Spitfire is concerned the performance situation eventually became so critical that the 'federal' version had to be given a 1,493 cc engine for

1973. Even the 75 bhp developed by British and European Spitfires has degraded over the years due to tighter noise regulations and rationalisation with export derivatives. By 1973 the latest Spitfire was down to a mere 61 bhp (DIN) and was virtually no quicker than it had been way back in 1962. It may be a much more civilised car, but doesn't compare for excitement with an early Mk 3 Spitfire. Building yourself the best performing Spitfire now would mean buying a Mk 4 to get the new body style, the latest rear suspension and the all-synchromesh gearbox, then re-building the engine to 1968 specification. In America, the 1972 model represented an all-time low in performance, for emission limitations pushed power down to 48 bhp (DIN) and there was only a single-carburettor engine to show off when you opened the bonnet to demonstrate to your friends. Truly the Americans have had to lose a lot to gain ecological advantage in the 1970s.

1973 saw the product planners and the cost accountants gain precedence over the engineers at Triumph, for the GT6 and the Spitfire were further commonised. The Spitfire gained by having a wider rear track to bring it into line with the GT6, but the GT6 lost a lot when its 'lower wishbone' rear suspension was thrown away (after four years only) to be replaced by the Spitfire's cheaper and simpler pivoting transverse-spring layout. What will the future hold for these cars? Certainly they are now completely isolated at Triumph. Several years ago they were largely similar to Heralds and Vitesses, both of which have since been discontinued. They have a separate chassis frame, a unique design in itself, and only one other Triumph uses such a structure. Can British Leyland continue to tolerate a situation where similar cars are made in Coventry and at Abingdon? What will they find as cost-benefits from merging designs or even throwing one design away? By 1960s standards 25,000 cars a year was well worth encouraging, but will that figure make any profits in future? Are we, in fact, approaching the end of the second age of 'sporting midgets'? I certainly hope not.

When race-tuned for Le Mans a Spitfire engine looked like this. Later engines used alternators instead of dynamos and bigger Weber carburettors

CHAPTER 11

Back to competitions

STANDARD-TRIUMPH'S takeover by the Leyland company was followed by cut-backs in various areas, though far fewer in the engineering departments than many had anticipated. Leyland at that time, as to a modified degree since, did not agree that expense in a competitions programme was worthwhile – not, at least, unless the team was sweeping all before it at minimum cost. By the time that the Richardson era had ended in the middle of 1961 the rallying efforts had already tailed off, and the Le Mans programme was brought to a successful if uninspired conclusion when the three TRS cars won the team prize in the 24-hour race. In line with other economy measures taken at the time, the original Competitions Department was closed down swiftly.

One department that was most unhappy to see the closure was the sales division, which had always seen benefits for Triumph's sports car image from successful participation. By the end of 1961, with the Triumph Herald 1200 safely launched, the TR4 beginning to get into quantity production, and the British economy picking up, Standard-Triumph began to look profitable again. Consequently, the pressures to re-open a Competitions Department began to mount, particularly from Lyndon Mills' sales staff, and from Harry Webster, who had always had a soft spot for competition cars that would confirm or deny his many engineering developments.

The problem, at first, lay in Leyland's and Ken Richardson's thoroughness. When Richardson was shown the door in the summer of 1961 he had decided to take all his records with him. In fact much of the works preparation of rallying TR3As and Heralds had never been written down, being ingrained in the memories of Richardson's mechanics. Therefore, when thoughts of re-opening a department began to circulate, it became clear that a new manager would have to start from scratch. Similarly, Richardson's mechanics had been dispersed, and since one doesn't breed building and servicing expertise overnight it was apparent that the new department would have an uphill struggle.

During the autumn of 1961 Harry Webster began to formulate his plans for the new department. In view of the geographical and personality problems which latterly had existed with the original department, Webster was determined to keep a new operation tightly under his control, and more subservient to Engineering; in any case the proposed budget was going to be small, so there would be little opportunity for a new manager to get delusions of grandeur. The recently closed department had operated out of a gloomy workshop at the Radford factories, a couple of miles from the Fletchamstead engineering centre. Fortunately for Webster, a bright and airy department around the back of the experimental workshops was shortly to become vacant. At the time it housed a small department working on a new Standard tractor design which Dick had wanted to make in competition to the Ferguson once he had sold out his interests to Massey Harris. Leyland had decided, probably with some reason, that the tractor project should be cancelled, thus clearing the area for new activities.

Webster's next problem was to find an administrator (rather than a full-blooded Competi-

They do roll sometimes! In spite of the tough rally suspension the team cars reacted normally on corners. This was in Greystoke Forest during the 1962 RAC Rally (Picture: Autocar)

tion Manager) and it was here that the author was pitchforked into a new job. At the time I was working in the Standard-Triumph experimental department, but indulging (in my spare time and holidays) in club, national and international rallying. In fact, although it might sound strange, I was employed by Standard-Triumph during the week, but engaged to co-drive in works-entered Sunbeam Rapiers on international rallies! It was a very cosy arrangement that Harry Webster condoned and tolerated as long as there was no conflict of interests at Standard-Triumph, and in any case there was no question of extra leave being taken. My driver was Peter Procter, then one of the three musketeers (Harper, Hopkirk, Procter) in the Rootes factory team.

Harry Webster decided that the best way to harness my hobbies was to make me work on them, and accordingly one day I was summoned to his office and told to start planning for a new Competitions Department! First I had to make a survey of the company's products – and the opposition – so that the best cars could be chosen, and look around for the most suitable tiny team of mechanics. The first year's budget was to be a completely derisory £12,000 – not enough even to build a set of works rally cars for their first event these days – and the department would be under John Lloyd's overall control. We could call on engineering services for the construction and modification of mechanical components, and have body-builders on loan whenever they were needed. I was to have the title of Competition Secretary, but with no assistants and no secretary!

Before putting on my new hat I took part in my final event with the Rootes factory team, when Peter Procter narrowly missed an outright win in the 1962 Monte Carlo by sliding off the road on the Col du Cucheron special stage and puncturing a tyre (he went on to finish fourth overall). It was here, incidentally, that I realised the power of persuasive public relations men; Procter's accident on the Monte was described as being 'due to a puncture' when in fact it had been an accident first, followed by the puncture! Either way, going off the road certainly robbed him of an outright Monte win – which would have been a spectacular achievement in the good old Sunbeam Rapier. From time to time I tried to lure Procter into the Triumph team, but by the time we had competitive cars for him to drive he had been drawn into the Ford net, subsequently winning the 1964 Tour de France in a Mustang.

The new Triumph Competitions Department was made known to the press at a most unprepossessing occasion when they were invited to a London reception to have a look at two new Standard vans! In the meantime I had been looking for drivers, but in view of the tiny budget to which we were restricted there was no question of handing out fees or buying men from other teams. For the whole of that first year the three drivers were to be John Sprinzel, Mike Sutcliffe and a young Swiss called Jean-Jacques Thuner, who had already won the Geneva International Rally in a TR3A and who had been surprisingly fast on the recent Monte Carlo Rally in his own TR4. A look around the company's cars had shown that the Heralds would not be competitive with their existing engine, and that the TR4s in suitable lightened form seemed to be the best bet. Professionalism had arrived in rallying in a big way since Richardson's TR3As had last appeared, and it was clear that such cars as the latest 2-litre four-overhead-camshaft Porsches were going to be very serious competition. The rallies, too, had changed. Whereas Richardson's cars were fast and rugged enough to deal with such gruelling events as the Alpine Rally, the RAC Rally when it had been run on tarmac, and the Liège-Rome-Liège when it had not ventured into darkest Jugoslavia, the TR4s would have to cope with much rougher events like the revamped RAC Rally and a 'Liège' which now went to Sofia and back.

1962 was a year of moderate success for the works cars. Ray Henderson, who had learned so much in building the twin-cam Le Mans cars in the Engineering Department, had only four mechanics to maintain the cars, and a preparation programme that started with suggestions from anyone with TR experience, but soon evolved into the production of some very rugged cars indeed. The team's first event was the Tulip Rally, where the cars were very narrowly beaten by a much-modified MGA from Abingdon, mainly because the engines were still virtually standard.

Almost as soon as the new department had been opened, it became clear that the old department had never consulted experimental engineers over tuning details and consequently, the engine men had to start from scratch while the department looked around for items which could swiftly be homologated. Only weeks after the Tulip Rally, however, four-branch exhaust systems had been homologated and high-lift camshafts installed and these, along with the decision to run 2.2-litre cars on the Alpine Rally, produced much quicker machines. The Alpine, indeed, was much like old times, and though the entry was none too large it lacked nothing in quality. Sprinzel's car was shunted out of the event by a non-competing car, but Sutcliffe and Thuner retained their clean sheets right up to the final stages. Mike Sutcliffe came through the final serpentine *Quatre Chemins* sections without losing time to win his class, take a still rare *Coupe des Alpes* and finish fourth overall, but poor Thuner spun at an impossible place on the same section, had to reverse to find a turning place, and lost his own *Coupe* by a miserable 90 seconds.

Every time the TR4s appeared on an international event they were faster and lighter (aluminium skin panels were supplied, at great inconvenience, from the presses at Standard-Triumph's Liverpool plant), but this didn't help on the Liège. As in 1961 it was a rough, rock-strewn obstacle course which was a graveyard for sports cars. Sprinzel's and Sutcliffe's cars battered themselves to destruction in the Jugoslavian hinterland, though Thuner's car struggled through in a dreadful state to finish ninth of 18 finishers. The only other low-slung sports cars to make it to the finish were a couple of Austin-Healey 3000s from Abingdon.

Thuner then took his car on the Geneva Rally, where one of the fashionable class handicap systems robbed him of any high placing, even though he was consistently second fastest overall on all the stages behind Hans Walter's four-cam Porsche Carrera, which won the event. In earlier years Thuner's performance would have been acclaimed, but in 1962 with its stupid handicaps it went almost unnoticed.

The TR4s finished their year on the RAC International Rally, which was as rough, tough and glutinous as usual. Thuner's TR4 finished ninth, with the usual brace of Austin-Healey 3000s just ahead of him, and because of the way the class divisions were made his 2.2-litre car had to give best to the big Healeys in an over-1600 cc class as well. But some consolation for a run of such administrative *malchance* came when the team won the GT team prize.

Much more significant on this event, however, was the fact that the Triumph team was joined for the first time by a determined young man called Vic Elford. He had already made his name as a co-driver with David Seigle-Morris in TRs and Austin-Healeys, then as a saloon car racing driver with his own Mini, but unfortunately had earned something of a reputation both as a crasher of cars, and as a 'loner' who could not fit into a team. To their eternal credit, Triumph chose to ignore both these supposed failings and gave Elford his chance in a modified version of the Triumph Vitesse, which had only recently been announced. It is only fair to Vic, who always appreciated the start given him by Triumphs, to record that he quickly gained a reputation for being the most dedicated driver the team ever saw and that he proved to be a very good 'team man' as well. He worked his Vitesse up into sixth place overall on the RAC Rally at one stage – ahead of all the TR4s – until gearbox failure let him down towards half-distance.

For the 1963 season, when the budget was no more realistic than it had been before, a set of the new Vitesse saloons were prepared for rallying. John Sprinzel left the team after the Monte when it became clear that his talents didn't suit these cars, and Vic Elford became the un-stated number-one driver. 1963 was not a year that the Competitions Department would like to remember, mainly because there wasn't a single major success to report, and because of the depressing series of crashes and breakdowns that occurred. But one thing which became abundantly clear was that Vic Elford was an extremely capable driver, and that unless lots of money could be waved under his nose it was unlikely that his services could be retained for more than one year.

The TR4s reached their final tune, with twin-choke Weber carburettors helping output up to over 130 bhp, and cars lightened as much as driver sanity would allow. Limited-slip differentials were also adopted – an advantage proved in the Tulip Rally when all three cars went off into the same ditch on a stage; the single car which didn't have a limited-slip mechanism had to be pushed out while the other two motored out! Handicap systems still afflicted European events, so Elford's fine performance right behind the Morley twins on the Tulip Rally went unrecognised, while Thuner's second-fastest aggregate performance on the Geneva Rally was also submerged. The Liège was more of a disaster than in 1962 as all the works cars were forced out, and not a single car finished the Alpine Rally. Indeed, on the Alpine Mike Sutcliffe crashed badly on the lower slopes of Mont Ventoux, an accident in which co-driver Roy Fidler broke a leg. Elford had been chasing the Austin-Healeys for a couple of days and had worked his car up to third overall before he overdid it and shot off the road. The RAC Rally was also a disappointment for Fidler's car looped the loop in Wythop Wood, near Keswick (this being Sutcliffe's painstakingly rebuilt Alpine car!) and Elford's car blew a gasket, a very rare occurence indeed on the Vanguard-based engine.

As had been anticipated, Vic Elford could not be enticed to stay with the team for 1964, in spite of the new cars then being developed, and after trying both Rovers and Fords he eventually joined Ford at Boreham. It is worth recalling that Elford was not above 'going to the top' in the search for perfection. During 1963 it became clear that a much-modified Vitesse, with 2-litre engine, TR4 gearbox and stronger rear axle might succeed on the Liège, yet no amount of

Works TR4s were light, fast and strong, but the rough forest rallies hit them pretty hard — Roy Fidler's car in the 1963 RAC Rally
(Picture: Autocar)

persuasion could convince the Triumph management that this should be done. Nothing daunted, Elford then contacted Sir Donald Stokes to talk him into the idea and as a result a car was built in double-quick time; the sad end to this tale is that the car was very well placed (fourth overall) during the third night when a carburettor fire burnt it out.

The sad story of 1963 proved to the Competitions Department that several changes would have to be made if more success was to be achieved in 1964. Cars more suited to rough roads and to the class handicap system that was still rife in Europe were required. It would also be necessary to look carefully at classes where 'homologation specials' from other companies could be avoided, and ideally Triumph needed a comprehensive homologation programme themselves so that the cars could be made as quick as possible. With a budget as small as had been imposed in the previous two years, this looked unlikely, but the turning point undoubtedly came when Harry Webster's desire to send cars back to Le Mans became too strong to be resisted.

During the summer and autumn of 1963, when the TR4s were being hurled against terrible roads in Jugoslavia, several important decisions were made, one being that Triumph would return to Le Mans in 1964, and another being that a much larger competitions budget would be made available, which would allow more effort to be put into engine development.

As far as new cars were concerned, it seemed obvious that fully-developed Spitfires would provide the answer for fast tarmac rallies and where the handicap system was still used, and that the soon-to-be-announced Triumph 2000 might form a very good basis for a rough-road rally car to match the Rovers and Fords which seemed to thrive on such events. All this, of course, would have to wait until the development programmes had been completed, and in the meantime it was decided to do one more event with the TR4s. Incidentally, throughout two full seasons there were only four team cars – carrying the numbers 3VC, 4VC, 5VC, and 6VC – though each had a new chassis frame and many new components before every event. The bodies soldiered on through two very busy and rugged seasons and the same engines were rebuilt time and time again. Only once– in Sutcliffe's 1963 Alpine Rally crash – did a car have to be written-off, and this one (4VC) was resuscitated using as much of the badly shattered body as possible.

The 1963 Monte Carlo Rally; even with studded tyres you slide a lot on ice. The wing vents were to get heat out of the engine bay

The cars' final fling was to be in Canada, in the Shell 4000 Rally which, had Triumph known it, was to be just about as unsuitable to sports car motoring as any other which the cars had entered in the previous two years. Like so many such operations the Shell 4000 entry was bedevilled by company politics, and an international team of drivers were chosen (including Jean-Jacques Thuner and Roy Fidler) of whom none was a Canadian rallying specialist. The cars were prepared in Coventry, then shipped via the USA competitions base in Los Angeles before being sent up to Vancouver for the start. The Shell 4000 that year went all the way across Canada from Vancouver to Montreal, using all sorts of horribly unmade prairie tracks on the way. The Triumph 2000s would have been much more suitable for the conditions, particularly if specialist Curta-weilding navigators had been installed in each car, but North American publicity had its way – the TR4s were selling well in the area and needed a boost – and a rag bag of drivers were chosen (including an American press man who had never done a rally, and probably didn't do another one after that!). This stated, the TR4s did remarkably well in an event where lots of ground clearance and navigators with computer-minds were required. All three finished, winning a team prize, and showing that the TR4 was an extremely strong car indeed. Back at home the happiest man of the moment was company test driver Gordon Birtwistle, who had spotted that the fourth car was not going to Canada and had stepped in with an offer to buy which was quickly accepted.

1964 was to be a big year for factory competitions activities. Not only were new sets of rally cars – Spitfires and Triumph 2000s – to be prepared, but a completely separate set of Le Mans Spitfires were also to be built. With an ambitious engine development programme to be completed in only six months, and the need to make everything as light and reliable as possible, it seemed reasonable to separate the Le Mans programme completely from the rest of the competitions activity. It was therefore decided to build and prepare the Le Mans cars in the experimental workshops, still under the control of Chief Mechanic Ray Henderson, but with a new set of mechanics whose sole job was to build racing cars. It was a system that worked well, and no inter-section rivalry developed.

If ever there was an authenticated case of a silk purse being developed from a sow's ear, it was probably in the complete transformation of the Spitfire from a cheeky though mild little sports car into a formidable racing or rallying machine. Without the decision to go to Le Mans in 1964 it is doubtful if the Spitfires would ever have been competitive, but of such sentiments are little prodigies made! With the Le Mans project in mind, a very powerful engine would be needed and work began during 1963. Nicknamed the '70X project' (the Spitfire's engine being, conveniently, 70 cubic inches), the original Standard Eight-based unit was reworked from top to bottom. Interwoven in all these decisions was the fact that at the time Appendix 'J' Group 3 GT cars were required to be built at a rate of not less than 100 units a year, or have their special items – camshafts, cylinder heads, gearboxes and so on – sold at the rate of 100 sets in the same period. It was absolutely vital to the legality of the works rally cars that duplicate equipment should be made available to private owners, and since no sort of selling arrangement such as the Ford and BMC tuning departments used existed at Coventry, it was decided to sign a marketing agreement with Sid Hurrell's SAH Accessories firm to do the distribution job. This mainly took the form of a Stage II engine conversion for the Spitfire. Unfortunately this gave rise to the impression that the SAH concern not only designed the race and rally engines but were also the official 'factory tune-up' specialists. Though this was demonstrably untrue – all the 70X engine work was done by Standard-Triumph engineers – there is little doubt that Hurrell's company was one of the few to understand this engine thoroughly, and backed up Stage II kits with a variety of suspension and lightweight body items of their own. Only the minimum number of sets of Stage II engine parts were made to satisfy homologation requirements, and a goodly proportion of these were used on factory-owned cars.

The Le Mans cars in the paddock in 1964. Very little air intake area was needed for Le Mans' high speeds

A service point on the 1964 Tour de France. Jean-Jacques Thuner aiding brake-bleeding work, John Gretener and the author looking on, and Robbie Slotemaker (far left) waiting his turn. The mechanic is Mick Moore

It may be argued (and was so, often, within the factory) that engines such as the Triumph Stage II design had no place even in pseudo-production cars, especially as the publicity spin-off would, at best, be marginal. But in the face of similar exploits from BMC, Ford and Alpine-Renault there was little choice if the cars were to be successful. The Austin-Healey 3000s, for instance, used triple twin-choke Weber carburettors that were in themselves legal, but that they were used with aluminium cylinder heads that could almost be equated in value to their weight in gold was of more doubtful legality. BMC always claimed that the aluminium head was only used to cut down the weight over the front wheels – which was nonsensical in such a big car – whereas the real reason was that much higher compression ratios and more extreme valve timing could be entertained in the search for yet more horsepower. In the case of the Triumph Spitfires similarly borderline methods were used, but apart from their limited use in competitions much of the knowledge gained in the 1964-1966 period was eventually put to good use in later versions of the Spitfire or the GT6.

Work on the engines started from the premise that the Le Mans cars would have to be capable of 130 mph at least (which was asking a lot when one remembers that the Spitfire's body shape was only to be altered in detail); even with the more smoothly contoured body then being considered it looked as if the little 1,147 cc engine would have to produce at least 100 bhp! Since this was 37 bhp, or nearly 60 per cent, in excess of the advertised horsepower of the Spitfire's production engine, which was itself a tuned version of the Herald unit, it was clear that a lot of work would be needed.

The engine had started life a decade earlier, displacing a mere 803 cc and producing only 26 bhp in the chunky little Standard Eight saloon, and Standard-Triumph was suffering from a dearth of knowledge about the engine in super-tuned form. Through no technical failing of its own the Herald engine had never been seriously developed for the Formula Junior and Formula Three racing classes which had proved to be technically so beneficial to BMC and Ford. The 1,147 cc engine's capabilities and limits, therefore, were largely unknown, and in spite of rumblings from the Competitions Department on the subject, Harry Webster was not prepared to authorise sending the engine for race-tuning by an outside firm. Early studies, carried out among other people by Olympic swimmer Graham Sykes, showed that the existing SU carburettors would have to go, that the existing cylinder head would have to be persuaded to breathe much more deeply, and that the rev range would have to be extended.

The full story of how the engine became a Le Mans contender was the subject of an absorbing article by Ray Bates (later to become Harry Webster's deputy at Longbridge) in *Autocar* on February 5th 1965, before the later 1965 improvements were made known. The biggest single change was to the engine's breathing arrangements. The existing cylinder head was known within Standard-Triumph as the 'six-port' head – that is to say it had four separate exhaust ports but only a pair of siamezed inlet ports. No amount of gas-flow experimenting could persuade the six-port head to produce the required power, so a completely new 'eight-port' head was commissioned, to fit on to the existing cylinder block. This was to be fed by a pair of large twin-choke Weber carburettors, and had a free-flow exhaust system. The camshaft timing promised to be wild indeed, and was expected to produce peak horsepower at around 7,000 rpm. Right from the outset it was decided to try cylinder heads in both cast iron and aluminium, though in the end it was the cast iron head which was chosen both for the Stage II 'customer engines' and for the Le Mans race cars. The aluminium head, which produced several more bhp than any other version, showed up minor problems connected with valve-gear life on the test bed, and was never used at Le Mans. The most powerful engines, therefore, found their way into the rally cars, where their reliability record was good!

For a time the Achilles' heel of the engine was centred in the improbably narrow main and big-end bearings, which at first broke down under the extremely high loads imposed, but a diligent series of modifications in association with Vandervell produced new bearings and re-profiled crankshaft machining details. Considerable piston development was required, but by the time the first Le Mans engines were delivered to the department the power was up to 98 bhp at 6,800 rpm. The compression ratio was an astonishing 11.75-to-1, but even so the fuel consumption was prodigious at racing speeds. Engines for the works rally team were delivered shortly afterwards, and because they had opted for the aluminium cylinder head were producing about 5 bhp more than the Le Mans units. The first 1,147 cc engines thus prepared had virtually no low-speed torque at all, and were never happy when being driven at anything less than 3,000 rpm. Factory torque curves never started below this figure, and it is doubtful if the engine would have run smoothly if pressed! The rally cars were

Even with a limited-slip differential, wheel spin round tight corners was usual. Slotemaker at Clermont-Ferrand in the 1964 Tour de France

a real pig to drive in traffic, particularly with the later close-ratio gearbox and high overall gearing for high-speed events, and there is little doubt that a really experienced independent engine-tuning specialist could have improved the shape of the curve. Certainly, by present standards, the inlet ports of the eight-port cylinder head look too large, but at the time it was only in this fashion that maximum power (thought to be all-important at Le Mans) could be obtained in such a brief development period. At first the camshaft timing included 104 degrees of overlap and 42DCOE Weber carburettors were used. A year later the overlap had gone up to 120 degrees and the carburettors to 45DCOEs, raising the maximum power to 109 bhp at 7,300 rpm for Le Mans. Apart from the use of aluminium cylinder heads and a slightly milder camshaft the rally cars used identical engines, apart from on one occasion. For the Alpine Rally in 1965 prototype 1,296 cc units were preferred, when power output went up to 117 bhp at 7,000 rpm with much improved torque and consequently drivability.

Production-type Stage II engines used a milder camshaft than either of the works engines, along with smaller Weber carburettors and a 10.6-to-1 compression ratio, but they still produced really sparkling performance. The kit of parts retailed at £193, and even carried a factory guarantee, though this was wisely withdrawn from the rest of the power train and transmission. *Autocar* tested an otherwise normal Spitfire with the Stage II engine and gearbox, finding a maximum speed of 104 mph, and acceleration to 60 mph in 11.2 seconds. It was a very cheerful little car in this guise as the road test comments made clear:

'Everyone on our staff who drove the test car came back looking years younger and full of enthusiasm for it. We would readily add it to our stable, if funds permitted, as a means of relieving depression; someone even suggested it should be available on the National Health.'

To go with all this power, the rally cars were equipped with the close-ratio Vitesse gearbox, though with long-term reliability in mind the Le Mans cars had the much heavier TR4 gearbox instead. Getting the suspension right was not too difficult, especially as there were to be no concessions to riding comfort. Lowered rear swing-axle spring settings, stiffer front springs and revised damper settings were soon finalised for the Le Mans cars, but for the rally cars the problem was more serious. Even though the cars were not intended for rough-road use, the Alps and Dolomites can produce surface and profile changes that require as much wheel movement as possible. To allow for over-exuberant drivers who like using the grass verge from time to time it was also thought desirable to keep the noses well up in the air. A large 18-gallon fuel tank, when fitted, was placed over the rear suspension and could give rise to a 140 lb difference in laden weight. In these conditions the car's basic final-oversteering behaviour was hard to tame, but after much hilarious testing (including one occasion when the author put a Spitfire backwards through a MIRA fence when trying an unsuccessful scheme!) the traditional methods of lowered transverse leaf spring and carefully-tuned dampers did the trick. Another aid to instant oversteer had been the spinning inside rear wheel on hard corners, but a Salisbury limited-slip differential soon put paid to that.

The Le Mans cars had bodies constructed entirely of aluminium apart from the coupé top which was in glass-fibre. In the days when craftsmen were cheap and time plentiful these might have been hand-beaten, but for 1964 every pressed panel was supplied in aluminium from the tools at the Forward Radiator company; the difficulties in programming perhaps a dozen panels through any particular tool (which may not be in commission all the time) can be imagined. Getting all the panels together took several weeks, and because there was no question of re-setting the tools to take account of the less ductile aluminium sheet quite a lot of panels had to be rejected due to tears and splits. Assembling them was also something of a major exercise, so it must have been heartbreaking for the bodymakers to be told that two cars had been destroyed in their first race. The rally cars, by dint of more severe regulations, were more nearly standard, only the skin panels being aluminium, welded or bolted on to a normal steel shell. The rally cars used normal production hardtops for their first event.

Future historians no doubt will be happy to know the way in which the Le Mans Spitfire's body shape was evolved, allied to its relationship to the GT6 production coupé, which didn't appear until a couple of years later. When the Le Mans cars were being built, even though they were to be entered as prototypes, the Triumph publicists were most anxious that they should look as near to a standard car as possible, though it was clear that a completely unaltered shape would look out-of-place and be aerodynamically undesirable. In addition, Le Mans at that time laid down a certain minimum vertical windscreen depth, which could only be satisfied on this car by keeping to the standard shape and size. With such a deep screen, and the near-standard shape requirement, it appeared that the only two areas which could be altered were the hardtop shape (an extra, in any case, on the production cars) and the nose of the car.

When the cars first appeared at Le Mans for the test session in April 1964 they retained a standard bonnet profile, but sported a very attractive fast-back coupé top grafted on to the standard windscreen, doors and rear quarters. In spite of any impressions which were given at the time, this shape had not been anywhere near a wind-tunnel, but had – conveniently – been taken from a Spitfire prototype car that Michelotti's Turin studios had completed the previous winter. The Le Mans tops were of glass-fibre, and made by the simple process of using the prototype car as a mould! The fact that the shape was aerodynamically good for the sort of speeds the Le Mans engine could confer was pure chance, and to this day no-one at Triumph knows what the drag figure actually was. Indeed, that of the standard car was also unknown.

The six-cylinder GT6 sports coupé, when announced in October 1966, was assumed to have been based on the successful Le Mans cars, while in fact the reverse had been the case. Naturally, the production car had a large opening rear window/loading door and opening rear quarter windows, while the Le Mans cars used flush-fitting perspex, and a 'posting slot' below the fixed window through which the spare wheel could be inserted or removed.

That the coupé shape was a success became abundantly clear at the test days, when the cars were timed at 130 mph on the Mulsanne straight, and lapped at around 4 minutes 55 seconds (102 mph) – a lap speed almost identical to the out-

On the grid for the hour-long race at Rouen in the 1964 Tour de France. Slotemaker's re-bodied rally car is alongside Cheinisse's Alpine-Renault, and Andrew Hedges' works MGB. Thuner's Spitfire and Bianchi's Alpine are in the second row

right record set by Louis Rosier's winning $4\frac{1}{2}$-litre Talbot only 14 years previously! Between test day and race day the bonnet was reshaped to give a very Jaguar-like profile. This item similarly was not the result of deep aerodynamic study, but merely a case of fairing forward the existing bonnet line to enclose more powerful headlamps retained in the standard position. Race lap speeds were not published in 1964 for any of the Spitfires (though Triumph pit staff recorded 4 minutes 53 seconds on occasion) but a maximum speed as high as 136.7 mph was published for Jean-Francois Piot's car. There had been minor engine power increases since April, and of course one cannot say that the cars were being driven flat-out on both occasions. However, as far as Triumph were concerned, their own technical advances had been truly remarkable. The twin-cam TRS, when last used in 1961 with a 160 bhp 2-litre engine, had lapped at 4 minutes 47 seconds, probably with a little more frontal area, but with at least 50 per cent more horsepower; light weight and aerodynamic efficiency had almost made up for a very significant power deficiency.

In the 1964 race three cars started but only one finished. Of the other two, Mike Rothschild's crashed at the Dunlop Bridge on the curve just after the pits, which was flat-out for a Spitfire, so the accident could either have been due to driver error or (more likely) to having been blown off line by a bigger car, while Jean-Louis Marnat's car also crashed near the pits when the driver became asphyxiated due to the entry of exhaust gases following the rupture of a body panel in an earlier brush. David Hobbs and Robbie Slotemaker finished well in their car, covering no less than 2,273 miles and averaging 94.7 mph; the best TRS had averaged 98.9 mph three years previously. What gave Triumph particular satisfaction, however, was to beat a special-bodied works Austin-Healey Sprite by 5 mph and 125 miles. As Le Mans clashed with the Alpine Rally, the 24-hours race became a John Lloyd exercise, with Harry Webster and Lyndon Mills showing their keenness by being co-opted as pit staff.

In spite of the fact that two expensive race cars had been reduced to scrap – very expensive scrap because of the all-aluminium body shells – the results certainly vindicated all the work put in by Ray Bates and the rest of the engine design team. On reflection after the race it seemed that the use of the heavy TR4 gearbox would no longer be necessary, especially as all-synchromesh prototype GT6 gearboxes could now be made available.

For 1965 the old registration numbers were resuscitated and two new cars built to replace the write-offs. Thinner-gauge chassis frames, the GT6 gearboxes, and attention to detail pared no less than 100 lb off the weight, and a further year's engine work pushed the power up to 109 bhp. Some of these modifications had been incorporated into a car taken to Paris for the 1000 kilometres sports car race, which won its class. Three cars were sent over to Sebring in March 1965 for the nine-hours race, two of them finishing second and third in class.

Le Mans that year was very much a repeat performance of 1964. All four race cars started, one originally having been a reserve, and two finished. It was the reserve car, driven by Simo Lampinen and Jean-Jacques Thuner, which won its class at 95 mph, finishing 13th, with the Piot-Dubois car 14th. Of the other two, Slotemaker crashed his car at White House after dipping his lights at the wrong time to aid an overtaking car, and the Bolton-Bradley car split its oil cooler. Once again the Spitfires had the satisfaction of blowing off all the competing Alpine-Renaults. However, as far as the rest of the race traffic was concerned the Spitfires were a problem, for with their 130 mph maximum speed (though very creditable for such a small car) they were no less than 70 mph slower in a straight line than the big Fords and Ferraris which were scrapping for the lead. Another incidental difference between the 1964 and 1965 entries was that the later cars ran in the GT rather than the prototype category. Lap speeds in practice in April had shown that the 1965 cars were significantly faster than before, with the best lap times recorded at 4 minutes 49 seconds.

Following a post-Le Mans strip-down, to inspect the engine and transmission components in search of lessons for future production sports cars, a study of the trends at Le Mans suggested that the Spitfires might not even be allowed to take part in 1966 unless they could be made much faster. Certainly they would have to be fitted with larger engines, and since the Triumph 1300 unit (1,296 cc) was not projected for the Spitfire just yet a return to prototypes was indicated. The arch-rival – the Austin-Healey Sprite – had now appeared at Le Mans with a very special non-standard bodyshell in search of higher maximum speeds, and it looked as if a similar exercise would be needed at Coventry. Triumph therefore faced a real philosophical problem, which was coupled with the knowledge that the general regulations covering the modifications of GT cars was going to be tightened up in 1966 in any case. The problem could

Two of a kind, parked at a Monte Carlo Rally control in 1965. Valerie Pirie's SMART-entered car is on the left, with normal hardtop, a team car on the right. The bonnet-mounted auxiliary lights allowed quartz-halogen headlights to be used

be summed up by one question: 'Why did Triumph go racing?' Without the ulterior motives of advancing engineering knowledge, and of racing a quasi-standard vehicle, there didn't seem to be much reason for carrying on. Added to this was another shift of opinion within the Leyland organisation about the worth of competitions, and the expense of being properly represented, with the result that Competitions were requested to look into the future and report back. Ray Henderson, who had taken over administrative as well as preparation duties when the author left the company early in 1965, summed it all up by saying that more success could be guaranteed with more money and more specialised cars, but without development the cars would become less competitive.

The outcome is well-known. Triumph pulled out of sports car racing, and a few months later out of rallying too, but two projects which carried on are worth mentioning in passing. A very special Spitfire was built up from unused Le Mans components, but kitted out with an open body incorporating a Jaguar-type headrest and wrap-around windscreen. Known as the Macao car, this was built at the request of the Triumph importers in the Far East for use in the free-formula events which took place out there. The other in effect was a Le Mans GT6 prototype built on the lines of a Le Mans Spitfire. Using most of the existing components from a Le Mans car, it was powered by a GT6 2-litre engine which was installed in the normal GT6 fashion, and which in final race tune was expected to give at least 175 bhp. Maximum speeds of over 150 mph seemed certain, but as far as is known this car was never completed, and certainly never driven at racing speeds to prove the forecasts. The Le Mans cars were never sold, though one was built up for British club racing and loaned to Bill Bradley for his own use; in due course it was comprehensively written-off in a racing accident, and replaced by another car also based on an old Le Mans shell, this time with an experimental MacPherson strut type of independent rear suspension and a much-modified chassis frame.

The rallying programme got under way at about the same time as Le Mans with three cars entered in the Alpine Rally for Terry Hunter, Roy Fidler and Jean-Jacques Thuner. A related programme, though not actually within the works team, was Valerie Pirie's green Spitfire, entered by the Stirling Moss Automobile Racing Team (SMART). Success in rallying was almost immediate, for Terry Hunter's normal-bodied car missed a *Coupe des Alpes* by only a minute on its very first event, which showed that the cars were quick and nimble enough, even if they suffered from the lack of syncromesh on first gear, which could not be rectified without new parts being homologated.

After the Alpine the rally cars were to be entered for the ten-day Tour de France, probably the longest and most gruelling of any road event in Europe. Since more than 4,000 miles of road work was involved in addition to racing circuits all round France and in Italy, the rally cars were thought to be more suitable than the Le Mans cars. However, since Le Mans had proved the efficiency of the fastback bodies, these were quickly fitted to the rally cars as well. Although the cars now began to look distinctly non-standard, FIA regulations which applied at the time were perfectly clear on the subject; special bodies were allowed without any guarantee as to the numbers made. For rallying there was always the problem of getting at tools or the spare wheel through the rear 'letter box' – one usually solved by taking the required items out through a door – but as far as the crews were concerned this was far outweighed by the extra volume of storage space, provision for the huge 18-gallon fuel tank, and the extra snoozing room. By the time the cars had their special bodies and their developed engines they were pretty ferocious little beasts, where passenger comfort came a very poor second to pure effectiveness. Eventually the only similar-size cars capable of beating the Spitfires were much-modified Mini-Cooper Ss from Abingdon, which could also compete as GT cars when suitably non-standard. Valerie Pirie's car never had the fastback top fitted, though her car did use the faired bonnet on the Tour de France along with the works cars.

The Tour de France brought exactly the sort of result which Webster and the Competitions Department needed. In an event which should have suited the Alpine-Renaults and the Bonnets ideally as it was run on their home territory and used circuits with which they were familiar, the works Spitfires fought tooth-and-nail for ten days and finally saw off all the other works cars except Cheinisse's Alpine, which finished behind them! The event started badly for Triumph, as Bill Bradley's engine melted a piston at Reims, and Valerie Pirie's threw a connecting rod, but the Slotemaker-Hunter, and Thuner-Gretener cars proceeeded to beat the Alpines at circuits as varied as Le Mans, Rouen, Cognac and Albi. The Spitfires' biggest problem was that they had to run with very high gearing to attain their 130 mph maximum on the Reims, Le Mans and Monza circuits, which meant that starting from rest *uphill* on a speed hill-climb like the Col de Tourmalet was a distinct adventure! Thuner's car harried Slotemaker to the very last night when it, too, broke down spectacularly in the French Alps, and the Dutch skid-king's car nearly let him down when a raw edge in the bodyshell rubbed a hole in the big 18-gallon fuel tank! Fortunately for everyone the hole was above the half-way mark, so as long as less than six gallons were in the tank on the last day all was well; both of the crew were sick due to petrol fumes in the car, but suffered cheerfully for the glory and the piles of Shell-sponsored French francs. Even after some years of sober reflection it was a splendid show, particularly as the little Renault-engined French cars were thought to have had this part of the Tour de France all their own way; as it was only the Spitfire's third competitive event (after Le Mans and the Alpine Rally) the success was rather unexpected.

With big advances to be made in power, tractability and (hopefully) engine reliability there was much to look forward to in 1965, but in the meantime the team persuaded Webster to enter a couple of cars for the Geneva Rally, a European Championship qualifier, and of course dear to the heart of Thuner, whose business was in Geneva itself. As in previous years the event was run to a handicap system, but that suited the Spitfires extremely well. A series of very fast times in the speed hill-climbs, together with accurate navigation in the French Alps, all helped Terry Hunter and Patrick Lier to achieve a rousing second overall behind Henri Greder's 4.7-litre Ford Mustang, with Thuner's car fifth. Hunter's car also won the Grand Touring category outright – an astonishing performance for a 1.1 litre car.

Modified further for 1965, with extra headlamps let into their bonnets so that single-filament quartz-iodine headlights could be used, the Spitfires were expected to win many more awards, and to this end the young Finnish driver Simo Lampinen was signed for the season. Lampinen, though walking with a limp following childhood polio, was already famous for having won the Finnish Rally Championship in Saabs, and his signing followed a growing feeling in Britain that it was the 'In Thing' to have at least one Finn in your team. However, 1965 was not the year it had promised to be, as corporate thinking swung away from competitions, and though Lampinen was undoubtedly a great asset to the team he never achieved the successes that were thought possible. By the end of the summer, the best Spitfire result had been a very good class win on the Alpine Rally, when the prototype 1,296 cc engines and the all-synchromesh gearboxes had been fitted. Mechanical failures had been the downfall on the Monte Carlo and the Tulip Rallies, after a Monte class win had been confidently expected until it was discovered that BMC were going to enter a Cooper S as a GT car; Timo Makinen drove the car, won the event, and left a rather disgruntled Slotemaker behind him in the class as well.

To drive a Spitfire to its limit for long one had to be tremendously determined, and it helped to be partially deaf; the Spitfire was very noisy, particularly with its glass-fibre coupé top in place. During 1965 *Autocar* magazine started a series of tests called 'Given the Works', where well-known race and rally cars were tried out and performance figures which the factory had almost certainly never had time to take themselves were logged. Standard-Triumph loaned one of the rally team cars, and it is instructive to quote the comments of Geoffrey Howard, *Autocar's* Technical Editor, about ADU 7B:

'If ever a car needed to be driven with earplugs, the rally Spitfire is it. Outside it's not too bad (we sent someone else off round the block in it, so that we could stand and listen) and it may just conform to the limit set in regulations, but in there with it all is like a fiendish piece of Chinese torture.

'Part of the trouble is the plastic coupé shell which resonates at every frequency there is in the

By 1965, with 1,296 cc and 117 bhp, the rally cars were really quick. This is Simo Lampinen driving as near to the limit as usual in the Alpine Rally

whole of the rev range. At speed it's like travelling actually *inside* the silencer, with the noise coming in cyclic beats like in a ship's engine room or the power house of a generating plant. Then there's the vibration – that real teeth-hammering kind that hammers through the car and driver and reminds him of standing in the middle of a machine shop full of automatic capstans punching out rivets.

'A lot of the noise stems from the four unsilenced mouths of the twin-choke Weber carburettors, all gasping for air. Below about 4,000 rpm they feel gagged and the car will barely pick up from low down. But once under way and pulling cleanly the revs soar to the safe limit for sustained running of 7,500 rpm and even beyond.

'Gearing is strictly for special stages with top running out at 105 mph and first gear much too high for quick getaways. This combination of intractability and high indirects makes the car a real pig in traffic. . . .

'Acceleration from rest to 80 mph is almost exactly half that of the last Spitfire we tested three years ago (in fact it was 18.0sec on the rally car as against 36.9sec on the road car) but fuel consumption is double – sure proof you can't get something for nothing after all . . . . .

'Later one begins to get used to it in the same way as a cross-country run or a cold shower, for the exhilaration, the challenge, and – yes – the wonderful calm and relaxation of being warm by the fireside *afterwards.* Friends have to shout for the first hour or so until the buzzing in the ears stops, but who cares? We've been driving a racer.'

A lot of the above could be termed journalist's licence, especially as Howard is known to have a leaning towards Lamborghinis and Ferraris, but it does show just how different a fully developed competition car can be from the mild-mannered little sports car that forms its base.

Apart from the inevitable crashes and rebuilds there were only ever nine of the special-bodied cars. Of the four original Le Mans cars, two were crashed in 1964, and subsequently rebuilt from the ground up. Four works cars were converted in late 1964, and a fifth new left-hand-drive car for Simo Lampinen built-up during the winter. Valerie Pirie's car always had the latest mechanical build, but was never given the special hardtop, and was the only one ever officially to be sold; Peter Cox (one of the racing mechanics) bought it for his own use. With the help of Peter Clarke from the rallying workshop, the light green car was soon converted from a rally car into an out-and-out marque racer for British club events. Cox had an extremely successful season with it in 1966, after an early shunt at Oulton Park in 1965 when he finally discovered the limits of the swing-axle suspension; in 1966 his was probably the outstanding car in its class of marque racing, defeating all the good Sprites and Midgets at one time or another, including several with the larger 1,275 cc engine. None of the other cars was ever sold in full rallying or racing trim, the cars either being reconverted to standard for experimental and test use, or used in the construction of the loaned racing cars for Bill Bradley.

Bradley was extremely successful in his 1966 Spitfire, which was much more highly developed for circuit racing than his earlier car had been and was completely unbeatable in its class, often finding itself mixing it with Jaguar 'E' Types and Sunbeam Tigers in British events. At the end of the 1966 season, when Triumph's interest had lapsed, the car held class lap records at Goodwood, Brands Hatch, Crystal Palace, Snetterton, Oulton and Mallory Park, and the year brought no fewer than 14 class victories. Unfortunately the car was comprehensively written-off in the Nurburgring 1,000 kilometres race when leading the works-supported Sprites in the 1,300 cc class by many minutes at three-quarters distance in an accident which also involved the race leader! Peter Cox apparently bought the car after Bradley's arrangements had ceased, and with Richard Lloyd set up the Spitfire Gold Seal Racing Team in 1967.

The other car used by the Competitions Department in the 1960s was, of course, the Triumph 2000 saloon. As first used in the 1964 Liège-Sofia-Liège Rally, when all three cars retired within a few miles of each other with the same fatigue failure – a classic case of repeatable failures, which once cured never occurred again – the mechanical specification included 150 bhp Weber-carburetted engines, 15-inch road wheels and much larger disc brakes. Triumph kept going with the saloons rather longer than with the Spitfires, largely because they were not as specialised and therefore easier to maintain. Simo Lampinen put up some stirring performances, notably when he finished second overall to Roger Clark's Cortina-Lotus in the Welsh International Rally, while Roy Fidler used one to win the RAC Rally Championship series in 1966. When British Leyland decided to enter a team in the London – Mexico World Cup Rally in 1970, Peter Browning's choice of car fell on the Triumph 2.5 PI saloons, which had recently been shown in re-styled Mark II form. Most of the motoring press hailed this as a newly discovered rally car, which served to prove how short people's memories can become. Apart from the Triumph factory's considerable success in the middle 1960s, they had found time to prepare a pair of 2.5 PI prototypes for the 1967 RAC Rally; one was to be driven by RAC Rally Champion Roy Fidler, while the other was to have been handled by no less a personality than World Champion racing driver Denis Hulme (for whom the author was to act as co-driver). But the cars were never used, because the event was cancelled due to the rapid spread of foot-and-mouth disease in Great Britain at the time. In fact the World Cup Rally, in which Brian Culcheth's car finished second overall and Paddy Hopkirk's sister car fourth, was the second rallying appearance for the PIs; British Leyland had entered a team of the Mark I saloons in the RAC Rally the previous autumn, when Paddy Hopkirk gained much publicity for himself, if not for Triumph, by answering the question 'What is most difficult about the RAC Rally?' by, 'Winning it in this motor car!'. For the World Cup Rally the bodyshells were specially built by the Pressed Steel Company, with honeycomb structures in some sections, double skins in others, and the most meticulous welding at all points. The Abingdon Competitions Department actually built the car, but almost all the development, and the mechanical components, tuned engines, special undershielding and modified suspensions came from Ray Henderson's mechanics in Coventry. Abingdon gained all the praise for that valiant effort, but Coventry took all the sweat! That fine World Cup Rally performance in 1970, with cars basically no quicker than they could have been in 1967, gives an idea of what might then have been achieved by a Triumph-based department if it had been allowed to carry on. Brian Culcheth rubbed in the message of fuel-injected performance and Triumph 2000 structural reliability by winning the Scottish International Rally in a World Cup development car in 1970, and putting up a string of other fine PI performances in countries as far apart as Cyprus and Jamaica.

However, at the time these words were written a full-scale return to competitions looked as far away at British Leyland as ever. Harry Webster, though himself a considerable motor-sport enthusiast, was now reconciled to competitions being almost totally a PR exercise, with little rub-off to engineering, and to judge by his experience at Triumph, a great consumer of time:

'A racing programme within a normal production-orientated engineering department has always been, in my experience, a nuisance. Don't get me wrong, though, every engineer is an enthusiast, and there was nothing we enjoyed more than to be able to work on competition programmes in favour of the production stuff we ought to have been looking at. Sir William Lyons once spoke to me, at about the time we were

Built from a box of spares – the Macao racing Spitfire assembled for Triumph's Far Eastern distributors in 1965

going into Le Mans racing, and he was getting out. He said "Why ever are you trying to do this? You will spoil your engineering programme like I have done. If ever Jaguar is to go back into competitions again, I will engage professionals to do it, miles away from my factory, because before it ruined my development programme". We really had to stop the racing Spitfire programme, and I said we won't touch the damned thing again until we've finished our day-to-day stuff – *then* if we've got the capacity to spare, which you never do have again, then we'll go back in. . . .

'Nowadays it's more PR than engineering, in my opinion, and expensive PR at that. Particularly if you don't win. If you're going to do a competitions programme now, there's only one thing to do and that's to try to win outright. Those people who can advertise that they win this class with this car, that class with that – it doesn't work now, the public isn't interested. In the days when we were rallying the Spitfires we had the success advertising ready before the event. You know – Triumph First, but in what? Someone else might have won the rally, but by clever advertising everyone somehow managed to win something.'

Webster made the point that a company which could sell every car it made (and British Leyland had been in this happy situation for the past five years at least) didn't need competitions as an image builder, but that if they were in a free market, with cars to sell, then perhaps they would need to polish their image up a bit.

Lord Stokes had clearly become completely opposed to an expensive competitions programme, and the final straw must have come on the World Cup Rally when even a budget of £100,000-plus could not guarantee success for the beautifully prepared Triumphs. In the course of a discussion about the future of Triumph, which I held with him during 1973, he had this to say about the value of competitions:

'I think that what has happened in the competitions business is that a few companies have removed it entirely from the realms of sport, and they put sporting activities merely into a matter of money. The Monte Carlo Rally (which British Leyland won for three or four years depending on who is arguing the case), and other events like the East African Safari, these have just become exercises in which certain companies have decided to spend enormous sums of money in attempting to win by any means, and this includes things like helicopters and planes overhead with spares; there's such a fantastic amount of money and resources behind it that I think the whole element of sport has gone out of it. I think this is what has ruined a sporting image, and I think the public is not so dim as some people think they are – I think perhaps they realise this now too. On the other hand I don't know how you put a limit on this – it's very difficult to say "You should only spend so much" because people do have a habit of going right up to the end of a rule, and people do have a habit of cheating unless everything is absolutely water-tight; but I must add that none of these companies has done anything improper, because they all acted within the rules of the game, even if they had broken the spirit of the thing.'

But what are Lord Stokes' views now on the value of a competitions programme to British Leyland in the future?:

'I think I'm very often misquoted on this question of competitions. I like competitions if I think I have a chance of winning them – that's just good business practice. I think also we have to consider what the purpose of competitions is. If we take Grand Prix racing, for instance, which interests a lot of people, it has no bearing on reality whatsoever, and I think it does practically nothing for the development of the modern car. You get as much spin-off from a Concorde as you do from a Grand Prix car, in spite of what people may tell you. We've got to design cars which are reliable, and which cater for the majority of people about their daily business. This is far removed from Grand Prix racing, though I wouldn't like to see Grand Prix racing stop, because I think it is all a tremendous challenge to drivers' skills, and for engineering skills, but not quite the sort we want. It is very interesting to think that the most successful firms in terms of production volume give very little support to racing as such. I believe that if you can arrive at a universal formula where a standard saloon can be raced, then this is much more interesting to the general public. It's much more interesting to us too, because this really does develop a motor car. We have done, and will continue to enter a number of rallies. We have developed and improved our cars a lot from these rallies, because we have put in cars which are standard production (or prototype production) cars. Other people enter souped-up monsters which have no relevance to what they are actually producing, and they have no intention of actually making any. Where we have entered standard cars, and where components have failed, because they have been on terribly rough roads, this is where we have had a good spin-off of knowledge which has benefited the production car, by driving a car under the stress of competition which is conceivably experienced by the most enthusiastic of private owners.'

Would Lord Stokes therefore be interested in supporting entries in standard production saloon, or sports car races?:

'Certainly here again I am not enthusiastic about big motor manufacturers cornering the business. It looks as if it is happening already, and if so it will ruin saloon car racing as it ruined rallies. It is all very exciting to know that the XYZ company is sponsoring a car, but here again this will eventually end up just as a money battle between giants. I feel that it is much better if you can keep it in the hands of the amateurs, with general support from the manufacturers. We don't have any reaction from our dealers at all. There's no pressure whatever on us from dealers to go back into motor sport. I think perhaps certain companies may need to do more to get a good image than we do! I think motor sport, if done on a sensible basis, is fun, and I like to see it, but I think certain companies are ruining it!'

Lord Stokes has therefore made himself fairly clear on his attitude to motor sport, and particularly to the necessity of entering radically modified cars if there is to be any chance of winning. Triumph have had their moments, both in Europe and in America, but if it needs lots of money and non-standard cars to repeat the successes then there will be no further involvement. Motor sport certainly improves the breed of a standard car, if a standard car is actually used in the sport itself, but Harry Webster is happy that modern testing techniques can cover all the development wrinkles that a rally car (for instance) might throw up, even if it takes a little longer. We may not agree with him in our hearts, but the facts speak for themselves. If there was, any longer, any evidence that companies indulging in heavy competitions programmes build more reliable cars, then Triumph would be back in. But if cars such as Jaguar, Mercedes Benz and Volkswagen can prosper who needs competitions?

CHAPTER 12

Triumph in America

NO POST-WAR company making sports cars in any volume could hope to survive without large-scale North American deliveries. This is truly a post-war phenomenon, of course, for Britain's between-wars sports cars were rarely exported to any country in significant numbers. The legend is that enough GI servicemen tried our funny little cars during their sojourn in Britain during the war, caught the bug of open-air motoring, took it home with them and started a trend that has seen no reversal. MG usually get the credit for satisfying the first demand; indeed, most European sports car builders should be thankful to MG for this one effort. Once demand began to explode, there was a big enough market for everyone.

Coupled with this was Britain's invidious economic position in 1945. In seeking to put to rights the dreadful economic ravages brought about by the war, it was necessary to 'export or die' (government phraseology, not mine), more than anything else to export to dollar-currency countries. The shocking sheet steel shortage brought a government-controlled licencing scheme in its wake, once again the favoured manufacturers being those who could send nearly all their finished product to the North American continent.

At Standard-Triumph, as we have seen, Sir John Black originally circumnavigated these restrictions by building the 1800 Roadster (and saloon) with tubular chassis and hand-beaten aluminium body panels. His first serious look at the North American market was with the Vanguard (itself a copy from current Plymouths which he admired so much), and it was not until the early 1950s that proper sports cars were ever sent over there. The Triumph distributive chain in the early 1950s, such as it was, had noted that MG could sell has many TCs and TDs as they could build, and that the much more expensive Jaguar XK120 was also popular. North America – the United States and Canada, that is – had become a happy hunting ground for sports car salesmen, and there was no sign of a dropping off

After two seasons of European rallying the works TR4s were sent to Canada for the Shell 4000 Rally in 1964. Roy Fidler and Jean-Jacques Thuner shared one of the cars which formed the only complete team of sports cars to finish
(Picture: Triumph – USA)

The start of a famous partnership – Bob Tullius in the Group 44 TR4 in 1962
(Picture: Triumph – USA)

in the demand for open-air motoring, in cars that actually went round corners on the line you asked of them and stopped when you pushed the brake pedal.

However, the Americans, although part of the richest country on earth, were not foolish enough to part lightly with their valuable dollars. Any company hoping to sell loads of cars to them would first have to prove that they had a good product. The story has grown that the vast majority of all TRs, Spitfires and the like have been sold in North America, and while this was substantially true of the 1960s and early 1970s, it was not always so. The TR2, while demonstrably fast, economical, and above all fun to drive, first had to prove itself, and the fact is that no more than 3,000 actually went to the United States. In 1955, for example, more TR2s were registered in Britain than in the States (1,504 against 949). However, 'oak trees from little acorns grow', and the TR2 founded the Triumph cult which expanded mightily later in the 1950s. The TR3 was better-equipped and better-known, while the TR3A was arguably nicer looking and benefited from the sporting reputation of the earlier cars. It is instructive to look at the sales figures for the TRs in the latter years of the 1950s:

		USA	Canada	UK
1955	TR2 and TR3	1,261	263	1,730
1956	TR3	2,900	421	613 *
1957	TR3 and TR3A	8,068	488	447 *
1958	TR3A	12,224	840	542 *
1959	TR3A	17,321	1,080	638 *
1960	TR3A	10,497	812	640 *

* Deliveries restricted because of export demand

Once the TR3A became the TR4, and the Spitfire was added in huge numbers, the

Ten years after his first win, Bob Tullius was still the fastest TR driver in North America. In the meantime the car had become a TR6, and had been pushed up two performance classes by the SCCA
(Picture: Triumph – USA)

Four Spitfires (a Mk 3 leading, a Mk 4 in second place) head a gaggle of Midgets and other Spitfires in the 1971 United States Road Race of Champions at Road Atlanta (Picture: M.L. Cook)

proportion of cars sent to North America at times reach 90 per cent. Over 150,000 TRs of all types, and more than 200,000 Spitfire/GT6s of all variants have now crossed the Atlantic. In recent years, Triumph have looked at their American market very carefully before making any changes to the specification. Styling, engineering and furnishings are all now subservient to their dollar-market customers, without whom it would simply not be worth making the cars at all. Selling 30 GT6s every week in England, plus perhaps 120 Spitfire 4s and 20 TR6s would never be profitable, and such buyers as exist should no doubt be grateful that American sales keep them going. In view of the large preponderance of sales to North America, it is doubly surprising that Triumph should have taken the trouble to develop a fuel-injected engine for the TR5 and TR6 (when only 10 per cent of the cars made have it fitted), or lower-wishbone rear suspension for the GT6 (when at least three-quarters of all sales went to North America where there was little adverse reaction). Should we complain if some fittings seem to be laid out for left-hand-drive – such as the handbrake on TR2s, TR3s and TR4s? On the other hand, would we be willing to pay for the extra safety equipment now compulsory in North America – including special safety belts, energy-absorbing bumpers, beams in the doors to guard against crash intrusion and headrests to guard against neck whip-lash injuries?

It is a mark of popularity for a particular make of car when a 'one-make' motor sport club is formed around it. Therefore it is no surprise to learn that the Triumph Sports Owners Association (TSOA) came into being in 1954 as soon as the TR2 started to be built. The American branch was formed almost at once, and is now more active in terms of events held and competition cars used than any other branch. In America, the TSOA publish a regular Newsletter, complete with technical information, service hints and reports on member activities all around the globe.

The story of Triumph in America is also a story of wide-ranging success in motor sport. Sports Car Club of America (SCCA) racing forms the background of most so-called 'amateur' racing, and it was in this that the TR2s and TR3s began to excel. The very first TR2s into California were entered in the production sports car races, took over, won and virtually controlled them. When the disc-braked TR3s arrived in 1957 the winning margins grew even wider. At Sebring in 1957, in the 12-hours race, for instance, two such TR3s walked away with the 2-litre GT class (Rothschild/Johns and Oker/

Pennybacker). Mike Rothschild, who was later to drive team cars at Le Mans, also placed in his class at Sebring the following year. It was in 1959, however, that the Triumph Racing Team was formed in California. The leading driver was a determined young man who refused to believe that AC Bristols and the like could ever be quicker than his TR3s – 'Kas' Kastner, who put together an incredible string of firsts in the Californian events to become the local SCCA champion.

Kastner was a very talented Californian who – for many years – was able to extract more horsepower out of any given Triumph engine than any other tuner. In his early days as Triumph's United States 'Competitions Manager' the Kastner engines were much more powerful than anything being used by the team in Coventry, mainly because Ken Richardson refused to have anything to do with super-tuning; it was Kastner's busy fingers and the talented driving of Bob Tullius in a TR4 which combined to make Triumph champions of their group in 1962. SCCA racing in America was then (and is now) organised so that cars of theoretically identical performance could race against each other, whether or not they were of the same engine size. Any driver winning his group in one season would have to be careful that the margin was not too wide, or his car would be moved up into a more difficult category the following year. The penalty of such success came to Triumph, for the TR4 was moved up in 1963, and had to fight even harder. Not that it mattered all that much. Tullius had won the SCCA 'E' group in his first TR4, and won again in the 'D' category in 1963. 1963 also saw a full-blooded factory (ie, Kastner-prepared) team entry at the Sebring 12-hours race, where pre-race scrutineering bothers were circumvented in time for the cars to take a 2½-litre GT class win and second place (Bolton/Rothschild, and Tullius/Kellner/Spencer). Not content with two wins, Bob Tullius made it three in a row when he won the 'D' Production group in 1964.

The TR4A was greeted with great delight for its new optional independent rear suspension, though not for its unchanged engine. It was still enough for Kastner's 2.2-litre cars, which produced around 150 bhp, to take all three class positions at Sebring in 1966, Pendleton and Froines being in the leading car. Not that it was all that smooth, because there was still much to learn about the chassis-mounted differential, and the class-winning car crossed the line at 10pm making a noise like a rock crusher, with almost every tooth on the pinion gear destroyed. In the meantime a TR4 had won its national championship again, Steve Froines' car beating Bob Tullius by only a few cars' lengths. 'D' Production in fact was becoming almost too much of a Triumph benefit, so it must have come as quite a surprise both to spectators and drivers when another car, a Porsche 911 no less, beat three TR4As in the sudden-death championship. Kastner found time to send a car to the

British Leyland in Britain might not support motor sport very actively, but there is no doubt of the interest in the States. This is the Group 44 rig used throughout 1972. Left to right is a Triumph Spitfire, an MGB (how did that get into this book?), a GT6 and a TR6
(Picture: Group 44 Inc)

Bonneville records event in the autumn of 1966, proving what no factory tester had ever bothered to find out, namely that a TR4A with all the race-engine modifications could reach nearly 130 mph with all equipment including bumpers and brightwork fitted. The TRs lost the edge in 1967 and 1968, particularly after the rather gutless TR250 appeared and was instantly upgraded into 'C' group, but once the 1969 season came around Kastner had managed to work the fuel-injection engine as an option (which it was, indeed, in every sensible country). Once again, Bob Tullius, who seemed to have been driving for ever, but still looked no older, was always the fastest man in his Group 44 TR5. This and the TR6 have always been to the forefront of SCCA racing in America.

The Spitfires and GT6s have also been in the thick of it, though the Stag is not the sort of car which one takes racing. Even after it had been out of production for some time, the TR3A was still raced regularly; it took the 'F' group championship in 1965 in the hands of Brian Fuerstenau, and again in 1967 driven by Lee Midgley, but after that the Triumph enthusiasts moved on to the GT6. Spitfires won national championships in two groups in 1968, and one group in each of 1969, 1970, 1971 and 1972. The GT6 started its race career in 1968 (Kastner had had no time for race-tuning in 1967), in 'E' Production group, where it had to fight against the older TR3A, but it was not until 1969, with the new wishbone rear suspension, that the car became competitive. In that year the GT6 Plus rubbed in its superiority over all comers by taking all three places in the group at the American Road Race of Champions meeting at Daytona at the end of the year. In 1970 Carl Swanson's GT6 missed a national championship by perhaps a car's length when his car shed a rear wheel on the final run-in to the chequered flag; this after the car had been kicked upstairs to Group 'D' following 1969's sweeping successes. Triumph thumbed their noses at this instant equalisation by taking the old 'E' group in a swing-axle GT6 (Don Devendorf).

Since 1962 Triumph participation in American racing has been as fierce as that. The North American importing company continue to take a deep interest in the sport, and for some years kept up with an assistance programme which paid bonuses to successful drivers. As recently as 1971, however, the effort was concentrated on two teams. Group 44, based in Falls Church, Virginia, of which Bob Tullius is the most talented driver, became the East Coast group favoured with British Leyland finance and development, while Kastner threw in his lot with John Brophy to form Kastner-Brophy Inc., racing from California. The irony of all this is that if a Triumph factory team was to be reformed in Britain tomorrow, they would take a long time to catch up with their private, but supported, teams in terms of razor-edge engine tuning, and roadholding tweaks. For since the Coventry competitions department closed down in 1967 there has been no parallel development of track cars in this country.

Lord Stokes approves of the type of racing carried on in the United States, and the way in which it is organised. The BRSCC in Britain is trying to rearrange sports and GT racing into the same sort of pattern, and if it follows the success of the American SCCA series it will be well worth watching. With so many makes of car on sale in America, from so many countries, every item of good publicity adds to the marketing potential of Triumph cars. Although Triumph only won a single SCCA championship at the end of 1972 (Rick Cline's Spitfire in 'G' Production) they also placed third in 'F' Production (a Spitfire), second in 'D' Production (a GT6, inches behind the winning McQueen's Datsun), and second in 'C' Production (Tullius' Group 44 TR6, just four seconds behind a Datsun 240Z). And there were no other groups in which Triumph cars were competing. It is this sort of success, and this sort of consistency, which have made such a name for Triumph sports cars in the last ten years.

CHAPTER 13

The Stag and the future

'WHAT IS a sports car?' is a rhetorical question posed by many a motoring enthusiast in the last 70 years. There was a time when discussion of this problem could be guaranteed to occupy an entire learned feature in a motoring magazine, and the conclusion such a feature reached was almost inevitably that a sports car was so in the eye of the motorist who thought it was one! From time to time writers have tried to quantify the sports car's breed – postulating power-to-weight ratios, seating capacity, frontal area, handling qualities, equipment – or even the maker's name. What then, would these people make of the Triumph Stag? Surely there would be few of the world's enthusiasts who would deny its sports car status (or – at the very least – Grand Touring status), but there are many ways in which it does not fall into the recognised categories. Yet Stag was Triumph's idea of the sort of car a particular sector of the market would buy, people who were not interested in luggage space, cheap spares, ultimate re-sale value or passenger accommodation, people who wanted performance and excellent appointments, and were prepared to pay for it. More than any other Triumph sports car, Stag is a sporting car for the 1970s, and from it we may draw all sorts of conclusions about the future product.

Like many other successful cars, however, Stag was not the result of many hundreds of hours of market research, though in truth a modicum of such probing was carried out after the first car was built. It was a car that took a long time to mature – one which was conceived before the TR5 even, and almost in parallel with the GT6, but which took its first public bow as late as June 1970. In that time there had been a change of company management, a change of Technical Director, a change of Managing Director (and another one brewing) and the massive onset of American safety regulations. Yet Stag changed very little in basic concept in those six years. It can all be traced back to the Leyland success in achieving financial stability from the wrecked company that was Standard-Triumph in 1960 and 1961. To get the company's products up-to-date a new medium-large saloon car was required to replace the old Vanguard Vignale, which was dead on its feet in spite of the fine new six-cylinder engine that it had recently offered. Under Alick Dick, Harry Webster's engineers had been searching for a Vanguard successor for some time. Webster's main regret about those years was that there never seemed to be enough money for new-model tooling, and once a large sum had been earmarked for the Herald there wasn't enough left to tackle the big car.

In 1958 and 1959 there had been an advanced project – coded 'Zebu' – with a separate chassis, independent rear suspension of the same type as the new car was eventually to inherit, plus a rear-mounted gearbox in unit with the chassis-mounted differential casing. Zebu's body style was first tackled by Triumph's Les Moore, and later re-touched by Michelotti, being chiefly distinguished by the use of a reverse-rake rear window. Triumph were not influenced by Ford thinking for their new Anglias and Classics, and indeed were completely astonished when one eminent motoring writer saw Zebu and commented that similar plans were afoot – plans that were certain to pre-date Standard-Triumph by up to a year. Alick Dick was shattered by this revelation, for he had thought that such a reverse-slope window would be unique to Standard-Triumph and a good sales feature. This, coupled with Triumph's already doubtful finances, led to Zebu being frozen before the prototype had even run.

It was tentatively replaced by the same chassis clothed with a stretched Herald saloon body: 'We quite literally chopped up a Herald body like a hot-cross bun, took the corners out to the edges of the bigger chassis, converted to four-doors and filled in the gaps to see what sort of a looker it was'. None of these project studies were far off the ground when Leyland took over, and Webster was greatly relieved to hear that he could design a unit-construction body again for the definitive car. It didn't leave him much time, for whole-vehicle layouts didn't begin until the spring of 1961, with mock-ups of the body style required during the summer, body tooling to be approved straight off the drawing board, and first production before the autumn of 1963.

The new car – 'Barb' to its designers – went ahead remarkably smoothly and without major snags. Pressed Steel were to make the bodies (as they had for the last of the Vanguards – and remember that Standard-Triumph still lacked enough of their own body-build facilities), while engines and gearboxes would be lifted out of the six-cylinder Vanguard with minor changes. MacPherson front suspension was adopted for the first time – it was fast becoming standard equipment in family cars from Ford to BMW, Rootes to Standard-Triumph – while the Zebu-type independent rear suspension was used. Much against its designers' wishes, there had to be 2-litre and 1.6-litre versions. The 2-litre would have none-too-much performance and therefore they expected the 1.6 to be plain dull.

The first prototype consisted of the correct underframe, along with its coil-spring independent suspension all round, braced with an angle-iron superstructure covered rather sketchily with canvas. This dreadful looking device, quickly dubbed 'birdcage' by its drivers, was soon set to work on the usual motor industry endurance routes around Wales, Derbyshire and the Cotswolds, where the industrial spies from other companies must have been very puzzled indeed; only the Coventry trade plates would give the game away, and even then there would be little else to indicate the car's intent.

The Stag was intended to have hidden headlamps, but a fear of changes in American legislation brought them out into the open on production cars

Right up to the spring of 1963 the semi-trailing light-alloy wishbones were bolted direct to the underside of the Barb's bodyshell, such that the lack of refinement and transmission roughness can be imagined. Every form of expert was thrown into the breach to tame the car to an acceptable standard, but eventually there came that terrible day in every designer's experience when a phone call had to be made to the Pressed Steel company cancelling the part-completed press tools for the car's underside, and substituting the revised layout. Refinement was achieved by fitting a rubber-mounted sub-frame to the bodyshell from which the semi-trailing arms could pivot. The axle casing was mounted to the sub-frame at its nose, but direct to the bodyshell by widely spaced pivots at the rear. Much to most people's relief the 1600 version was cancelled when it was realised that it would have to sell at virtually the same price, and after last-minute improvements to the internal trim of the car it was launched in October 1963 as the Triumph 2000.

Notwithstanding the simultaneous announcement of Rover's approach to the same market – also called the 2000 – the Triumph was an instant success, and sold very well ever after. The 1,998 cc engine was sufficiently powerful (90 bhp at 5,000 rpm) to endow the bulky car with a 95 mph maximum speed, the gearbox, like that of the TR4, had all-syncromesh gears, and there was an automatic option that did not actually reach production until the summer of 1964. Michelotti's styling had produced a spacious five-seater saloon car with a long nose and a rather short boot – a shape not thought particularly fashionable at the time, but one increasingly adopted since then. Above all the 2000 was refined, very middle-class, and (if sexes came into this) very definitely a lady.

Michelotti was very pleased with this, his first large-car style for Triumph, and thought he would like to create a more specialised, sporting, version of it for show on his own display stands at the motor shows of Europe. John Lloyd remembers that an old Triumph 2000 was requested for conversion, and that this was delivered to him direct from the Le Mans circuit after the 1964 race in which the very special racing Spitfires had first appeared. No-one at Triumph knew exactly what Michelotti had in mind, except that he was going to build a special for show, using the Triumph 2000 as a base. One can imagine Harry Webster's surprise, therefore, when on a routine visit to the styling studios in Turin to look at Michelotti's latest proposals for revised TR4s and Spitfires he was confronted with an unfamiliar four-seater coupé using Triumph parts.

'Michelotti had requested an old Triumph 2000 chassis, on which he wanted to do a coupé/sports car based on the 2000 chassis, and he wanted to use it for a piece of advertising for his own skills. I agreed to this on the proviso that he didn't put it into a show until I had a look at it. When I saw it I liked it, and thought this was a car that there was a need for, in Britain particularly, for the type of young manager who had some money to spare. It was the classic case of the car for a man who had a sports car when he married, then a family comes along. Soon he wants a car with a difference, get-up-and-go. Conversely there was the sort of man who, when the kids have left home and married, has quite a lot of money to spare, who still wants to feel young, and wants everyone else to know about it. I don't know where this would put me, but I thought I might want one of those myself. So I instantly made my own decision on behalf of the company, and told Michelotti that I couldn't let him use it in a show now that he had finished it, but that I wanted to keep it! In fact we then got it back to Coventry and kept it on ice for some time. It was the usual problem of priorities, and money to tool it. I'm afraid it had to wait – we were particularly pre-occupied with cars like the

The 1973 Stag – is this the way all future sports cars will have to look?

1300 and the TR5 at that time, and of course with the development of new engines.'

Stag was delayed several times, both at this stage, and at various phases in its development, either by the priority of getting other things done or – in at least one case – by a major change of policy over the car's basic specification. It took just six years from conception to birth, a very lengthy gestation period in all truth, but hardly as long as some other important models from the Midlands at that time. Hilarious motor industry gossip had it that by the time the Rover 2000 was eventually shown to the public the early prototypes had already been subjected to compulsory seven-year tests! Though this story was only slightly exaggerated, it looked like being repeated at one stage with Stag, which had at least one major bodywork revision, and no fewer than four different basic engine specifications before it was announced with the 3-litre V8 unit; indeed, the final revision upwards, from 2½-litre to 3-litre V8, caused a redesign of gearbox, axle, brakes and wheels. In fact, Stag was so long delayed that when it appeared several months after the restyled Triumph 2000 and 2.5 PI, most people could have been forgiven for thinking that Stag styling details had followed those already chosen for the saloons. The reverse was, in fact, the case, for Stag styling was broadly fixed by the end of 1964, with release at one time intended for 1968, to be followed by the revised saloons. Commercial considerations, including the fact that the saloons sold in far higher quantities, dictated the release of the saloons first even though their Stag-type nose styling and facia layouts had not been designed until 1966/67.

The very first Stag (its original code name, by the way) was based on the Triumph 2000 chassis and understructure, suitably chopped around and with a shorter wheelbase (8ft 4in instead of 8ft 10in) and had completely unaltered engine, gearbox, and suspension items. John Lloyd says: 'We were always going to alter the engine, of course, to a 2000 TS tune as first intended for the TR5, but we thought we could get away with modified tooling. By the time we had had to chop a bit off here, add a bit on here, and particularly because of the need for roll-over protection, there was precious little left of the original pressings. Our body design people then pointed out that new tooling could be as cheap as modified tooling, especially if we did most of it ourselves. Stag as it is now made doesn't have a single common panel with the 2000 saloons, even though it may look like it. Anyway, the saloon is made for us at Pressed Steel, at Cowley, while we make the Stag completely at the Liverpool factory.'

The Stag V-8 is a compact 3-litre design. Made in small quantities, it seems destined to suffer under the British Leyland rationalisation programme

Apart from the constant change of plan for the car's specification, another sizeable hold-up was because of Leyland's decision to build the car completely at Liverpool. There was not enough capacity at Coventry, anyway, and with a big new factory being built not far away from the original Hall Engineering plant, it was decided to assemble the Triumph 1300 and its successors, together with the new Stag, there. The Liverpool factory was late in being finished, as were the Toledo and 1500 which jointly replaced the 1300 and 1300TC, so Stag was also held up.

Engine development work aimed at Stag and the TR5 soon showed that the right sort of power and torque could not be achieved from a tuned 2-litre engine, so Harry Webster's next step was to enlarge the engine to 2.5-litres. How this was done by lengthening the stroke and generally improving the breathing has already been described in connection with the TR5. Like the TR5, however, it was thought that much more power was needed than could be provided with carburettors, so the cheaper type of Lucas fuel injection was tried instead. The next Stag prototypes, the first 'proper' prototypes, unlike the chopped-and-channeled car from Michelotti, accordingly had TR5 injection engines, and by all accounts were very rapid cars. Though not quite as powerful as the final product, the engine was light (and therefore didn't call for power steering because of too much weight on the front wheels) and very torquey. Stag with the TR5 engine was just about the last car with which Harry Webster was completely concerned, though his engine designers had been working away at a completely new family of engines for the 1970s, engines which eventually were destined to play a big part in Stag.

So important, indeed, to Standard-Triumph and now to British Leyland were these new engines that it is worth diverting to see how they were evolved and developed. Indeed, in the last few years, a lot of uninformed nonsense has been talked about the latest Triumph engines, which power the growing family of Dolomites and Stag. Many writers have attributed the engine's basic design to the consulting engineering company of Ricardo, or at least have given a lot of credit to Ricardo along the way. This, if true, would be a really romantic coincidence, as the first Triumph car used a Ricardo-designed engine in 1923, but it is quite without foundation, and it would be totally unfair to Triumph's gifted engine designers to let such assertions slip into authenticated history.

Triumph began their design studies into a new family of engines in the early 1960s, when their only corporate connection was with Leyland, and it was Lewis Dawtrey – who had been the original inspiration for Harry Webster's dream of becoming a great engineer – who was given the responsibility for this. Dawtrey, then not too many years from retirement, was directed to look at all the possibilities for a complete new range of engines that conceivably could cover the requirements of every Triumph car for the 1970s and probably beyond. It was his recommendation to Harry Webster that such a requirement could be covered by one range, if it should comprise a V8 engine, and a slant four-cylinder design derived from it. Note that the V8 was the kernel of the plan, and the slant-four came afterwards, even though Triumph then chose to make the four-cylinder engine their first priority. That the engine family has not yet grown as varied and as universal as hoped is partly because the formation of British Leyland altered a lot of people's thinking, and because there has been such a huge demand for the slant-four engine that production of the V8 has had to suffer in consequence.

With the basic engine layouts agreed, and Dawtrey already turning his thoughts to a different cylinder head to top the bare bones of the engine itself, detail design can then largely be credited to a young man called Ron Warwick, whom the author met several years previously at Jaguar, where he was to be found working on the latest racing tweaks for the racing Jaguar 'D' Types; there are several touches in the Dolomite/Stag engines which owe lip service to Jaguar, though there is no question of patents being infringed. Detail design of the engine was completed in 1964; Harry Webster and John Lloyd are adamant that at no time were Ricardo consulted, and that the engines were completely inspired and detailed at Coventry. If any one man is to become immortal because of this fine design, it should be Lewis Dawtrey; his was the recommendation that the V8 should displace between 2½-litres and 4-litres, which meant that the slant-four could displace between 1,250cc and 2-litres.

The first time the existence of new Triumph engines became known was when Saab announced that their next new car would have a Standard-Triumph-built engine. This was in the winter of 1964/65, and is where the Ricardo 'red herring' crept in. Saab, one remembers, had made their name from cars using exclusively two-stroke engines and front-wheel drive, and had no four-stroke engine experience of any nature when it became clear that such a power unit would be needed in the 1960s. Several of Europe's manufacturers were consulted about future supplies, urgently needed for the Saab 96, and in the meantime Saab started on a development exercise connected with new designs with Ricardo in Sussex. Ricardo, however, whose corporate ear was very close to the ground, had heard of Triumph's intentions, and recommended Saab to make contact. Initial approaches confirmed that such engines were, indeed, on the way and that sufficient supplies for Saab's new car, the 99, could be guaranteed in 1968/69. Saab and Triumph therefore did a lot of joint development work on this engine, but at no time was Ricardo further involved. Saab, for three years, were the only people to use the slant-four engine, which was not put in a Triumph until the much delayed Dolomite arrived in January 1972, and they have now completed their own manufacturing facilities at Trollhattan to make the engine themselves.

Chronologically, however, Dawtrey's V8 version was at least a year behind the slant-four, the first engine running towards the end of 1965, using similar cylinder heads, valve gear and connecting rods.

Just at the time when Stag should have been committed for production, with the TR5 fuel-injected engine, the first 2½-litre V8 engines began to produce very encouraging results. Triumph sales staff were very keen to project Stag as an all-new car and fastened on this V8 engine as another major advance. But would it even go into the car? But surely, one might say, hadn't the engines been designed to fit into existing bodyshells and engine bays? Astonishing as it might have seemed, they hadn't. When Dawtrey conceived his engine family, it was without reference to any existing car; enough time existed, it was reasoned, before the engines were needed to ensure that the cars would fit around them. Would one ever be able to accuse Ford, for instance, of such lax forward-planning? Probably not – however, much to Triumph's surprise, the V8 engine could be persuaded to fit into the engine bay of the Stag or the Triumph 2000. (In a parallel exercise they were not as lucky with the slant-four, now used in the Dolomite. Originally slanted for fitment to later front-wheel-drive developments of the Triumph 1300, the slant-four caused much embarrassment by failing to fit into the existing space; the Dolomite, when it came, even in classic rear-drive form, needed a restyle). Once the point had been made, and the V8 engine installed in Stag, Sales were prepared to sit back and wait for it. In hindsight, Harry Webster is still sorry that this happened: 'I left for Austin-Morris in 1968, so didn't have any power to alter policy after that. However, I always felt

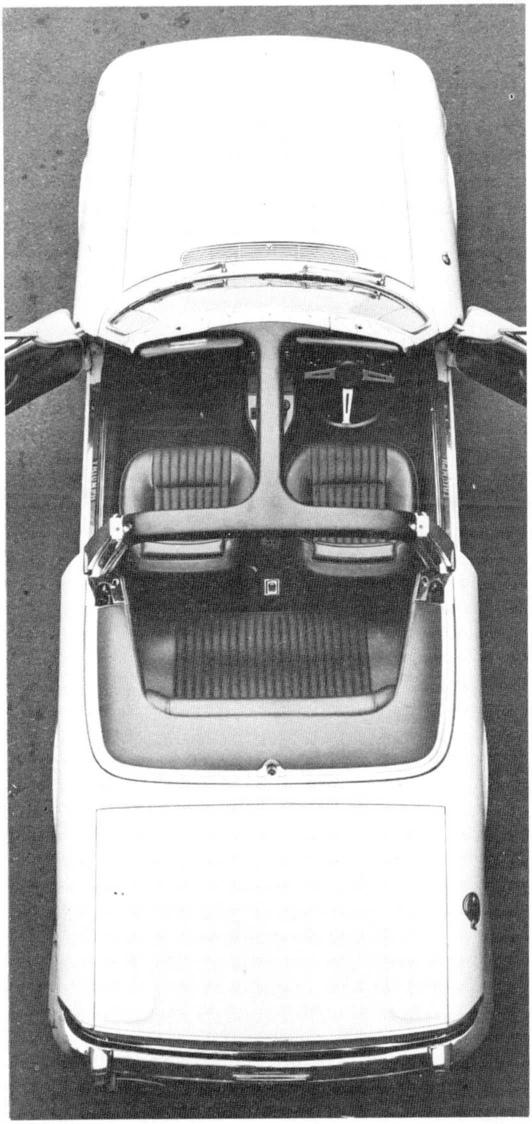

The Stag laid bare (above). The roll-hoop and strut is permanently fitted, whether under a hood or a hardtop (below)

that we could have introduced Stag with the 2.5 PI (or TR6) engine first, then brought in the V8 as an option, or even as a later facelift. There's no doubt that the biggest reason for the delay on Stag was because the engine wasn't ready.'

But what sort of a car was this prototype Stag, what sort of a car is the production car, and how significant is it to Triumph's future? More, much more, than any previous Triumph sporting car, Stag is civilised. With the single exception of reduced passenger space compared with the Triumph 2000, Stag is every bit as refined and as well equipped as the saloons. The days of the noisy draughty sports car are over, and there must be no question of water leaks through a poor hood, 'peaky' engines which need rowing along on the gear lever, or a ride which could cause an expert driver to differentiate between 'Heads' or 'Tails' on the penny his wheels have just driven over. Stag was designed to be very fast, with a top speed of around 120 mph in the right conditions. Its ride had to be equal to that of the saloons, and its appointments as cosy. It should be capable of getting from London to the Mediterranean in an untiring day, rushing round the Alps while one was there, or acting as a luxury carriage to take one to the social occasions on the spot. It was to be, in other words, a car to be matched against a Mercedes-Benz, an Alfa Romeo or a Lancia. The prototype cars exhibited two major styling differences from those which subsequently were made – in the nose the headlamps originally were hidden behind panels designed to swivel out of the way at night, and there was a simple but strong roll-over bar for accident protection. The engine was all set to be of 2½-litres, perhaps with Zenith-Stromberg carburettors or with Lucas fuel injection (that decision had not been taken), and – to the horror of the purists – there was to be the option of automatic transmission. Worse, perhaps, was the decision to fit power-assisted steering – but any enthusiast would soon have agreed that however 'cissy' this might seem, lugging around a reasonably direct steering without assistance, with all that weight of V8 engine sitting on top of it, would have been no joke.

Since Stag is the only Triumph sporting car to have the modern V8 engine, it is worth considering its 1973 specification and layout in some detail. Its cylinder banks are disposed at 90 degrees to each other, and each cylinder head has a single overhead camshaft, which operates a line of parallel valves through the conventional bucket tappets shimmed to ensure the correct valve clearances. The bore/stroke dimension is fashionably over-square (the original 2½-litre was even more over-square than the final job), and the compression ratio is 8.8 to 1. To reduce the overall width of the unit, though actually penalising its height, the valves are inclined substantially towards the vertical; this worked wonders for the shape of the inlet port shapes, while slightly penalising those of the exhaust system. One consequence of the valves being tilted so far away from the vertical in relation to their cylinder heads meant that both rows of cylinder head holding-down studs had to be aligned outboard. The outermost line remained truly vertical, while the innermost are angled in towards the centre of the head. Triumph made a virtue out of necessity on announcement by suggesting that this might make servicing and repairs easier. It may well, but stress paths in the cylinder block are not as ideally spread as would be desirable. The oil pump and distributor are driven from the rear of the engine, while all other auxiliaries including the alternator and the power steering pump are driven from the front. A jackshaft runs down the crook of the crankcase 'vee' connecting the two sets of drive, chain-driven *via* the double-chain arrangement in the engine's nose. Single-overhead-camshaft cylinder heads are really nothing to shout about in the technological 'seventies, but as far as British sports cars are concerned, only the V-12 Jaguars and the small-production Jensen-Healeys and Lotuses can do better.

It may not be generally known that the Triumph Stag engine, if available somewhat earlier than eventually transpired, might by now have been specified by Morgan. Ever since 1938 Morgan had remained faithful to Standard and later Standard-Triumph for the engines fitted into its fastest cars. However, when Peter Morgan learned in 1966 that the legendary old four-cylinder TR4 engine was due to be phased out of the factory cars in a year or so, he realised that a new engine would soon be necessary for his cars. No doubt he could rely on TR4 engine supplies from Standard-Triumph after they had dropped the engine from their own cars, but he was itching to push Morgan yet another step towards modernity. He found that the six-cylinder Triumph engine intended for the TR5 (not, at that time, equipped with its fuel injection, of course) was both too long, and somehow too 'soft' for the car's hearty image, and therefore he decided to break with a 28-year tradition to look elsewhere. Although the motor industry's grapevine had let it be known that there would soon be a lusty V8 engine from Rover, there was as yet no leak regarding Lewis Dawtrey's masterpiece. Peter Morgan then approached Rover for an engine, managed to squeeze it into a slightly lengthened and widened Morgan chassis, and decided that his future engine supplies should be from Solihull rather than from Coventry. Once a V8 car had been built, and partially developed, unavoidable delays in production supply built up at Rover (not the least because their new masters – Leyland – took some time to decide whether to kill off the project or let it go ahead) and at a crucial moment in February 1967 Harry Webster decided to complicate things by inviting Peter Morgan to Triumph to have a look around. Webster showed him the prototype of the new V8 Triumph engine, and asked if it might be of any interest to Morgan in place of the Rover engines that might not now be available. Peter Morgan then indulged in a short period of heart-searching, particularly as at that moment the Triumph engine looked more likely to go ahead than did the Rover, but eventually decided to stay with Rover's cubic inches rather than to opt for Triumph's technical sophistication. In the event, he may have been correct, for Triumph's engine was delayed, the Rover got the go-ahead, and the Morgan Plus-Eight appeared in the autumn of 1968.

Two things conspired to delay Stag even further. One, predictably enough, was the onset of the first batch of American safety regulations, which delayed everybody, and the second was the arrival of a new Technical Director, Spencer King, from Rover. Anyone interested in motoring must remember the panic and plain despondency which set in at almost every car factory which sold cars in America when the first Nader-inspired proposals appeared. Some were so ludicrous as to defy belief (MG for instance found that to comply with proposals for windscreeen wiped areas they would need to fit three wipers *and* fit a much deeper windscreen, while the proposals for minimum tail lamp dimensions had every stylist in the industry scratching for inspiration) though others, such as the first emission control regulations, were not so severe. The implications of the regulations which concerned headlamp performance, and what to do against failure, convinced Webster that they could not continue to use a covered-headlamp scheme. The neat, if rather sinister, style chosen by Michelotti therefore had to be modified to expose the headlamps permanently, as seen on the production cars. The stout roll-over bar was seen to be a very useful thing to have around in view of ever tighter regulations concerning crash-test integrity, though it was not thought at first to need further bracing. Pavé testing showed that there was a body shake problem common to all open four-seater cars, a problem easily solved by tying the roll-over bar to the screen rail. Triumph therefore made a virtue from necessity, while taking the eminently thoughtful step of *bolting* the T-shaped bar both to the body sides and to the screen rail; the reasoning was that anyone who felt very strongly about having safety thrust upon him might then work out his own solution. Triumph did not actually exert themselves to let anyone know that this was so, but a peep under the appropriate trim panels was all that anyone needed to know.

Spencer King's contribution to the delay was caused simply because he did not think the car had enough 'steam', and at a fairly late stage he persuaded his Board of Directors to agree to an enlarged engine, from the $2\frac{1}{2}$-litre of the prototypes to the 2,997 cc capacity used on all the production cars. In itself this would have been enough to cause delay, but the much beefier 3-litre engine caused wholesale design changes behind it. It brought in its train a stronger gearbox and a bigger axle mechanism, bigger brakes were needed to deal with the improved performance, and these had to be accommodated in wheels of an increased (14 inch) rim diameter. Once the power change had been made, no-one seemed to regret making it, but the production planners and specifications staff must have had

The Coventry-developed, Abingdon-built 2.5PI took second and fourth overall on the 1970 World Cup Rally. This is Brian Culcheth's car

several words to say at the time. After that trauma, it seemed only a minor matter when it was decided to call the production car Stag, like its engineering project code, rather than other names that had been bandied around for so long.

The Stag eventually reached its public in June 1970 and, it must be admitted, received a rather luke-warm reception from those journalists who at the time seemed determined to prove that British industry could not, never had, and probably never would produce anything as good as did the Continentals. It was also a time when the British Leyland empire was still in a state of flux, profit figures were down, and all was gloom. Stag in itself was different, different enough certainly from other Triumphs and other British sports cars, and it was probably asking too much of some writers to accept it as a viable proposition. There seemed to be only grudging acceptance of the car's many virtues, which were so numerous and so unobtrusive that there was almost unseemly haste to condemn the power steering out of hand, which was lacking in feel and definitely required getting used to before the car could be thrown around.

Delivery of early Stags was slow, principally because it was to take some time to get the Liverpool factory fully used to building fast high-quality cars like this. However, in August, Triumph had another change of top management when Lord Stokes gave up his Chairmanship, and appointed Bill Davis (ex-BMC and Austin-Morris) as the Triumph Division's new Chairman. One of Davis' first acts was to stop production of Stag for several weeks while the quality problems were rectified, after which production got under way rather more briskly. Originally there were two versions of Stag – an open car, which nevertheless retained the fixed roll-over bar under its hood and exposed it when the hood was folded down, and a hardtop version, where the hardtop once again fitted over the top of the roll-over bar. It was hoped that there would also be a fast-back coupe version of the car, but the usual question of priorities and tooling costs kept that one out of the line-up. Lyndon Mills, who has since retired as Triumph's Sales Director, was always disappointed that the fastback Stag never made it – there is only one car in existence, which is used for one-upmanship transport by Triumph executives. If one didn't want the overdrive transmission which was standard, there was always the optional Borg-Warner automatic in its place. Die-hard sports car enthusiasts might say that an automatic has no place in a sports car, but the people who buy Stags obviously don't know this, for over 50 per cent of all Stags are now built with automatic transmission, the majority of them going to the United States.

But how does Stag behave? How fast is it? How does it hold the road? How much of a sports car is it? Perhaps the best way to answer is not to accept what British Leyland advertising might say about it, nor even what a single road test covering perhaps 1,000 miles might show, but to look at the comments of a man who used a Stag for well over a year and was able to keep a careful check on its behaviour in that time. Maurice Smith, Publishing Director of *Autocar*, picked up his Stag from the local Triumph distributor in December 1970, which means that it was an early-build production car. Over a year, and 13,000 miles later, he commented about it at length in his publication. In his opening paragraphs the writer recorded: 'To the most pointed question "Would you have bought a Stag in December 1970 if you had known what you know now?" the answer, without hesitation, is "Yes". To a further question, "Has it turned out as expected?" the reply is, "Not entirely". Having owned two Sunbeam Tigers before the Stag, a Jaguar 'E' Type and an Aston Martin DB Mk3 before those cars, there was obviously quite a lot of cross-comparison to be made:

'One of the differences that you really notice (from the Tiger II) apart from the Stag being bigger, concerns the V8 engines of the two cars; the Tiger with 1.7 more litres and less weight, was always eager to go off like a rocket, and it encouraged the driver to do so. The Stag is not particularly eager or rocket-like, but can readily be wound up to give a lively burst of acceleration. It will cruise continuously nearly as fast as a Tiger – say 100 mph – and is quieter, more comfortable, softer sprung and more spacious.

'To live with, then, the Stag is much more relaxed and relaxing in nature. Its 3-litre V8 engine gives a very smooth and gentle burble of power in traffic but gets surprisingly wound up and whirring if you kick down and use all it has got.'

Not that the Stag was sluggish. Mr Smith's automatic transmission version could reach 112 mph (compared with perhaps 116 mph for a manual transmission car in overdrive top), while both versions shoot up to 60 mph from rest in around 10 seconds flat. Another nice thing about the Triumph gearbox, when fitted with overdrive, is the number of gears from which one can choose for any particular speed. In Britain, for instance, with its overall 70 mph speed limit, one could 'go illegal' in no fewer than four gears – third, top, overdrive third or overdrive top. You could break the law in built-up areas in Britain without shifting out of first gear (maximum 42 mph), or crack a 50 mph speed limit in second gear (maximum 61 mph). The automatic transmission car would provide no less than 54 mph in the lowest ratio when held in engagement, a speed matched for revs by 89 mph in the middle of the three automatic ratios. All this was available at an overall fuel consumption of around 20 – 22 mpg.

Was the choice of automatic justified? 'This is the first time we have opted for automatic transmission on a sporting car. It is a sign of the changing times – British automatics changing for the better and traffic congestion for the worse. We do not regret the choice but think it high time that a cruising overdrive were available with automatic. The automatic Jaguar XJ6 is another car that needs one. Motorways are here to stay.'

What about the four-seat package on a wheelbase six inches less than that of the Triumph 2000, and what about the open air motoring?: 'It is no good buying a Stag if you need limousine accommodation. This is a compact, convertible, coupé of the true plus-two kind. Average grown-ups can sit comfortably in the back without much to spare. Tall people will find that their heads touch the hardtop roof. Getting in and out of the back seats (front seat catches controlled by levers high in the seat back) is easy enough. With the hood up, back passengers have as much space, but of course feel a bit blinkered. Wind noise becomes considerable over 60 mph, though less than in most other open cars with the hood up. Many owners will buy their Stags intending to keep the hardtops on all year round. The folding hood is, surprisingly, an optional extra. Not so, us. Either you like an open car or you don't. There is something about that rush of air, even if Nader says it is polluted! Agreed, most people will not bother to wrap up like Eskimos to go motoring, so the days of the classic open tourer have passed. Of course, the weather has become much worse as a result of the Americans and the Russians piercing the earth's atmospheric crust with their rockets, so we also feel the need of the hardtop!'

As for roadholding: 'Some early talk of Stags "jacking up" and twitching on corners, owing to the half-shaft splines sticking under heavy torque and then slipping suddenly, has not been supported on this automatic car, although another manual Stag we had on test once showed signs of this in pretty extreme conditions. We followed a Stag fairly fast around Stowe corner at Silverstone during a recent test day and were interested to see the busy behaviour of the back wheels, and the early lift-off of the inside front one. It goes to show that the ordinary owner, even a fast-driving one, gets nowhere near the limits to which cars are tested when their ultimate behaviour is being investigated.'

On the question of reliability this Stag had not been good, with problems ranging from a hood whose mechanism stubbornly refused to work properly, through unreliable electrics, to doors which dropped and jammed at first.

This was, in fact, a fairly average summary of most people's opinions of their Stags. Because of the highish price, particularly when extras like automatic transmission and hardtop were added, many of them were inevitably older and more well-to-do, and not particularly interested in the last ounce of performance or the last fraction in the roadholding. The Stag is a success as far as British Leyland's accountants are concerned, and Triumph certainly have their usual delivery problem. In fact, if there was one marketing factor common to just about every Triumph in the last 20 years it is that supply has *always* fallen far behind demand.

Whatever the string-back-gloved brigade may hope, Stag and its relations point the way to future sports car design. Modern man likes his comforts much more than in the past (it is not only hooliganism that keeps people away from most football grounds these days, but the fact that they have to stand up for a couple of hours), likes everything to be civilised, and reliable. Many modern sports car buyers would rather not have more than a nodding acquaintance with a spanner, and as for tools to take out the plugs or adjust the brakes . . . The other side of the coin as far as future sports car design is concerned is what the American safety regulations will force upon our car makers. Even ten years ago they might have been prepared to suggest that America was unique, that the rest of the world was not interested in safety belts, roll-over protection, anti-crush doors and padded steering wheels; nowadays this would simply not be true. The next generation of sports cars will be safer, plushier, better-equipped and certainly not as idiosyncratic as before. There will be sports cars because there are people clamouring for them. There will certainly be more cars from Triumph, because the sports car market, especially in the United States, is as buoyant as ever.

When Leyland, who already owned Standard-Triumph and Rover, merged with British Motor Holdings, the British Leyland Motor Corporation came into being. As soon as the dust had settled, task forces were sent out in all directions to advise on future policy, and for a time there were the most horrifying rumours regarding rationalisation, model cancellations, factory closures and even the axeing of complete makes. Triumph were going to be merged with MG, or MG merged with Triumph, said some. They haven't been, and the major merger has been between Triumph and Rover. The Stag would be cancelled before it went into production, or at least sold with a Rover V8 engine, said others. It wasn't, and hasn't been. However it *is* known that making one Stag engine means losing three slant-four Dolomite engines, so on purely economic grounds this one made some sense at the time. The Spitfire competed head-on with the MG Midget – one of them would have to go, said some. They do, and neither has suffered. The TR6 fights the MGB – one would be killed, said others. They do, and neither has suffered. Worst of all, some suggested that British Leyland would stop making sports cars altogether. They haven't, and five years after the merger they looked as committed to sports cars as ever.

If British Leyland were soon to stop building sports cars, they would surely not have gone ahead with the changes seen in the last five years. Would there have been a TR6 at all, for instance? Would the Stag have appeared? Would there have been an expensive facelift on the Spitfire and GT6. Down at Abingdon, in the rival camp, would there have been any incentive to squeeze Rover's splendid 3½-litre V8 into the old MGB? Would such cars as the Dolomite Sprint (whose engine *must* one day be slotted into a sports car) ever have been made? However, as far as Triumph is concerned, the time for further big changes must be drawing near. With the Spitfire/GT6 family in its eleventh year, the TR family in its twenty-first year, and even Stag more than three years old, the new thinking must inevitably show through. The Spitfire's engine has its roots in the 1940s. The GT6 and TR6 engine's ancestors were built in the 1950s. The Stag V8 was drawn in 1964. Further, we have not yet seen a sports car fitted with either the Dolomite slant-four or the sixteen-valve Sprint version. Most sales will continue to be in the United States, where the regulations, if they have a bias at all, give a little more freedom to the open-top cars so long as they have good strong roll-over bars. Perhaps this book will qualify for another chapter in two years' time? Perhaps by 1975 several branches of British Leyland will have more to shout about than they do now?

What is going to happen at Triumph, and how it compares with what has been happening in the last few years, may still be locked in the confidential files, and the minds of the Product Planners. However, I thought it necessary to ask as many questions as possible about Triumph's future, and was able to talk to Lord Stokes about his plans and opinions. I can think of no more appropriate way to close this book than to let the architect of British Leyland, and the man who did so much to drag Triumph kicking and screaming into the 1970s, reassure the many thousands of Triumph enthusiasts about the future of the make. Reproduced below is the major part of a question-and-answer session I was able to hold with Lord Stokes during the Spring of 1973:

Author: When Leyland took over Standard-Triumph in 1961, how did you then view the sports car side of the business in relation to Standard-Triumph's future?

Lord Stokes: We've always felt the sports car operation was a fundamental part of Triumph, not only from its profitability point of view, but because of the image it gave the company, and I think continues to give the company.

Author: Have you always found sports cars financially valuable to the group – or would you rather be able to use the capacity for other more mundane cars?

Lord Stokes: Well, at that time, all of Standard-Triumph was in certain financial difficulties so you could say that it was one of the more attractive areas of the company.

Author: Did the fact that Triumph had sports cars make any difference to your desire to take them over, or did you view the Triumph company as, if you like, a company of products?

Lord Stokes: When we decided to take Triumph over we looked at it as a car-manufacturing unit which we felt could be slotted into our commercial vehicle activities, and we were rather learners in the car field then, but this was the only outfit that was going and that was readily available.

Author: How does a sporting image help British Leyland at the moment, or even how does it help Triumph alone? Would you like to see, for instance, British Leyland not making sports cars? Does the existence of a TR or Spitfire mean anything significant to Austin or Morris for instance?

Lord Stokes: Very much so. I think that sports cars are a very necessary part of our business. They're profitable in themselves. After all we make cars for people, and there are a lot of people who seem to want sports cars. I think one has to define what exactly a sports car is. Motoring correspondents have one interpretation, but the buying public seem to have an entirely different one, and I think we have got to aim ourselves at the majority of the actual buying public. If you take it here, in Europe and in America particularly, I think you'll find that the buying public tends to go towards a car in which they can enjoy themselves in a sporting manner. I don't think they're looking for all-out racers. It so happens that Triumph in particular win an enormous number of local races and rallies in the States, and have a very good image. They're all little events in which there is an enormous amount of fun. This is the sort of car we're interested in and we mustn't make this car too expensive to take it away from the chap who is looking for a piece of fun equipment, in the same way that you or I might buy a sailing dinghy.

Author: What sort of sports car will be developed

in the future within British Leyland? Will marques come closer together?

Lord Stokes: Obviously we are going to try to cover the market for sports cars and saloon cars, to cover what we think is 90 per cent of the market – obviously there is a fringe at the top and bottom of the market which is not attractive to us, maybe to other manufacturers but certainly not to us. I think there will be, I'm sure there will be a rationalisation of models, but we do not intend to leave any area of the market uncovered. I think the development of the sports cars as such is going to be dictated to a certain extent by legal requirements, particularly in regard to safety in various countries. You know that we've started a trend with Stag – roll-over bars and so on. I think most people like open cars – that is to say that people who want sports cars want open cars – but I'm frankly not sure if we're going to be allowed to perpetuate open cars. It may be that you will get a car with roll bars, or some other form of head protection in the interests of safety. This may mean that you get a sort of sports coupé with sliding roof, so that you still get fresh air, but that is the general way that our new cars will go.

Author: Does the life and history of any particular make within British Leyland have any bearing on your future plans for it?

Lord Stokes: If you're saying what I think you mean – are we going to keep on, for instance, with Triumph because they have a sporting background, yes, of course we are. The names we have got in this corporation are among the most valuable assets we have, and certainly the envy of I should think nearly every other manufacturer in the world. Names like Jaguar, Rover-Triumph and MG really are household names with everybody, and we will perpetuate this. We will allow companies to develop their own identity, their own personality. But to gain the benefits of a large firm we have cross-fertilisation of ideas, and we also have commonality of development in certain areas such as pollution control, safety and so-on, and a lot of development work rubs off from one company to another. I think it's terribly important *not* to have an overall engineer who says "We will do this for sports cars and that for passenger cars."

Author: Rover and Triumph appear to be drawing closer all the time. Is this as you intended?

Lord Stokes: This is fact. Rover and Triumph are being merged. We have one executive in charge now – Bill Davis. This is because we believe that Rover and Triumph are complementary, and by coincidence we have both the Rover 2000 and Triumph 2000, both of which were designed before we took over Rover. I think it makes sense not to perpetuate that in the future. Rather we're going to put all our resources at Triumph and Rover into making a better car for the future. But there will also be future Triumph sports cars as well.

Author: But this doesn't mean, presumably, that Rover engineers will be encouraged to get involved in sports cars themselves?

Lord Stokes: It might. We've got one Technical Director for two companies. Spencer King, a very brilliant chief engineer, was at Rover, went over to Triumph, and now heads up the two engineering teams. I think I can say this, though, that Triumph will probably concentrate on sports cars, and the Rover people on developing successors to the Rover and Triumph 2000s, which will take on a world-wide reputation.

Author: How logical is it, then, that you have Rover-Triumph, and then MG which is in a separate part of the corporation?

Lord Stokes: Well, it's just a fact of life, whether it is logical or not. MGs are developed from Austin-Morris products. The whole of the MG line has been developed from basic Austin-Morris parts, though it is built at Abingdon as a completely separate car.

Author: Does that mean that we can look forward for MG and Triumph to continue to compete with one another for some time to come?

Lord Stokes: Well obviously they will continue to do so for some time to come, but again I think our intention is not to make our own products compete head on with each other; we like to slot them in one above the other. You'll just have to wait and see for the answer to that one!

Author: You yourself, or those around you, have been in charge at Triumph for about 12 years. Is there anything you have not been able to do at Triumph that you are sorry about now? For instance, in the early 1960s, when things were a bit tight, were there new models you would have liked to make and didn't?

Lord Stokes: I think we had great fun at Triumph. It was a very exciting and exhilarating team, and with the money available at our disposal I think we worked wonders. We produced some absolute winners – like the Triumph 2000 for instance. I think the only mistake we made was that we couldn't afford to put down sufficient plant to make the cars in the volume that we could have sold. I think the sports cars have been a great success. No, I think that, looking back, we made the right decisions. There are quite a lot of things at Triumph that I would have liked to do, but nothing to do with new models.

Author: Have you always had a volumes problem at Coventry?

Lord Stokes: No, actually at first, when we took over, we had a problem selling the cars. It was only when we started to change the models, and got engineering and quality improved, that we began to build a volume and production difficulty. We still have that difficulty – we're not making enough Triumph cars, not as many as we can sell. But there's a limit to the rate of expansion here. We have suffered from an inheritance of rather antiquated factory facilities and inability to expand due to the government's policy of making us go to the development areas.

Author: Do I presume that you are not allowed to build any more in Coventry now?

Lord Stokes: Well, it has been relaxed now, but we couldn't build for a long time. It has only been in the last six to twelve months that we've been allowed to expand in the Midlands, which includes Coventry.

Author: Have you, or will you, be making Triumph/MG dealer rationalisations in America?

Lord Stokes: We are already on a very big programme of dealer rationalisations. The States is a huge country and there are such complicated laws regarding dealers and distributors and so on that you just cannot do it at the stroke of a pen, but it is roughly our policy to control about half of the distribution ourselves and have the other half in the hands of competent distributors. Generally speaking we're aiming to get the whole of the British Leyland range together, so that one dealer handles the whole lot. This is not always possible, because of old customs and practices, and there may still be odd cases where you might get separate dealers for MG and Triumph. Sales are going very well; providing nothing ghastly happens on this regulations business we're fairly optimistic about our position in the United States. Our big problem at the moment is in meeting the demand for our cars from all over the world.

Author: Do you have any thoughts on the way the Americans are squeezing sports car specifications? Is it all fair, or just yet another engineering challenge that you have to meet?

Lord Stokes: I suppose everything's fair in love, war and business . . . . I think there's a great danger that countries will impose legislation as a form of tariff. This is unfortunate, and I think there is a question of import deterrent that can arise. How much should one make regulations on a safety basis that could be described as a constraint on trade . . . I don't know, this is a very difficult marginal area.

Author: Do you see a streak of nationalism in this?

Lord Stokes: I think there is a streak of nationalism in nearly every country – except this one at the moment! But we do get a fair run from the Americans. But there is this rather 'going overboard' approach to safety and pollution requirements. No-one can object to making cars free from obnoxious fumes, but I think we have got to get it into perspective. In the United States they never do things by halves, and now they're making the motor car the bogey of all pollution, whereas pollution is from a variety of sources of which the motor car is but a small one. I think you've also got to count the cost against the available natural resources. All these anti-pollution requirements are going to put up the fuel consumption and make motoring more expensive. I think one has to balance up the benefits one gets as well as the disadvantages.

But the Americans have been very fair on their import policy. It must have been shattering for them to find themselves, the world's major producer of motor vehicles but with negligible exports, suddenly swamped with small cars, Japanese cars, sports cars and what have you.

Author: There have been press suggestions recently that British Leyland are not going to 'make it' for future pollution requirements. Surely this is not correct?

Lord Stokes: I find that a most odd sort of remark. There are an awful lot of people who are not all that well informed, and make all sorts of irresponsible statements. To the best of my knowledge the state of the art on pollution control is pretty well known, and interchanged among professional engineers. All of us will depend on hang-on catalysts, reactors, air-pumps and so on to take away the obnoxious gases, and as far as I am aware if anyone solves this problem the bits will be sold to British Leyland as freely as they would to any other company, so I can't see how we can be behind. I think we're honest in that we do say that we've got a problem though.

Author: Ending on a happier note – may I presume that the name of Triumph will be around in the future?

Lord Stokes: We don't intend to drop any of our important brand names. A lot of people would give their eye teeth to have them – such as Jaguar, Rover, MG or Triumph. Triumph *is* going to be there for another 50 years. It is an extraordinarily good name, it has an extremely good reputation, a tremendous customer loyalty both in this country and overseas. Some of the new Triumphs that are coming along now, not just the sports cars but the sporty variety such as the Dolomite and Dolomite derivatives, are really very attractive cars. They're better value for money *and* better engineered than most of the competition. Triumph is a name and a company that I would hate to lose at any price.

Finally, a look back at perhaps the most attractive of all the TR sports car series – the TR5

Appendix I : They used Triumph bits

In Britain, more than in any other car-producing country, there has always been a thriving specialist car industry. Most of these cars are built for a tiny market, usually take the form of sports cars, and have mainly been distinguished by their very fragile financial and service structure. A few – Lotus in particular – have survived their amateur origins, and blossomed forth to become worthy second-division producers behind the Big Four. Without exception, a specialist firm must look around the Big Four (or Big Six as it was not too many years ago) for the major components which they could not possibly afford to develop or tool-up for themselves. Triumph, even when faced with direct competition, have rarely refused to supply major components to a small concern, and a list of the cars using Triumph components makes interesting reading.

Oldest and least 'modern', but certainly well respected and very sound, is Morgan. This famous old family concern has been making completely individually-erected sports cars in the sleepy spa-town of Malvern since 1911, four-wheelers since 1935. First Standard, then Triumph, acted as benefactors to the Morgan firm, the association only being broken off in 1968 when the Rover V8 $3\frac{1}{2}$-litre engine was fitted to the Plus-Eight. The first Morgan to fit a Standard engine was the 1939 Four-Four, which threw away its 1.1-litre Coventry Climax inlet-over-exhaust unit (itself quite closely related to the Climax-inspired Triumph Gloria and Southern Cross engine of 1931 to 1937) in favour of an overhead-valve Standard engine of 1,267 cc. This Standard engine had been developed from the original side-valve Standard Flying Ten unit, and was never used in a Standard car. (As recalled in an earlier chapter, according to Peter Morgan, John Black's very first contact with the Morgan motor company came in 1909/10. Black was then working for patent agents Stanley Popperwell, and helped prepare patent drawings for the first Morgan three-wheeler!). After World War Two, Morgan continued making the Standard-engined Four-Four, but a desire to produce a much faster car led to the development of the Plus-Four, which used the Vanguard engine in completely standard form, remotely mounted from the proprietary Moss gearbox.

The Plus-Four immediately became a rally winner and an effective club-racing car, and it was this model which prompted Sir John Black to approach H.F.S. Morgan with takeover proposals in the autumn of 1951. Morgan had already experimented with tuned versions of the 2,088 cc engine themselves, racing a twin-SU-equipped Plus-Four at Le Mans in 1952, which unfortunately retired with valve-gear problems. Morgan had to make some changes to the basic Vanguard engine, principally because it was a very tight fit under the slim bonnet. Adoption of the TR2 engine was logical just as soon as Standard-Triumph were prepared to supply; the first TR-engined Plus-Fours were built in 1954, and were manufactured continuously until the car was phased-out in favour of the Rover-engined Plus-Eight in 1968. Apart from the classically-styled Plus-Four, there were also 50 of the glass-fibre-bodied Plus-Four-Plus models, which also used the TR engine. Engine specifications for Morgan always ran parallel with those in use at Coventry, the change from 1,991 to 2,138 cc taking place in 1962 as the TR4 finally replaced the TR3B. Morgan also produced a Super Sports version of their car, with an engine modified by the Lawrencetune concern to incorporate two twin-choke Weber carburettors, a four-branch exhaust manifold, gas-flowed cylinder head and re-profiled camshaft. Morgan, it will be remembered, were refused a start at Le Mans in 1961 because the scrutineers suggested that the car was old-fashioned and therefore (by rather convoluted French logic) unsafe. Yet an identical car returned to Le Mans in 1962, was allowed to start, and succeeded in winning the 2-litre GT class at an average speed of 93.96 mph, which compares well with that achieved by the best twin-cam Triumph TRS in 1961. A total of 778 Vanguard-engined Plus-Fours were built, and 3,732 were equipped with TR engines.

About the time that Morgan took delivery of their first TR2 engine came the announcement of another sports car to compete with the TR2 – the Swallow Doretti. At first sight one would have thought it suicidal for Standard-Triumph to sell kits of TR2 components to any company which was determined to produce and sell a competing sports car. Yet this is precisely what happened when Triumph agreed in 1953 to supply the Swallow Coachbuilding Co (1935) Ltd with parts for their new Doretti. It was in testing a prototype Doretti with Ken Richardson that Sir John Black was involved in the car accident outside Banner Lane that was officially supposed to hasten his departure from Standard-Triumph.

Perhaps Black had retained some sort of liking for the Swallow name, for it was to SS Cars Limited (which incorporated Swallow sidecars) that Black had supplied chassis and engines for the first SS1 car in 1931. It is often stated that the Swallow company which made Dorettis was nothing to do with William Lyons' Swallows, but whilst this is a broadly correct remark, there is no doubt that the Swallow Coachbuilding Co (1935) Ltd of Walsall Airport in Staffordshire was a descendant of the original firm. Once the car business of SS built up sufficiently to make sidecar production a nuisance, Lyons sold out the rights to Messrs Mills-Fulford, who in turn sold-out to Grindlays of Coventry. They re-registered the company to its 'Doretti' title in 1935, later selling out to the Helliwell Group, who in turn disposed of it to Tube Investments Ltd. It was the TI group who finally settled the Swallow company at Walsall Airport, and decided to make sports cars with it. So there is a tenuous link after all – yet another of the business tentacles which seem to abound in the motor industry around this time.

The result of Black's agreement with Tube Investments gained its first public showing in January 1954 soon after the first TR2s were actually delivered, when Triumph dealers were rather horrified to see the sleek and attractive Swallow Doretti. This was a car that looked good and was certainly structurally strong, but it had not been laid out by experienced motor industry body engineers, and suffered quite badly from lack of passenger leg room, shorter seats and a much smaller luggage boot. All the power train, transmission and suspension components were from the TR2; the tubular chassis frame (naturally, with the parent company being Tube Investments) and the steel-panelled body with aluminium skins was manufactured by Swallow. Compared with the TR2 the engine and gearbox were set back several inches in the chassis, which explains in part the lack of passenger leg room. In addition to the TR2 rear suspension, there was also an 'A' bracket formed by twin radius arms converging on the axle nose-piece. Compared with the TR2 the instrument layout was much less functional, for the large speedometer and rev-counter were disposed one on each side of the full-width facia – thus the driver could not see the rev-counter which faced a bemused passenger. The whole car was five inches longer than the TR2 though the wheelbase was seven inches longer.

The complete car was about 60 pounds heavier than the TR2, and in spite of a slippery-looking bodyshell it was considerably less aerodynamic. *The Autocar*'s road test car could only attain 97 mph compared with the TR2's 103.5 mph, and overall fuel consumption, at 28 mpg, was well down on the TR2. The testers were less than fair to the Doretti's suspension, which they described as 'inclined to be hard by modern standards, and this is particularly noticeable when the car is driven over rough surfaces . . .' because it was to all intents and purposes the same as that of the TR2, which *The Autocar* had liked. The Doretti's acceleration was also down on the TR2 (0 to 60 mph in 13.4 seconds compared with 11.9 seconds for the TR2).

That the Doretti was a 'good try' by a company not previously used to making complete cars could not be denied. But it was heavier, slower and less economical than the TR2, and lacked the character of the Morgan. In addition, its British retail price was £1,102 when the TR2 sold for only £844. No car, however nicely styled and competently engineered, could be expected to overcome a 30 per cent price penalty. Very few were sold, and in spite of the fact that some enthusiasts revere the name in a Doretti owner's club, it cannot be seen in retrospect as a significant car.

Another British car that looked strangely like the TR in many engineering respects, had no common parts, but nevertheless told an intriguing development story was the Daimler SP250. When the TR3A was approaching the height of its sales and competitions success, Daimler decided to get in on the sports car scene by producing a new car of their own. The SP250 – or Dart, as it was

Thought to be a serious rival to the TR2, the 1954 Swallow Doretti used the TR2 engine, gearbox, axle and suspensions. It was pretty but heavy, and this chassis/body frame (below) explains why
(Picture: Autocar)

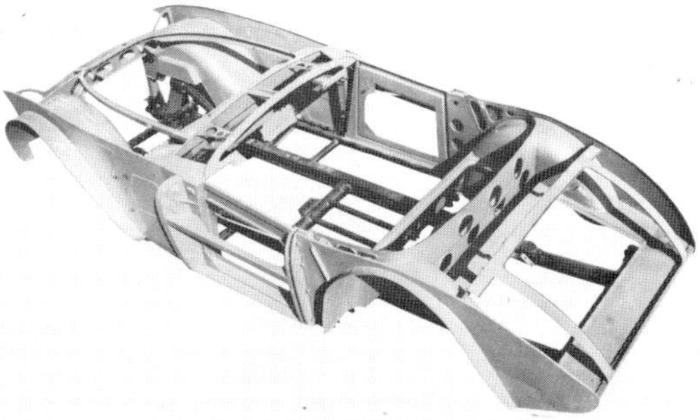

known at first – was first shown at the New York Motor Show in the spring of 1959. Nothing remarkable about this, especially as Daimler were known to be anxious to get away from their old 'limousine' image. Commercially, certainly, there could be nothing but curiosity from Triumph – until Triumph engineers had a look at the Daimler SP250 chassis and discovered that at first glance it appeared to be almost a straight crib of the Triumph design!

Although writers in the past have thought that Daimler actually purchased mechanical components from Standard-Triumph to help them assemble SP250s, I regret that this was simply a good tall story. Though there were many basic similarities between the SP250 and the TR3A, the only common items were purchased from the same supplier of suspension parts. For a start the basic dimensions of wheelbase and track were quite different. The TR3A's wheelbase was 7ft 4in, the Daimler's 7ft 8in; the TR3A's front track was 3ft 9in, the Daimler's 4ft 2in. The Daimler, of course, used its own V8 engine, and four-wheel disc brakes. Nevertheless, it was quite obvious that the Daimler's chassis layout had been inspired by the TR3A.

The actual design link was forged in 1958, but one must go back many years – to the Triumph motor-cycle company – for the start of the story. After the Triumph car and motor-cycle interests had finally parted company, the re-born motor-cycle company was absorbed by Ariel, who already employed Edward Turner as their Technical Director. Ariel and Triumph eventually were sold to BSA, in 1951, who also owned the Daimler and Lanchester car companies. Edward

Turner eventually became Managing Director of the automotive companies in the BSA group, and it was his decision to expand the marketing horizons of Daimler. The key to this strategy was that a new engine would be needed. Even though Turner was Managing Director (and thus could be accused of having better things to do) he found time to sit down and sketch out the outlines of a new 2,548 cc V8 engine, whose pushrod and general cylinder head layout were developed versions of his original Triumph motor-cycle unit. It was thought that the sports car to take this engine could be designed at a reasonable pace once the V8 engine had started its prototype development.

The engine ran for the first time in August 1958, and required so little modification and development that the requirement for the total design became more urgent; the Daimler design staff therefore were instructed to get on with the rest of the design in a hurry. To obtain endurance and road experience of the new engine, one was fitted to a Daimler Century saloon, first with automatic transmission and later with a manual gearbox from an Austin-Healey 100/6; at that point a TR3 gearbox was not fitted, nor even considered. Meanwhile, a survey was made of the competition (which presumably included the TR3A, the MGA, and the Austin-Healey 100/6) after which it was decided that the basic layout of the TR chassis was the one most suited to the Daimler, especially as the entire front suspension could be purchased from an independent supplier – Alford and Alder – without infringing patents or having to deal with Triumph themselves. All the SP250's chassis guidelines, therefore, were the same as those of the TR3A, including the method of building up stiffness around the front suspension towers, the bolt-on cross-member ahead of the engine to brace these towers, the cruciform arrangement, and the general layout of main chassis members. Like the TR3A, the chassis was underslung at the rear axle, and the dampers were Armstrong piston-type mounted on top of the main side-members. Gearbox mountings, handbrake positioning and other details were remarkably similar.

The SP250's production gearbox also bore a striking similarity to that of the TR3A, with its aluminium casing, remote-control gearshift and light-alloy bell-housing. It also had synchromesh on top, 3rd and 2nd gears, though the ratios within the box were different to match it with the high-revving engine, and the fact that overdrive was not then available. The front suspension was identical to that of the TR3A except for spring and damper settings, and even the instruments chosen bore similarities. Shortening the design time in this way saved Daimler many months, such that prototypes were on the road early in 1959 (looking sleeker than the car that was to be produced in some quantity), and the first show car was seen in New York in April 1959, only eight months after the V8 engine had first run.

A well-developed car from the outset could have spelt trouble for Triumph, especially as the V8 engine was very much more powerful than the Triumph four-cylinder unit. That the price in this country was so much higher, at £1,395 total instead of the TR3A's £991, was a relief. Unhappily for Daimler, and no doubt to the grateful thanks of Triumph, the SP250 had an unreliable early life, mainly due to lack of structural rigidity in the glass-fibre bodyshell, and because the somewhat way-out styling was not to everyone's tastes. By the time Jaguar took over Daimler in 1960, and set about improving the body strength, the damage to the car's reputation had been done, and it died in the middle 1960s. No-one, as far as is known, ever shoe-horned a Daimler V8 engine and gearbox into the TR3A or TR4 structure. This combination would have been very much more powerful than anything Triumph were then contemplating, and no heavier – the result could have been an extremely desirable car.

The only other car to take reasonable numbers of TR engines and transmissions was the glass-fibre-bodied Peerless GT car. This was a worthy attempt to provide a close-coupled four-seater closed car at a time when such things didn't exist, but foundered under the usual problems of lack of financial control, and inability to provide service and spares back-up. The Peerless was reborn as the Warwick, building almost precisely the same car, but this didn't last long either, and the design team then went on to evolve the much more exciting and even more drastically under-financed Gordon-Keeble GT.

A special version of the TR4 that was

The Bond Equipe 2-litre GT was a bold attempt by a small car manufacturer to produce a distinctive four-seater based on Triumph Vitesse components *(Picture: Bond Cars)*

mechanically entirely standard apart from relocation of the petrol tank, was the individualistic Dove GTR4. By 1963 Triumph had not become convinced of any demand for a fast-back GT version of the TR4 or the Spitfire, preferring to stay with the removable hardtop concept for both cars. Although there was not a great demand for converted fastback cars – as Harrington had discovered with their Sunbeam Alpine conversions – one Triumph distributor, Dove's of Wimbledon, decided to sponsor such a car themselves.

Taking over a normal soft-top TR4, Dove arranged for the rear portion of the bodywork between the rear wings to be removed, the fuel tank to be discarded, and a rather angular fast-back coupé body to be constructed which utilised the existing TR4 windscreen, doors and drop windows. Let into the sloping tail of this conversion was a large opening rear window (which doubled as a loading door), hinged at the top and self-supporting when raised. A new 15-gallon petrol tank was located in the extreme rear across the car in the base of the old boot pressing. There were a pair of very occasional rear seats, which were admitted to be only suitable for the use of small (and presumably legless) children. Long rear quarter windows could be opened slightly to improve the through-flow ventilation. The enterprising Triumph distributors then christened it with the rather odd-sounding title of 'Dové' – which all buyers instantly called Dove and forgot all about the French pronunciation.

To maintain headroom all the way to the location of the occasional seats (which were somewhat high because of their position near the rear axle) the roof line could not start its customary gradual fall from the screen rail; in consequence the car looked humpbacked from some quarters. The bodies were to be made by Harringtons, who had now abandoned their own specially-bodied Alpines, and who could therefore be adjudged to know a thing or two about this sort of conversion. The car went on the market during 1963 at an asking price without extras of £1,250, compared with £907 for the open TR4, and £949 for the hardtop TR4, as sold by Triumph. This 32 per cent price penalty was undoubtedly one reason for the GTR4 being a flop, and because the advantages of a full-length hardtop and very occasional rear seats did not seem to transform the car's appeal.

Yet, as so often with other features found on TRs, it seems that such a layout might have been ahead of its time. With a bit of attention from factory stylists the rather awkward roof line could have been refined, and with proper tooling and production the price brought down. Would it have been a success? Let's just give as an example the MGB GT, which didn't arrive for a couple of years after the GTR4, and has since provided a very substantial part of the MGB sales volume from Abingdon.

Once the TR lost its four-cylinder engine,

Triumph were not prepared to continue making small quantities for other firms, though they were prepared to supply various types of six-cylinder engine, with or without fuel injection. Morgan, as we have seen, could not be persuaded to fit the 2.5 unit in place of the TR4 engine, mainly because it was too long, and because Peter Morgan was yearning for a lot more horsepower. One might mention, in passing, that Standard-Triumph made one disastrous attempt to make a sports saloon out of the bulbous Phase II Standard Vanguard, and fitting a slightly modified TR3 engine, in 2,088 cc form, to the car. Equipped with a Triumph-style grille, but precious little else in the way of roadholding or appearance improvements, the Standard Vanguard Sportsman, as it was called, was a complete flop. Announced in the autumn of 1956 at a time when Britain's motor industry was about to slip into a decline helped along by post-Suez petrol rationing, the Sportsman lasted only a couple of years, though there is evidence to suggest that cars were only made in 1957. This was one of Standard-Triumph's rare miscalculations, as originally it had been intended as a new Triumph Renown, to replace the elegant Callaby-styled car which had been discontinued in 1955.

The TR5 fuel-injection engine, or the emission-controlled version with Zenith-Stromberg carburettors, has now found its way into the TVR 2500, the TX-Fairthorpe TX-GT Mk 11, and the Trident Tycoon. It also found its way into the very strangely-styled Marcos Mantis, a much-modified car between conception and announcement which only received its Triumph 2.5 injection engine at the very last moment when it was apparently decided that the 3-litre Ford V6 engine was not powerful enough. The Mantis was one of the contributory causes of Marcos' financial failure, and would never have been a car with which Triumph would have been proud to be associated.

One could be excused for thinking this to be a TR chassis with someone else's engine. In fact it is a complete Daimler SP250 chassis and mechanical components. The frame was a close copy of the TR3A (Picture: Autocar)

Spitfire and associated engines have found a home in a variety of cars. Air Vice-Marshal Don Bennett's Fairthorpe cars have remained faithful to Spitfire and other Triumph engines, while his son Torix' advanced TX GT cars used either Spitfire or 2000 units in various states of tune. Latterly TVR have marketed a Spitfire-engined version of their car, using the same body shape and chassis as for all the other TVRs, though this was no ball of fire because of its overall size.

The plucky little Bond company from Preston decided to make the big step from three-wheelers to proper cars early in the 1960s, choosing to base their Equipe GT 2 + 2-seater on the Triumph Herald. But it was a Herald with a difference, for not only was the body carved about so that a distinctive coupé body shape and newly styled bonnet were included, but a Spitfire engine was specified in place of the normal Herald engine. The Equipe was a nice enough little car, and benefited by being sold through selected Triumph dealers with a good guarantee and an ideal spares situation, but once again it was expensive and sold in small numbers. Bond supplemented the Equipe GT with the 2-litre GT in the mid 1960s, which used the GT6 engine and gearbox in a completely new style of coupé bodywork that still managed to use some of the Vitesse inner panels. Bond advertised this car by the slogan 'Is this the most beautiful car in the country?' but wisely refrained from answering. Bond, like so many other specialist car producers, continued to lose money, however, and were absorbed by the thriving Reliant concern in 1969. Reliant continued to sponsor production of the Equipes for a time, but soon closed down the Preston factories and started making a new three-wheeler Bond in Tamworth.

The strangest car ever to use Triumph engines might indeed be called a sports car – if by sports one means activities outside the normally required run of things for a family car. For Triumph Herald engines (untuned) were specified by the German company who made an amphibious car called the Amphicar. Unlike the flying car, this floating car really did exist, and could buck against the tide on nothing more exposed than an estuary if the tidal flow was less than four knots! The Amphicar had a rear engine and propellers. When driven on land the propellers didn't revolve, and the Amphicar looked like a rather ungainly mittel-European attempt at American styling. In water the door sealing strips were brought into play and the car wallowed along using the front wheels as rudders, with the water line not too far below the top of the doors. The Amphicar was open, by the way, which made things very embarrassing, and probably nerve-wracking, if the waves broke over the side, though there was a sort of bilge pump to dry things out up to a point. An Amphicar sounded ideal – say – for anyone living on the Thames around Richmond or Hampton Court to use for commuting, but with a still-water speed of not more than five miles an hour, a commuting journey to central London would have taken rather a long time.

While discussing supplies to small-production companies, one must not forget to mention that Triumph Spitfire front suspension units used to grace a majority of the small cheap single-seater racing cars in the early 1960s. Alford and Alder (then a part of Standard-Triumph, now of the British Leyland group) used to supply un-machined items – usually stub-axles, ball-joints and brakes – to the constructors, who found them ideal for the front suspension of their Formula Junior, Formula Three and even Formula Two chassis.

Pre-war Triumph components found very little outlet, as most small firms looking for engines, gearboxes and axles could go to the still-thriving companies such as Coventry Climax, ENV, and so on. Coventry Climax engines similar to the small four-cylinder Triumph unit went to a variety of customers (including Morgan before they used the Flying Standard Ten unit), but these were supplied direct, not from Triumph themselves. The Vale Special, produced in tiny numbers in the 1920s and 1930s, used a Triumph Super Seven engine, gearbox and axle in a sporting body, but was never an inspiring performer.

Certainly the largest customer yet for Triumph components has been Saab – who launched their all-new Saab 99 model at the end of 1968 with Triumph's new slant-four overhead-cam engine unit. Saab, in fact, were granted exclusive use of this engine for a time, for Triumph were not ready to use it in one of their own models. The engine was originally built as a 1500, then a 1600, before Saab found that the great weight of their new car would need a 1700 cc version to give it adequate performance. The engines were made in Coventry, and shipped to Sweden for the first three years, while Saab decided whether or not to instal their own production lines. (Saab had not, up to that time, ever made a conventional four-stroke engine of their own, for the original 92, 93, and 96 had used a two-stroke engine, while the 96 V4 used a German Ford which was bought in complete). Saab's original engine supplies from Triumph were of 1,709 cc, with bore and stroke of 83.5 × 78 mm, a compression ratio of 8.8-to-1, one Zenith-Stromberg carburettor, and a power output of 80 bhp (net) at 5,200 rpm. To make the car more lively still they decided to take larger-capacity engines, and during 1971 changed over to a 1,854 cc version (basically identical to the Dolomite units) with a single carburettor, and 88 bhp at 5,000 rpm. Finally, in 1972 they installed their own engine plant to build 2-litre versions, which were first fitted in the four-door saloons and in the automatic-transmission variant. At the time of writing the two-door saloon retains its 88 bhp engine, the four-door saloon has a 1,985 cc engine (with dimensions of 90 × 78 mm unlike Triumph's Dolomite Sprint engine), but boasts 95 bhp at 5,200 rpm because of its single carburettor breathing system. The 99EA4 is an automatic-transmission version of the car which is married to a unique version of the engine. Of the Saab-built 1,985 cc capacity, its fuel is fed *via* a Bosch injection layout, and the power output is boosted to 110 bhp (net) at 5,500 rpm. To all intents and purposes the Saab-built engines are structurally the same as those built in Coventry, but whereas the Saabs either have single carburettors or fuel injection, the Triumphs use twin carburettors exclusively.

Appendix II : Standard-Triumph sports car production figures – 1946 to 1972

		Home	Export	Total
1800 Roadster	(1946-1948)	1,750	750	2,500
2000 Roadster	(1948-1949)	1,816	184	2,000
TRX Roadster prototype	(1950 only)	3	-	3
TR2	(1953-1955)	3,115	5,521	8,636
TR3	(1955-1957)	1,286	15,561	16,847
TR3A (including TR3B)	(1957-1962)	1,896	56,201	58,097
TR4	(1961-1965)	2,592	37,661	40,253
TR4A	(1965-1967)	3,075	25,390	28,465
TR5PI	(1967-1968)	1,161	1,786	2,947
TR250 (USA only)	(1967-1968)	-	8,484	8,484
TR6 PI	(1969 to date)	5,020	4,647	9,667
TR6 Carb. (USA only)	(1969 to date)	-	39,571	39,571
Spitfire Mk 1	(1962-1965)	9,104	36,649	45,753
Spitfire Mk 2	(1965-1967)	9,002	28,407	37,409
Spitfire Mk 3	(1967-1970)	16,785	48,535	65,320
Spitfire Mk 4	(1970 to date)	13,603	31,432	45,035
GT6 Mk 1	(1966-1968)	2,663	13,155	15,818
GT6 Mk 2	(1968-1970)	1,251	10,815	12,066
GT6 Mk 3	(1970 to date)	3,019	7,605	10,624
Stag	(1970 to date)	6,195	2,950	9,145

Production figures for the TR6PI, the TR6 Carb., the Spitfire Mk 4, the GT6 Mk 3, and Stag are corrected up to 31 December 1972.

Not strictly a sports car, maybe, but the Dolomite Sprint is the first of a family of high-performance Triumphs which will include cars with more sporting bodywork

Appendix III : Standard-Triumph total car production figures – 1946 to 1972

The totals listed below include all Standards and all Triumphs. Tractor production on behalf of Ferguson is not included.

Financial Year	Cars produced	Financial Year	Cars produced
1946-47	37,363	1959-60	138,762
1947-48	36,923	1960-61	78,735
1948-49	41,004	1961-62	78,383
1949-50	54,490	1962-63	100,764
1950-51	65,444	1963-64	119,937
1951-52	50,693	1964-65	121,405
1952-53	42,697	1965-66	118,398
1953-54	72,926	1966-67	117,350
1954-55	96,941	1967-68	139,488
1955-56	86,466	1968-69	132,322
1956-57	48,835	1969-70	112,127
1957-58	76,539	1970-71	134,350
1958-59	85,926	1971-72	138,666

The ingenious valve layout of the 2-litre overhead-camshaft Sprint engine contributes to an impressive power output of 127 bhp at 5700 rpm. This engine is a 'natural' for future Triumph sports cars

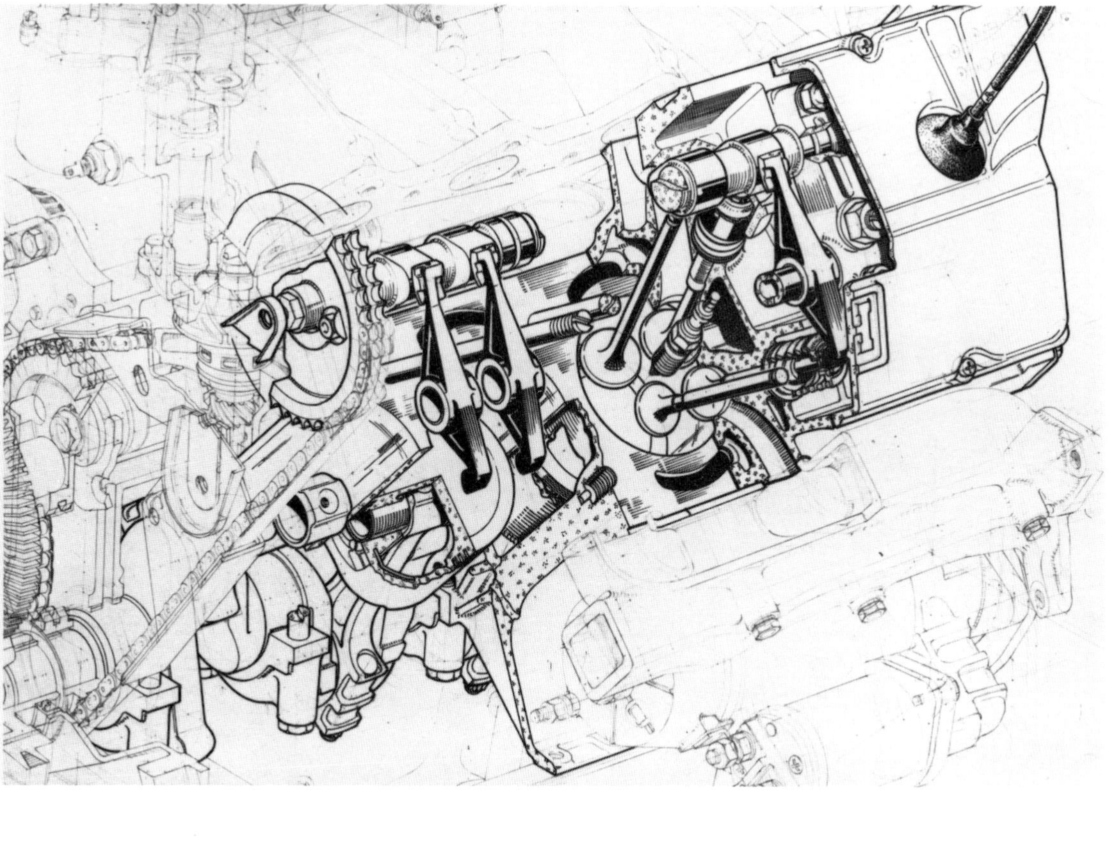

Appendix IV : Technical specifications of all Triumph sports and sporting cars – 1923 to 1973

The main features of each of the Triumph sports, coupé, or sporting tourer models are listed on the following pages. Features of pre-1940 models have been compiled by reference to handbooks and contemporary magazines, as all factory records have been destroyed. All post-war details have been checked with the factory.

No production figures exist for the pre-1940 cars which can be quoted with any confidence. Post-war production figures have been supplied by the Triumph factory. In the case of the Spitfire Mk IV, GT6 Mk III, TR6 PI, TR6 Carb. and Stag, production figures are corrected to the end of the calendar year 1972.

Until the 1960s, it was often difficult to define how a particular quoted maximum power output rating was derived; unless stated, therefore, it must be assumed that power and torque figures are gross – ie, maximum test bed figures.

Competition cars and prototypes exhibited at Motor Shows have been included. One-off prototypes are omitted.

Model	Year(s)	Total made	Best Year	Engine	Transmission	Suspension steering	Structure	Brakes	W'base & length	Unladen weight	Body Options
10-20 Sports	1923-1925	-	-	4-cyl, sv, 63.5 x 110mm, 1393 cc, 23.5 bhp/ 3000 rpm,Zenith updraught carb	4-speed No synchro	Front beam axle, ½-elliptic springs. Rear live axle, ½-elliptic springs. Worm & wheel steering	Pressed-steel chassis, wood-frame bodyshell, aluminium panelling	Rear only, drums, mechanical	8ft 6in 11ft 8in	1625 lb	3-str tourer, 4-str tourer, 4-str saloon
Super Seven Sports ('Gnat')	1927-1932	-	-	4-cyl, sv, 56.5 x 83mm, 832cc, Zenith updraught carb	3-speed (4-speed after 1929) No synchro	Front beam axle, ½-elliptic springs. Rear live axle, ¼-elliptic, later ½-elliptic springs. Worm & wheel steering	Pressed-steel chassis, wood-frame bodyshell, steel or aluminium panelling	Lockheed hydraulic, 9½ inch drums	6ft 9in 10ft 9in	1375 lb	Various 2-str sports, 4-str saloon and tourer
Super Seven Super-charged Sports	1929-1930	-	-	4-cyl, sv, 56.5 x 83mm, 832cc & 56.5 x 74.5mm, 747cc. Cozette s'charger, Zenith carb	3-speed (4-speed optional) No synchro	Front beam axle ½-elliptic springs. Rear live axle, ¼-elliptic springs. Worm & wheel steering	Pressed-steel chassis, wood-frame bodyshell, aluminium panelling	Lockheed hydraulic, 9½ inch drums	6ft 9in 10ft 9in	1375 lb	-

Super Nine Southern Cross	1932-1934	-	-	4-cyl, oh inlet/ s exhaust, 60 x 90mm 1018cc, later 63 x 90 mm, 1122cc. Solex horizontal carb.	4-speed No synchro	Front beam axle, ½-elliptic springs. Rear live axle, ½-elliptic springs. Worm and nut steering	Pressed-steel chassis, wood-frame bodyshell, aluminium panelling	Lockheed hydraulic, drums	7ft 8¼ in 12ft 0in	1790 lb	Various coachbuilt
Monte Carlo Sports Tourer (Gloria Sports)	1934-1935	-	-	4-cyl, oh inlet/ s exhaust, 66 x 90mm, 1232cc, 48bhp/4750 rpm, or 62 x 90mm, 1087cc, 40bhp/4500 rpm. Two Zenith downdraught carbs.	4-speed No synchro	Front beam axle, ½-elliptic springs. Rear live axle, ½-elliptic springs. Worm & nut steering	Pressed-steel chassis, wood-frame bodyshell, aluminium panelling	Lockheed hydraulic, 12 inch drums	9ft 0in 12ft 10in		
Dolomite straight-eight	1934	3	3	8-cyl, twin-ohc, 60 x 88mm, 1990 cc, 140bhp/5500 rpm. Roots s'charger, Zenith (later SU) carb.	4-speed Armstrong-Siddeley/ Wilson box	Front beam axle, ½-elliptic springs, radius arms. Rear live axle, ½-elliptic springs. Worm & nut steering	Pressed-steel chassis, wood-frame bodyshell, aluminium panelling	Lockheed hydraulic, 16 inch (later 12 inch) drums	8ft 8in	2128 lb	-
Gloria Southern Cross (4-cyl)	1934-1937	-	-	4-cyl, oh inlet/ s exhaust, 66 x 90mm, 1232cc, 50bhp/5000 rpm One horizontal, one down-draught SU carbs.	4-speed No synchro	Front beam axle, ½-elliptic springs. Rear live axle. ½-elliptic springs Worm & nut steering	Pressed-steel chassis, wood-frame bodyshell, aluminium panelling	Lockheed hydraulic, 12 inch drums	8ft 0in 11ft 8in	2016 lb	-
Gloria Southern Cross (6-cyl)	1934-1937	-	-	6-cyl, oh inlet/ s exhaust, 69 x 100mm, 1991cc, 55 bhp/4500 rpm Two Solex horizontal carbs. Two SU from 1936	4-speed No synchro	Front beam axle, ½-elliptic springs. Rear live axle, ½-elliptic springs. Worm & nut steering	Pressed-steel chassis, wood-frame bodyshell, aluminium panelling	Lockheed hydraulic, 12 inch drums	8ft 8in 12ft 6in	2350 lb	-
Dolomite Roadster Coupe (4-cyl)	1938-1939	-	-	4-cyl, ohv, 75 x 100mm, 1767cc, 65 bhp/4500rpm, Two SU horizontal carbs	4-speed Synchro on 2,3 & 4	Front beam axle ½-elliptic springs. Rear live axle, ½-elliptic springs Worm & nut steering	Pressed-steel chassis, wood-frame bodyshell, aluminium panelling	Lockheed hydraulic, 12 inch drums	9ft 2in 14ft 9in	2800 lb	-

Model	Year(s)	Total made	Best Year	Engine	Trans-mission	Suspension steering	Structure	Brakes	W'base & length	Unladen weight	Body Options
Dolomite Roadster Coupe (6-cyl)	1938-1939	-	-	6-cyl, ohv, 65 x 100mm,1991cc, 75bhp/4500rpm, Three (two on first cars) SU horizontal carbs	4-speed Synchro on 2,3 & 4	Front beam axle, $\frac{1}{2}$-elliptic springs. Rear live axle, $\frac{1}{2}$-elliptic springs Worm & nut steering	Pressed-steel chassis, wood-frame bodyshell, aluminium panelling	Lockheed hydraulic, 12 inch drums	9ft 8in 15ft 3 in	3149lb	-
1800 Roadster	1946-1948	2500	935	4-cyl, ohv, 73 x 106mm, 1776cc, 65bhp/ 4500rpm, 92 lb ft/ 2000rpm. Solex downdraught carb.	4-speed Synchro on 2,3 & 4	Front independent, transverse leaf spring, wishbones. Rear live axle, $\frac{1}{2}$-elliptic springs. Cam & roller steering	Tubular-steel chassis, wood-frame bodyshell, aluminium panelling	Girling hydraulic, 10 inch drums	8ft 4in 14ft 0$\frac{3}{8}$in	2540 lb	4-door saloon
2000 Roadster	1948-1949	2000	1845	4-cyl, ohv, 85 x 92mm, 2088cc, 68bhp/ 4200rpm, 108 lb ft/ 2000rpm. Solex downdraught carb.	3-speed all-synchro	Front independent, coil springs, wish-bones, anti-roll bar. Rear live axle, $\frac{1}{2}$-elliptic springs. Cam & roller steering	Pressed-steel chassis, wood-frame bodyshell, aluminium panelling	Girling hydraulic, 9 inch drums	8ft 4in 14ft 0$\frac{3}{8}$ in	2460 lb.	4-door saloon
'New' Roadster	1950	3	3	4-cyl, ohv, 85 x 92mm, 2088cc, 71bhp/ 4200rpm, 108 lb ft/ 2000rpm. Two SU horizontal carbs	3-speed all-synchro	Front independent, coil springs, wish-bones. Rear live axle, $\frac{1}{2}$-elliptic springs, anti-roll bar. Cam & roller steering	Pressed-steel chassis, aluminium bodyshell	Lockheed hydraulic, 11 inch drums	7ft 10in 13ft 10in	2716 lb	-
TR or TR 1 Prototype	1952	1	1	4-cyl, ohv, 83 x 92mm, 1991cc, 75bhp /4300rpm 105 lb ft/2300rpm. Two SU horizontal carbs.	4-speed Synchro on 2,3 & 4	Front independent, coil springs, wish-bones. Rear live axle, $\frac{1}{2}$-elliptic springs. Cam & lever steering	Pressed-steel chassis, pressed-steel bodyshell	Lockheed hydraulic, 9 inch drums	7ft 4in 11ft 9in	1708 lb -	-

TR2	1953-1955	8628	4891	4-cyl, ohv, 83 x 92mm, 1991cc, 90bhp /4800rpm, 117 lb ft /3000rpm. Two SU horizontal carbs	4-speed Synchro on 2,3 & 4 Overdrive optional	Front independent, coil springs, wish-bones. Rear live axle, ½-elliptic springs. Cam & lever steering	Pressed-steel chassis, pressed-steel bodyshell	Lockheed hydraulic, 10 inch (front) drums	7ft 4in 12ft 7in	1848 lb	Removable hardtop from Oct 1954
TR3	1955-1957	16847	7386	4-cyl, ohv, 83x 92mm, 1991cc, 95bhp/4800rpm, 118 lb ft/3000rpm Two SU horizontal carbs	4-speed Synchro on 2,3 & 4 Overdrive optional	Front independent, coil springs, wish-bones. Rear live axle, ½ elliptic springs. Cam & lever steering steering	Pressed-steel chassis, pressed-steel bodyshell	Lockheed hydraulic, 10 in. drums Girling front discs from Oct 1956	7ft 4in 12ft 7in	1988 lb	Removable hardtop
TR3A	1957-1961 and TR3B to early 1962)	58097	21298	4-cyl, ohv, 83 x 92mm, 1991cc, 100bhp /5000 rpm, 118 lb ft/3000rpm, or 86 x 92mm, 2138cc. Two SU horizontal carbs	4-speed Synchro on 2,3 & 4 Overdrive optional	Front independent, coil springs, wish-bones. Rear live axle, ½-elliptic springs. Cam & lever steering	Pressed-steel chassis, pressed-steel bodyshell	Girling hydraulic, discs and drums	7ft 4in 12ft 7in	2128 lb	Removable hardtop
Le Mans TR 'S'	1959-1961	4	4	4-cyl, twin-ohc, 90 x 78mm, 1985cc, 156bhp/6500rpm, 139 lb ft/5000rpm, Two SU twin-choke horizontal carbs	4-speed Synchro on 2,3 & 4	Front independent, coil springs, wish-bones, anti-roll bar. Rear live axle, ½-elliptic springs. Rack & pinion steering	Pressed-steel chassis, glass-fibre bodyshell	Girling hydraulic servo, all-discs	7ft 10in -	2127 lb	-
TR4	1961-1965	40253	15933	4-cyl, ohv, 86 x 92mm, 2138cc, 100bhp/4600rpm, 127 lb ft/3350rpm, or 83 x 92mm, 1991cc. Two SU horizontal (later Zenith-Stromberg) carbs	4-speed all-synchro Overdrive optional	Front independent, coil springs, wish-bones. Rear live axle, ½-elliptic springs. Rack & pinion steering	Pressed-steel chassis, pressed-steel bodyshell	Girling hydraulic, discs and drums	7ft 4in 13ft 0in	2128 lb	Hardtop with detachable roof panel

Model	Year(s)	Total made	Best Year	Engine	Trans-mission	Suspension steering	Structure	Brakes	W'base & length	Unladen weight	Body Options
TR4A	1965-1967	28465	13735	4-cyl, ohv, 86 x 92mm, 2138cc, 104bhp/4700 rpm, 132 lb ft/3000rpm. Two Zenith-Stromberg horizontal carbs	4-speed all-synchro Overdrive optional	Front independent, coil springs, wishbones. Rear independent, coil springs, semi-trailing arms (USA live axle, ½-elliptic springs). Rack & pinion steering	Pressed-steel chassis, pressed-steel bodyshell	Girling hydraulic, discs and drums	7ft 4in 13ft 0in	2240 lb	Hardtop with detachable roof panel
TR5	1967-1968	2947	2797	6-cyl, ohv, 74.7 x 95mm, 2498cc, 150bhp/5500rpm, 164 lb ft/3500rpm. Lucas fuel injection	4-speed all-synchro Overdrive optional	Front independent, coil springs, wishbones. Rear independent, coil springs, semi-trailing arms. Rack & pinion steering	Pressed-steel chassis, pressed-steel bodyshell	Girling hydraulic servo, discs and drums	7ft 4in 13ft 0in	2268 lb	Hardtop with detachable roof panel
TR250	1967-1968	8484	6127	6-cyl, ohv, 74.7 x 95mm, 2498cc, 104bhp/4500rpm, 143 lb ft/3000rpm. Two Zenith-Stromberg horizontal carbs	4-speed all-synchro Overdrive optional	Front independent, coil springs, wishbones. Rear independent coil springs semi-trailing arms. Rack & pinion steering	Pressed-steel chassis, pressed-steel bodyshell	Girling hydraulic servo, discs and drums	7ft 4in 13ft 0in	2268 lb	Hardtop with detachable roof panel
TR6 PI	1969-on	9667 (to 1972)	2420	6-cyl, ohv, 74.7 x 95mm, 2498cc, 150bhp/5500rpm (124bhp DIN/5000rpm), 164 lb ft/3500rpm (143 lb ft DIN/3500rpm) Lucas fuel injection	4-speed all-synchro Overdrive optional	Front independent, coil springs, wish-bones. anti-roll bar. Rear independent, coil springs, semi-trailing arms. Rack & pinion steering	Pressed-steel chassis pressed-steel bodyshell	Girling hydraulic servo, discs and drums	7ft 4in 12ft 11½in	2473 lb	Removable hardtop

TR6 Carb. (USA only)	1969-on	39571 (to 1972)	9900	6-cyl, ohv, 74.7 x 95mm, 2498cc, 104bhp/4500rpm (1972: 106bhp/4900rpm), 143 lb ft/3000rpm (1972: 133 lb ft/3000rpm). Two Zenith-Stromberg horizontal carbs	4-speed all-synchro. Overdrive optional	Front independent, coil springs, wish-bones anti-roll bar. Rear independent, coil springs, semi-trailing arms. Rack & pinion steering	Pressed-steel chassis, pressed-steel bodyshell	Girling hydraulic, servo, discs and drums	7ft 4in 12ft 11½in	2464 lb	Removable hardtop
Spitfire Mk 1	1962-1965	45753	20340	4-cyl, ohv, 69.3 x 76mm, 1147cc, 63bhp/5750rpm, 67 lb ft/3500rpm. Two SU horizontal carbs	4-speed, Synchro on 2,3 & 4 Overdrive optional from 1963	Front independent, coil springs, wish-bones, anti-roll bar. Rear independent, transverse leaf, swing axles. Rack & pinion steering	Pressed-steel backbone chassis, pressed-steel bodyshell	Girling hydraulic, discs and drums	6ft 11in 12ft 1in	1568 lb	Hardtop from 1963
Le Mans Spitfire	1964-1965	4 plus 4 rebuilds		4-cyl, ohv, 69.3 x 76mm, 1147cc, 99bhp/6800rpm (1965: 109bhp/7300rpm), 87 lb ft/5000rpm (1965: 86 lb ft/5500rpm). Two Weber twin-choke horizontal carbs	4-speed all-synchro	Front independent, coil springs, wish-bones, anti-roll bar. Rear independent, transverse leaf, swing axles. Rack & pinion steering	Pressed-steel backbone chassis, pressed-aluminium bodyshell, glass-fibre roof	Girling hydraulic, discs and drums	6ft 11in 12ft 1in	1480 lb 1380 lb (1965)	-
Spitfire Mk 2	1965-1967	37409	19520	4-cyl, ohv, 69.3 x 76mm, 1147cc, 67bhp/6000rpm, 67 lb ft/3750rpm. Two SU horizontal carbs	4-speed Synchro on 2,3 & 4 Overdrive optional	Front independent, coil springs, wish-bones, anti-roll bar. Rear independent, transverse leaf, swing axles. Rack & pinion steering	Pressed-steel backbone chassis, pressed-steel bodyshell	Girling hydraulic, discs and drums	6ft 11in 12ft 1in	1568 lb	Removable hardtop
Spitfire Mk 3	1967-1970	65320	16330	4-cyl, ohv, 73.7 x 76mm, 1296cc, 75bhp/6000rpm (USA 1968: 68bhp/5500rpm), 75 lb ft/4000rpm (USA 1968: 73 lb. ft/3000rpm). Two SU horizontal carbs	4-speed Synchro on 2,3 & 4 Overdrive optional	Front independent, coil springs, wish-bones, anti-roll bar. Rear independent; transverse leaf, swing axles. Rack & pinion steering	Pressed-steel backbone chassis, pressed-steel bodyshell	Girling hydraulic, discs and drums	6ft 11in 12ft 3in	1600 lb	Removable hardtop

Model	Year(s)	Total made	Best Year	Engine	Trans-mission	Suspension steering	Structure	Brakes	W'base & length	Unladen weight	Body Options
Spitfire Mk 4	1970-on	45035 (to 1972)	20790	4-cyl, ohv, 73.7 x 76mm, 1296cc, 75bhp/6000rpm (61bhp DIN/5500rpm)(USA: 58bhp DIN/5200rpm; 1972 48bhp DIN/5500rpm), 75lb ft/4000rpm (68lb ft DIN/2900rpm)(USA: 72lb ft DIN/3000rpm; 1972 61lb ft/2900rpm). Two SU horizontal carbs (USA one Zenith-Stromberg)	4-speed all-synchro Overdrive optional	Front independent, coil springs, wish-bones, anti-roll bar. Rear independ-ent, pivoting transverse leaf, swing axles. Rack & pinion steering	Pressed-steel backbone chassis, pressed-steel bodyshell	Girling hydraulic, discs and drums	6ft 11in 12ft 5in	1814 lb	Hardtop
Spitfire Mk 4 1500 (USA only)	1973-on	-	-	4-cyl, ohv, 73.7 x 87.5mm, 1493cc, 57bhp DIN/5000rpm, 74lb ft DIN/3000rpm. Zenith-Stromberg horizontal carb	4-speed all-synchro Overdrive optional	Front independent, coil springs, wish-bones, anti-roll bar. Rear independent, pivoting transverse leaf swing axles. Rack & pinion steering	Pressed-steel backbone chassis, pressed-steel bodyshell	Girling hydraulic, discs and drums	6ft 11in 12ft 5in	1708 lb	Hardtop
GT6 Mk 1	1966-1968	15818	7909	6-cyl, ohv, 74.7 x 76mm, 1998cc, 95bhp/5000rpm, 117 lb ft/3000rpm	4-speed all-synchro Overdrive optional	Front independent, coil springs, wish-bones, anti-roll bar. Rear independent, transverse leaf, swing axles. Rack & pinion steering	Pressed-steel backbone chassis, pressed-steel bodyshell	Girling hydraulic, discs and drums	6ft 11in 12ft 1in	1904 lb	-
GT6 Mk2 (USA: GT6+	1968-1970	12066	6033	6-cyl, ohv, 74.7 x 76mm, 1998cc. 104bhp/5300rpm (USA: 95bhp/4700rpm), 117 lb ft/3000rpm (USA: 117 lb ft/3400rpm. Two Zenith-Stromberg horizontal carbs	4-speed all-synchro Overdrive optional	Front independent, coil springs, wish-bones, anti-roll bar. Rear independent, transverse leaf, lower wishbones. Rack & pinion steering	Pressed-steel backbone chassis, pressed-steel bodyshell	Girling hydraulic, discs and drums	6ft 11in 12ft 1in	1904 lb	-

GT6 Mk 3	1970-on	10624 (to 1972)	4725	6-cyl, ohv, 74.7 x 76mm, 1998cc, 98bhp DIN/5300rpm, later 95 bhp DIN/5250rpm (USA: 90bhp/4700rpm, 1972 79bhp DIN/4900rpm), 108 lb ft DIN/3000rpm, later 106 lb ft/3000rpm (USA: 116 lb ft/3400rpm, 1972 104 lb ft DIN/2900rpm). Two Zenith-Stromberg horizontal carbs	4-speed all-synchro Overdrive optional	Front independent, coil springs, wish-bones, anti-roll bar. Rear independent, transverse leaf, lower wishbones. (1973 pivoting transverse leaf, swing axles). Rack & pinion steering	Pressed-steel backbone chassis, pressed-steel bodyshell	Girling hydraulic, discs and drums	6ft 11in 12ft 5in	2030 lb	-
Stag	1970-on	9145 (to 1972)	-	V8, single ohc, 86 x 64.5mm, 2997cc, 145bhp DIN/5500rpm (USA 1972: 127bhp DIN/6000rpm), 170 lb ft/3500 rpm (USA 1972: 142 lb ft/3200rpm Two Zenith-Stromberg semi-downdraught carbs	4-speed all-synchro Overdrive optional (standard from 1972) Borg-Warner automatic optional	Front independent, coil springs, MacPherson struts, anti-roll bar. Rear independent, coil springs, semi-trailing arms. Rack & pinion power steering	Pressed-steel monocoque shell	Lockheed hydraulic servo, discs and drums	8ft 4in 14ft 5$\frac{3}{4}$in	2807 lb	Hardtop

INDEX